DATE DUE

HUGO WOLF

Letters to Melanie Köchert

Hugo Wolf (1895)

HUGO WOLF

Letters to Melanie Köchert

EDITED BY
Franz Grasberger

ENGLISH EDITION AND
TRANSLATION BY
Louise McClelland Urban

FOREWORD BY
Martin Katz

SCHIRMER BOOKS
A Division of Macmillan, Inc.
NEW YORK

Collier Macmillan Canada
TORONTO

Maxwell Macmillan International
NEW YORK   OXFORD   SINGAPORE   SYDNEY

Schirmer Books
A Division of Macmillan, Inc.
866 Third Avenue, New York, N.Y. 10022

Collier Macmillan Canada, Inc.
1200 Eglinton Avenue East, Suite 200
Don Mills, Ontario M3C 3N1

Library of Congress Catalog Card Number: 90-41667

Printed in the United States of America

printing number
1 2 3 4 5 6 7 8 9 10

Library of Congress Cataloging-in-Publication Data

Wolf, Hugo, 1860–1903.
    [Briefe an Melanie Köchert. English]
    Hugo Wolf : letters to Melanie Köchert / edited by Franz
Grasberger ; English edition and translation by Louise McClelland
Urban ; foreword by Martin Katz.
      p. cm.
    Translation of: Briefe an Melanie Köchert.
    Includes bibliographical references and index.
    ISBN 0-02-873021-6
    1. Wolf, Hugo, 1860–1903—Correspondence. 2. Köchert, Melanie.
3. Composers—Austria—Correspondence. I. Grasberger, Franz.
    II. Title.
ML410.W8A4 1990
782.42168′092—dc20
    [B]   90-41667
                                        CIP
                                        MN

CONTENTS

ILLUSTRATIONS

FOREWORD

by Martin Katz

Who more appropriate to introduce a collection of letters by Hugo Wolf than a pianist who has centered his entire career on bringing poetry and music together in song? It is this very appropriateness that has persuaded me to accept this unaccustomed assignment of writing rather than playing. My enthusiasm for this repertoire, which displays equality for voice and piano, has outweighed my inclination to decline the publisher's invitation. I write from the pianist's perspective, just as Louise Urban speaks from that of the singer in her own introduction. This music itself demands equal representation from both partners.

Obviously there is more to Mozart than that which a knowledge of his relationship with his father reveals, but the additional glimpse we gain of his thoughts and feelings via his letters is incontestably valuable. So, too, with Wolf. Uncensored letters never intended for publication catch the composer in an unguarded moment, and offer insight that biography and even autobiography cannot approach. Wolf had only two real outlets for expression: his music has been readily available to us for a long time; at last those who speak English have the other. Although we have only Wolf's half of this dual correspondence picture, we come to sense his most private thoughts, ranging from the smallest details of his daily life to the largest concepts of human existence. We become acquainted with the intensity of his feelings regarding music, poetry, and the monumental task of launching a career as a composer. In these letters, the entire range of his emotions is virtually on parade. Performers surely sense a composer's emotional nature through a relationship with his music, but I know I experience it more palpably and personally having read his words to his dear friend. This enrichment is not purely intellectual: within months of my acquaintance with these letters, I found my interpretive choices at the piano directly affected by them, and this in music which I've known and played for twenty years!

Wolf's name on a program strikes simultaneous chords of joy and terror in any accompanist. Joy, because of Wolf's ability to synthesize music and text in a way that allows both to emerge, not merely uncorrupted, but enhanced. Terror, because, if one is thorough, the technical execution of even his simplest measures is a formidable task . . . and then there are the difficult ones! Wolf's concept of the marriage of voice and piano puts an unusual focus on the latter, at times going so far as to create a complete, independent entity for the keyboard. Thus being thrust into the spotlight is wonderful for the ego, but it also presents a challenge considerably different from the sublime modesty of our role in Schubert. As these letters will show the reader, Wolf was not uncomplicated or general in his approach to anything. As a pianist, I must rise to his complexity and try to enter the labyrinthine world of his mind—sometimes attempting to portray four characters, three forces of nature, and a keenly observant narrator . . . all in one song!

The extended moments before and after the singer voices the text are another daunting but grateful task for those of us at the piano. Wolf's ability to penetrate the poet's psyche is unsurpassed and, indeed, equaled by very few. You will follow his journeys to this understanding in these letters. Earlier, Schumann had raised the piano's postlude to a protagonist's moment; now Wolf extends this to each solo event for the keyboard, which consequently must embrace both external pictures and internal feelings. He is never content simply to set the text expertly; he demands, in addition, that it be framed and accompanied by the underlying human emotions. These feelings, which lead to, through, and from the words, must fuse together in the pianist's hands. It is thus easy to understand why pianists both smile and perspire at the mention of Wolf's name.

The translator has been kind enough to acknowledge my help in her own introduction, but at this point I must risk creating that tiresome institution that is the mutual admiration society by thanking her in return. When I met Louise in 1967 I already had a healthy respect and ardent love for Hugo Wolf's songs. What was new for me, however, was partnering someone in this repertoire who spoke fluent German *and* had lived for a time in Wolf's Austrian world. Formerly his songs had existed for me—now they lived! Her zeal for this repertoire is shared by all lovers of fine German poetry who marvel and rejoice at Wolf's ability to create perfect and equal partnerships for music and text, and for voice and piano. Louise's fervor infected me as might the most contagious of diseases; its potency must have rendered me a carrier, for I see my own students "suffering" in the same delightful way that I did.

This translation has been no easy job, I assure you. The German-speaking mind's ability to add clause after clause to a sentence, using a distinctly different syntax from our own, can create an insomniac of any translator. At the other extreme and particularly troublesome in letters to intimate friends, the translation of brief, colloquial, yet heartfelt expressions from any language to another offers challenges and ensures compromises of another kind. Yet Louise has dealt successfully with these problems, and with this volume of letters she provides a valuable new source of information and inspiration—for all of us who would find the world a much poorer place without Wolf's songs and for all those lucky enough to still await that discovery.

TRANSLATOR'S
INTRODUCTION

Hugo Wolf and I have spent a performer's lifetime together. As a young singer I was attracted to his songs by their interpretive possibilities, ideal for expressing my passion and exuberance. With my developing interest in the German language came appreciation of Wolf's literary judgment and his unique gift for combining the poetic and melodic line into a meticulously crafted musical entity. The artist's challenge of bringing to life the broad palette of vocal colors concentrated within a Wolf song continues to be irresistible. As I guide singers in performance classes and in the studio, my delight in the composer's musical concepts, realized in rich and varied detail, is renewed with every phrase. Truly, the well-performed Wolf song is one of my greatest pleasures.

Translating *Letters to Melanie Köchert* has been a labor of love in the truest sense of both words. I began a casual reading of the collection several years ago when the German publication, in print since 1964, was sent to me as a gift from a Viennese friend. The letters proved to be entertaining and enlightening, revealing an astonishingly clear portrait of the Austrian composer, whose songs I had enjoyed performing for many years.

More recently, I returned to the *Letters* in preparation for teaching a graduate performance seminar on Wolf. After a closer reading, I determined that their translation would provide interesting and useful information about the composer otherwise unavailable in English. Those who know and enjoy Wolf's songs recognize in them the culmination of the German lied, which had its first flowering in the songs of Schubert. Singers readily program his songs in concert and competition, yet there is precious little material in English on Wolf other than British musicologist Eric Sams's twenty-seven-page article in the New Grove Dictionary of Music and Musicians. In my own research I have relied on Frank Walker's definitive biography, *Hugo Wolf*, for reference. Originally published in 1951, revised and reprinted in 1968, it is now out-of-print, although it can be found on the shelves of good music libraries. English-language books on Wolf's songs are more accessible (see Bibliography), notably Sams's excellent *The Songs of Hugo Wolf*. An indispensable guide for singer and pianist, it is, alas, not always in print.

Reading the private letters in search of information about a great artist provides a perspective not always available in biographical accounts and discussions of the works. Regardless of their literary value, letters inevitably reflect the writer's inner self and an important sense of the life-style at the time.

Wolf's letters to Melanie Köchert were written toward the end of the nineteenth century in the shadow of Vienna, the capital of the Austro-Hungarian Empire. It was the era of Freud, Hofmannsthal, Mahler, Klimt, Hanslick, and Crown Prince Rudolf and the Mayerling incident, which foreshadowed the imminent downfall of the Austrian monarchy. The convergence of reigning philosophical ideas and the clash of political and cultural movements were to have far-reaching consequences. These were indeed heady times.

As a reflection of his inner self, however, Wolf's letters take on a special significance. He writes with passionate intensity. His uncompromising nature finds no need in letter writing for the finely tuned literary expression of his feelings so evident in his musical expression. The reader is subjected, rather, to a direct onslaught by the notorious Wolf temperament, dictated by the mood of the moment. He was a prolific correspondent, to judge from the number of letters to family and friends (see Bibliography: Letters). Those to friends contain substantial information about his music and give testimony to the respect and devotion accorded him by those of stature in their respective communities (see Glossary of Frequently Mentioned Names: Grohe, Faisst, Kauffmann, Müller, Potpeschnigg). However, it is the letters to Melanie Köchert, with whom he had the longest and most intimate friendship, which provide the closest look at the composer. She was the person who knew and understood him best and whose artistic judgment and personal wisdom he trusted completely. The wife of the prominent Viennese jeweler Heinrich Köchert of the firm Hofjuwelier (court jeweler) A. E. Köchert on Neuer Markt, Melanie became the key figure in Wolf's lifelong struggle to compose—nurturing, supporting, and in the end sustaining him. A woman of beauty, intelligence, and great sensitivity, she was knowledgeable in literature and music, in every way Wolf's intellectual equal and emotional counterpart. He entrusted the manuscripts of all his songs to her. Her devotion remained constant through the difficult final years of his life, when she visited him faithfully several times a week in the asylum. Three years after his death in 1903, Melanie ended her own life by leaping from a fifth-story window of the Köcherts' apartment above the family business.

This collection represents only a portion of a lengthy correspondence. Melanie burned the more intimate letters; *all* of Melanie's letters written to Wolf have been destroyed, in accordance with Wolf's own wishes expressed in an unpublished letter (see Walker, p. 347 n.). Regrettable as these acts are to historians, they were performed as a discretionary measure in keeping with the times. To Vienna and the world beyond, Melanie Köchert was the happily married wife of a respectable Viennese jeweler. (The firm continues to be listed as a family business in travel magazines and brochures.) Hugo Wolf was a devoted friend of the family; dearly beloved by the three Köchert daughters—Ilse (1879–1958), Hilde (1880–1961), and Irmina (1882–1972); and on friendly terms with Heinrich, who occasionally gave the penniless young composer financial assistance (often anonymously). The content of these extant letters thus reflects a close friendship acceptable to Viennese society at the time. Wolf's writing contains none of the passionate rhetoric and ardent declarations of love found in his subsequently published letters to the mezzo-soprano Frieda Zerny, with whom he had an intense affair in 1894. The alert, sensitive reader will, however, find ample expression of "hidden" feelings between the lines.

Wolf's death at the early age of forty-two (one month before his forty-third birthday) was caused by the progressive general paralysis that gradually overtook him at the State Insane Asylum (discussed more fully below by Dr. Franz Grasberger). This was the long-term result of syphilis, which he had contracted in his late teens soon after his arrival in Vienna. (Some accounts date the infection to early 1877; Grasberger gives 1880.) At that time there was no cure for the disease, although Wolf is thought to have consulted a physician and sought treatment, which included adopting specific health regimens to avoid infecting others. Less clear to the Wolf biographer and the contemporary medical researcher is the connection between the disease and the composer's erratic behavior patterns, chronicled from the time of his childhood by family, friends, and Wolf himself. Early evidence of emotional instability is recorded in accounts of his tyrannical outbursts as a young boy within the family circle, his frequent mood swings, and his constant change of schools during these years. All this predates the infection of syphilis and supports the theory advanced more recently that Wolf may have suffered from manic-depression, a strongly genetic form of mental illness. Little is known about the Wolf family medical history to support this diagnosis other than a few fragmentary accounts attesting to his mother Katharina's energetic, vital, explosive personality and his father Philipp's temperamental moodiness. For those who wish to consider the appropriateness of the diagnosis, I include a medical description of manic-depressive symptoms, taken in part from a discussion with Dr. Kay Redfield Jamison, an associate professor of psychiatry at the Johns Hopkins University School of Medicine. Dr. Jamison was the executive producer of the PBS television program "Moods and Music," which presented the music of composers considered to have suffered in varying degrees from cyclothymia: Robert Schumann, Hector Berlioz, G. F. Handel, Gustav Mahler, and Hugo Wolf:

> Greatly increased energy and productivity levels, decreased need for sleep, sharpened and unusually creative thinking, the ability to experience a great depth and variety of emotions, and increased sexual desire are the general

symptoms of the manic state in the creative individual. These are accompanied by either an expansive, gregarious mood or, conversely, an irritable, paranoid mood. There is also an inflated sense of self-esteem, along with strong conviction about the correctness and importance of ideas; this contributes to poor judgment, which, in turn, can lead to chaotic patterns of personal and professional relationships.

Depressive symptoms (minimum duration: two to four weeks) include apathy, lack of energy, sleep disturbance, hopelessness, slowed physical and mental processes, loss of pleasure in normally pleasurable activities, and suicidal thoughts.

After Wolf's arrival in Vienna and contraction of syphilis, his behavior became increasingly erratic. His letters to Melanie Köchert chronicle this very clearly. One may say that they contribute to a growing body of evidence to suggest that Wolf suffered from manic-depressive illness, possibly complicated and intensified by the effects of syphilis. Thus, his spasmodic, explosive bursts of creative activity alternating with severe bouts of depression during nonproductive periods have a broader medical basis than was initially presumed.

"Insight into the Personality," written by the late editor of the German edition, Dr. Franz Grasberger, is an important preface to a reading of the letters. As director of the music collection at Vienna's Nationalbibliothek from 1970 to 1980, he was able to provide pertinent biographical and other background information to the letters, writing in the respectful, discreet tone of his generation. Occasional gaps between the letters are noted here and to some extent explained. It should be mentioned that all of the letters, with the exception of the first few, were written *after* Wolf composed most of the songs on which his fame rests— that is, the settings of Mörike, Eichendorff, and Goethe poems and more than half of the *Spanisches Liederbuch*. Dr. Grasberger has added, in brackets, the missing dates and origins of several letters. All other bracketed information is mine. In preparing this translation for publication I have honored the express, written wishes of the editor and those of the German publisher,

Hans Schneider, by preserving the format of the original letters as they appear in the German publication. The date and place of origin, however, have been moved from the end of each letter to the beginning. Substantive annotations (those of Dr. Grasberger and myself) are provided as endnotes following the final epilogue. It is hoped that this arrangement will allow an easy, conversational reading of the letters, as they were intended to be read by their recipient. Words and expressions in German underlined by Wolf have been italicized, as have those in other languages. At times, German titles of works in other languages are translated to aid recognition. Names of Köchert family employees and friends appearing in the letters are omitted in the Annotations, as well as those persons otherwise untraceable. To help the reader, I have included a glossary of people frequently mentioned in the letters and a brief chronology of Hugo Wolf's life. For an extensive listing of Wolf's compositions in addition to those mentioned in the letters (see Index of Compositions), the reader is referred to Frank Walker's biography, *Hugo Wolf*, and Eric Sams's entry in the New Grove Dictionary.

A word of explanation is in order here about my approach to the translation itself. I have proceeded in two different ways, each determined by the writing style of the author. The philosophical tone of Dr. Grasberger's essay seemed to require a free, paraphrased English rendering to express most accurately the coherency of the author's views. Conversely, Wolf's letters mandated a literal translation to retain his personal writing style; therefore, their translation is as close to the original German as syntax would allow, using his copious dashes and variations in spelling. Minor changes were made only when deemed necessary to avoid ambiguity. This approach offered interesting challenges and rewards. Thus, the greetings and closings of the letters are awkward in translation, but the English accurately reflects the degree of formality expressed in German, even though it may often appear stilted within the context of the letter. The texts of the letters present a different case, for the seemingly complex structure of the notoriously extended German sentence yields the direct, readable tone of the German-language letters in literal English translation without sacrificing the personal style of their writer. In the letters I have therefore refrained at all times from altering the translation simply to improve readability.

I would like to extend my appreciation to all those who gave so willingly and generously of their time to help me with this translation, most particularly the German scholar Alice Kennington, the translation coordinator at the United States Department of Justice; my treasured friend and colleague Martin Katz, the distinguished professional coach and accompanist; and my supportive, helpful husband, Gerhard, who is himself Viennese. I am especially grateful to Dr. Hans Jancik, the Viennese editor of the recently published *Complete Works of Hugo Wolf,* for his encouragement and considerable assistance in this project. My thanks, too, to Helene and Kurt Otley, who proved to be excellent sources of reference; to Barbara and Bill Walters, for teaching me to use a word processor; and to Brenda Smith Barrett, who led me gently into the starting gate.

INSIGHT INTO THE PERSONALITY

by Franz Grasberger

Musical genius can be fully understood only after thorough study of a composer's work and a close look at the personality that created the enigmatic world of sounds. While it is indeed possible to examine the influence of a composer's life and personality upon his work, it is difficult to ascertain the effect of one upon the other. True creativity is much too complicated and ambiguous to be comprehended solely through the simple formulaic phrase "the person expressed in his work." The relationship between the person, the artist, and the composition is subordinate to the divergent and compelling force of the total personality. The existential expression of this personality encompasses both person and artist, yet its essential message lies in the higher unity of music. To what extent does this relationship exist or can it be recognized? How strongly is the person's character reflected in what is created? How much has the work been influenced by life itself? These are factors that vary greatly with each artist and are subject to the exhaustible breadth of the human spirit, which, particularly in genius, nurtures the growth of its most beautiful, yet most mysterious, blossoms.

The reflection of life and its experiences in the creative work of many great musicians may be viewed as a determining force in their artistic self-realization. To this observation one must add another: the more contradictory and divided musicians may appear to be as people, the more logically consistent they are as composers. Very often there is a clear artistic coherence—evident especially in their compositional style—that contrasts with their personal tendencies. It almost seems as if psychological imbalance and its stabilization were an essential requirement for musical creativity.

In order to see the characteristics of the creative personality as a whole, one must examine the interdependence of human and artistic events and establish a frame of reference for the inner life. One must also keep in mind that there is no established order of emotional sensitivities and that the disposition of the composer's psyche is subject to its own restless change.

Letters and diaries are the most important sources of immediate evidence of the personality's nature and development. Just as highly gifted talents have certain similarities, so are there recurring tendencies in the letters of musicians.

Great composers do not write insignificant letters. Their correspondence speaks with a fresh impulse of warm, human involvement and embraces even trivial events with vivid expressiveness. Mozart's letters, closely approaching the grace and depth of his music, represent a pinnacle in this respect. The letters of Beethoven, Brahms, Verdi, Wolf, and Bartók, however, are equally lyrical, despite their dissimilarities. Witty, warmhearted innuendo is another characteristic of musicians' letters: Brahms, in reluctantly condensed form, elevated it to a personal leitmotif, and Schumann, to that of a literary epistle; in Wagner's letters, it reached the point of self-admiration, a tendency other masters avoided. Revelations about creative methods are seldom found, but certain characteristics of the letter-writing styles allow one to draw some relevant conclusions regarding principles of the compositional process.

Rarely has a composer's life so embodied the genius' tragic turn of fate as that of Hugo Wolf (1860–1903). Like a comet gleaming in the distance, then sinking into the darkness of night, he completed his mission, despite the brevity of his thirty-eight years on earth. [Translator's note: Wolf died a month before his forty-third birthday. Dr. Grasberger has presumably discounted Wolf's final years in the asylum.] The most significant accomplishments were compressed into the short span of a decade. Within these few years of "true creative time," a single three-year period witnessed the thrust of his creative soul to its primary target: the lied. The time before 1888 was one of despair, of strong self-criticism, and of searching and struggling for his own style, which, once revealed, gushed forth in feverish creativity. Three years of inner stagnation followed, bringing Wolf to the brink of total despair before he was able to express the meaning of his life again in operatic form. What gripping irony that the artist's achievement shone brilliantly only at the time of his painful demise!

The knowledge of his calling had taken full root in Wolf's nature even as he was growing up, providing a secure sense of his own worth that remained undiminished throughout the years of apparent disappointment. Then came the moment of realization that his life was already cruelly fated to end in tragedy. It sounds as if a metamorphosis has occurred when Wolf writes to his mother at the beginning of 1898, "Until today, you have been a witness only to my struggle, my misfortunes, my defeats. But the time will come when the laurel wreaths of victory will decorate my brow, along with the palms of failure that I have brandished to date. May you only live to experience that time! This is my most fervent wish."

The exceptionally sensitive spiritual temperament, which inclines to passions and extremes in personal life, is an important prerequisite in the artistic world. In the creative process, that unique susceptibility to feelings is accompanied by a visible reflexive control. This fortunate union fully realizes the innermost core of talent.

Wolf once said about himself. "What I am, I am because of myself, and I am obligated to no other." But this "I" was divided and often hard pressed to assert itself in the conflict of his feelings. Oskar Grohe heard Wolf say, "Oh, you lucky one! How much more pleasantly I could live if I had only a portion of your even temperament." "I am a person," he admitted once to Joseph Schalk, "who acts on impulse in all matters, and when a sufficient amount of electricity has accumulated inside of me, something happens, either in 'thoughts, words, or deeds', be it good or bad.''

Hermann Bahr remarked that "it seemed he could not consciously achieve any mood. It always had to take hold of him." Wolf needed a medium to express himself. In the lied, he wanted to subjugate himself to the personality of the poet, relinquish his own musical identity, and feel sheltered. In so doing, he avoided falling prey to his own inner conflict; with the poet he was never alone.

From within the depths of the poetry, Wolf sought the personal nature of its creator, experienced the creative process of the poem once again, and found the hidden source of the poet's inner motivation. Only then did the musical formulation begin. What was "new" in Hugo Wolf's songs arose from his ability to ignite a reflection of the poet's personality in the content of a single poem and give it expression that went beyond the musical. He saw language as a necessary connecting link, which demanded at least as much attention to metric declamation as the music required to unify the voice and piano in a symphonic-thematic development.

Given the small form of the lied, it is clear that such a multifaceted, far-reaching creative process demands the utmost concentration. It is equally clear that such a process unfolds only gradually. But when the long-desired fusion of the psychological groundwork and musical inspiration is finally achieved, the result is a gift of intoxicating pleasure experienced to the limits. This ecstatic method of working is a natural result of a compositional process that relies completely on an empathetic relationship with the poet. As soon as Wolf found himself in the poet's presence and had made his first contact with him, he wanted to remain in the spiritual realm of this personality—hence the concentrated outbursts clustered together in short periods of time. When he was composing the fifty-three *Mörike-Lieder,* two songs a day were composed on eight different occasions, and three songs were completed on one occasion; of the fifty-one *Goethe-Lieder,* two songs were composed daily on ten different occasions.

Considerable introspection and even more self-discipline

were required to await the arrival of the creative impulse. What finally released the vivid richness of this consummate song form is naturally outside the realm of observation. One cannot know what effect his father's death (May 9, 1887) had on Wolf's state of mind. It is possible that, as a result of his father's death, Wolf's sense of obligation and his strong resolve never to disappoint him were intensified. (His father had seen only Wolf's difficulties, none of his successes.) It is far more certain, however, to assume that Wolf's success in finding a publisher, after many years of searching, gave the twenty-eight-year-old an inner momentum. The first public performance of two of his songs was also approaching. These were significant events for a young artist who had experienced many failures.

Delivered from a long period of confusion, Wolf went to Perchtoldsdorf in February 1888, feeling certain that he had found the right path. There he composed forty-three Mörike songs by the end of May. Thirteen Eichendorff songs followed, composed in Vienna and Unterach from the end of August to the end of September. Ten more Mörike songs were written from [early] October through November. He needed only four months of working time (October 1888–February 1889) to complete fifty settings of Goethe texts (one Goethe song was added in October 1889).

Breathing spaces within such periods of exertion were merely natural swings of the pendulum that moved continuously toward and away from new artistic expression. However, when exhaustion took over after the overwhelming productivity of three years, it signified personal catastrophe for Wolf.

An artist's way of life must become the reflection of his creative work. In Wolf's case, this way of life remained fully and exclusively bound to his work. For him, composing was the only justification for existence. He never considered his own personal situation to be of importance. His view of life was always optimistic, and every external loss was borne without grief.

Wolf firmly rejected bourgeois security for his existence. His attempt to fulfill a position as *Kapellmeister* ended miserably. His inner unrest manifested itself in his daily routine as well: until he was thirty-six years of age he changed his residence numerous times, sometimes living in a hotel, occasionally in a rented apartment, and often spending the night with friends. Finally, he was given a place of his own. Wolf had to sacrifice his sense of freedom now and then for the uncomfortable awareness that he was dependent upon family and friends. His lack of concern regarding financial matters is both characteristic and touching. For example, after he had left the proceeds (admittedly not a great deal of money) from the premiere of *Der Corregidor* lying in a drawer in Mannheim, he responded with a "Let the devil take it" when the money was not found. On the other hand, he toiled his entire life giving lessons—from his early years through the time of his strongest compositional efforts and into 1892, according to his pocket calendar. Everyday concerns were lessened as a result of his steadfast adherence to a modest life-style, indicative of his fanatical devotion to work.

It is obvious from the nature of Wolf's composing activities that his interests were diverse. Reading, which was actually a component of his work, largely defined his intellectual pursuits. He read every book to the end as a matter of principle, even when he initially found it objectionable or decided it had little to offer.

Meticulous order was his credo. His manuscripts, for example, are of a clarity seldom seen. He protected them against any disfigurement, raising sharp objections if a manuscript was returned crumpled. His work desk was always well organized, and his personal appearance, immaculate.

"Inconspicuous, modest, indeed almost threadbare in dress, Wolf always looked 'as if he had stepped out of a bandbox.' Everything about him was neat, trim, and orderly. There was also no one as particular about his possessions. He was a true fussbudget. If, to his dismay, he found a stain on his clothing, a rip, a small tear, a button that had become loose, nothing was more important or more urgent than repairing the flaw. Everything had to be cleaned, darned, or sewn immediately; he watched with a critical eye and was not easily satisfied, no matter how hard the women tried" (Edmund Hellmer).

Hugo Wolf was a man of very small stature, "but a sturdy frame—broad-shouldered, powerful, and short in the neck—the small hands and feet almost delicate. The head slightly lowered—face and hands the color of aged ivory—the thin face from which the muscles boldly protruded, furrowed and crisscrossed by a thousand tiny wrinkles, vertical, fine wrinkles even on the half-opened full lips—the eyes, dark as inkblots, radiated an inner fire. The close-clipped hair soft and blond—the sparse whiskers on the lip and chin more brownish" (Hellmer).

Wolf was not spared the noise and vexation of the real world. The overall tension between concerns of everyday living and the quiet, self-contained nature of his genius caused him many problems. His extreme sensitivity made it very difficult for him to adjust to his surroundings. Every noise, animal sound, and birdcall became his enemy when it distracted him.

Wolf seems to have placed himself continually above the commonplace. He tried to enfold it and his external life in an aura of poetry, and thus appeared to be inexperienced in worldly matters. This was not actually the case. He could be domineering and unfeeling when someone tore apart the poetry of his temporal existence from lack of understanding and disrupted the continuity of his routine. Wolf could not easily remove himself from the importance of his work, except possibly with humor. His friends report that to see Wolf rejoice was to know him as he really was. In the presence of strangers he remained silent, suspicious, and aloof.

Wolf was first known to the public as a critic and only later as a composer. "Your struggle is reflected in your critical essays," wrote his father in one of his last letters to his son. One cannot characterize Wolf better as a critic. His stern lectures were actually nothing other than an altercation with himself and all that did not correspond to the image of his own ideal. "The highest principle in art" was, for Wolf, "strict, harsh truth, unbending to the point of cruelty." This principle also guided his work as a critic. Wolf was obsessed with his own task and pursued it fanatically. Much of this obsession and fanaticism was also poured into his attacks on Brahms. Perhaps Wolf matured as a result of this altercation. In any event, he worked intensively on *Penthesilea* during his years as a critic (1884–1887) and was able to put aside the last uncertainties, for at the beginning of 1888 his "true creative period" set in.

The same year brought his first public appearance as a composer and his first round of applause. The lieder were introduced to the world by a group of friendly supporters. At first the Wagner Society of Vienna took up Wolf's cause, acting as an escort to his songs. Hardly were the first successes recorded when the countercurrents also began. Even within the Wagner Society there were those who wished to restrain the "Wolf cult." Already Wolf's double-edged attitude toward the public erupted: "Do I want to be a famous man?" he wrote to Joseph Schalk. "Yes, I was on the way, striving for this goal with full power! Madness! Folly! Stupidity! As if the appeasement of the most vulgar vanity offered a substitute for the manifold sacrifices, efforts, infamies, insults, and crimes that are connected with the achievement of such a goal. . . . No more of this. I want nothing more to do with the public." While a South German circle of enthusiasts was organizing a new sphere of activity, the disapproving critics in Vienna were gathering strength. The composer would now have to atone for what he had perpetrated during his years as critic. Wolf was compensated by successes in Germany, which in turn exerted an influence on his homeland and gradually earned public recognition for his songs there as well.

Despite his misgivings, Wolf expended considerable energy on gaining recognition. He was willing, if not always eager, to accompany singers at the piano. Admittedly this never took place without friction, for in his exacting insistence on artistic truth, he could become dictatorial to the point of tactlessness. During the period when his songs were being published, the composer of the finely tuned musical image displayed a vigor no one would have thought possible. Indeed, his friends handled negotiations with the publishers because Wolf was impulsive and sometimes capable of ruining a favorable agreement. When it came to the printing process, however, he would not be thrust aside. The format, choice of paper, print size, line spacing, title page, and binding were all precisely determined by him and were executed exactly as he dictated.

A major aspect of Wolf's critical work was his support of Richard Wagner. It must be acknowledged that his encounter with Wagner was a very significant occurrence for him. It did not involve an "influence" in the usual sense. Nothing could be more inaccurate than to speak of Bruckner as the "Wagner of the Symphony" or of Wolf as the "Wagner of the Lied."

Even before he had heard one of the composer's works, young Wolf was seized by the general Wagner rage of the time. When Wagner visited Vienna in November 1875, the life of the fifteen-year-old took on new meaning. After experiencing *Tannhäuser*, Wolf stood face to face with the maestro in the Hotel Imperial in Vienna. For Wagner, the meeting with the boy was a completely inconsequential episode. Even the compositions set before him (Op. 1 and Op. 2) made no impression. Yet the young music student was spiritually accompanied from that moment on by his true role model.

Wagner's intensification of musical statement to the point of ecstasy expanded the possibility for musical expressiveness in a way never before imagined, setting off one of the greatest revolutions in music as the embodiment of spiritual processes. Like Bruckner, Wolf then went his own way. And, like Bruckner, he needed time to find it. He did not resort to dependency on Wagner, except for occasional harmonic similarities that have little significance. Wolf's attempts to confine spiritual unrest and passionate excitement in absolute music did not turn out to his satisfaction. Only when he entrusted himself to a poet's individuality did his confidence grow. This was the solution. Just as Wagner sought the framework of the music drama for his ecstatic sounds and Bruckner wove his mystical, fervent visions into the logical structure of the symphony, so Wolf needed to anchor his musical ecstasy on a psychological foundation.

The power of Wagner's works unquestionably created a feeling of oppression in Wolf from which he could liberate himself at times only with difficulty. Although he knew that his own opera would be very different from a music drama by Wagner, the artistic totality of it burdened him. "What remains here for me to do?" he complained in 1882. "He has left me no room. . . ."

In a letter to Emil Kauffmann, Wolf speaks quite explicitly of finally bringing his song into a context of opera: "The opera, and again and again the opera! Truly, I already have a horror of my songs. The flattering recognition as 'song composer' grieves me to the innermost depths of my soul. It can only be interpreted as a reproach that I compose nothing but songs, that I have mastered only one small form and that one only partially, since in it one finds only the beginnings of dramatic work." In his early years he had intended to write the text himself, but later he desperately sought libretti, without much success, among the poets recommended to him by friends. He distinguishes his project very clearly from the mission of his great model [Wagner]. "I want to be content within myself," he admits to his friend Grohe, "I am not striving for 'world-redeeming' happiness; that least of all. We can easily leave this to the great geniuses. Wagner has already achieved so powerful a work of redemption in and through his art that we can only be glad it is not necessary for us to storm heaven, since it has already been conquered for us. The smartest thing to do is to seek a truly pleasant little spot for ourselves in that beautiful heaven. And I'd really like to find such a cheerful little place, . . . in happy and imaginative company, with guitars strumming, sighs of love, moonlit nights, champagne frolics, etc., in short—a comic opera. . . . For that and only for that do I need a poet."

The search for an appropriate opera subject was pursued with particular vigor in the years 1892–1894 in the hope of finding a dramatic work that would break through the spiritual dearth of these years. Eventually, the already familiar *Three-Cornered Hat* [by Alarcón] material satisfied the need. In nine months *Der Corregidor* was completed, beginning, so its creator thought, a new creative period devoted exclusively to opera.

In the midst of work on his second opera [*Manuel Venegas*, also by Alarcón], Wolf was forced to lay down his pen and relinquish his claim to an artistic existence. He had had a homeland among his friends, for scarcely a portion of his life had gone untouched by their hands. Their belief in Wolf's genius would not in itself have been sufficient reason for so many people to have taken such an interest in his destiny: he was also a fascinating personality, straightforward, without the least conceit, and openly devoted to his friends. Above all, he wanted to be understood, demanding unconditional devotion in matters regarding his work. In this he did not tolerate the slightest indifference.

In the history of the friendships of great men, Wolf's

friends must be given a special chapter. Without their help, which ranged from providing for basic needs to the promotion of his works, his life could have taken a different course.

Many of the existing sources identified up to now concerning Wolf's personality have been linked to his friends: the letters to Hugo Faisst, Oskar Grohe, Emil Kauffmann, Henriette Lang and Josef von Schey, Rosa Mayreder, Paul Müller, and Heinrich Potpeschnigg, and the memoirs of Viennese friends.

The letters are a splendid self-portrait. All their liveliness notwithstanding, they are simple, very restrained, well organized, and truly candid only in relation to an artistic problem. Outbursts are immediately brought under control and can only be regarded as aberrations. Overall mental vigor and trusting sincerity form their very substance. In addition, external situations are quite graphically depicted, with untiring pleasure in details and a dash of pithy, sometimes sarcastic humor. Dominating everything, however, is a forthright honesty that rejoices over the good and openly shares the bad.

For a poetic lifework of such intensity as is recorded in Wolf's songs, the tie to a circle of friends cannot have been the only inner bond. Here, too, as so often, Eros helped to give birth to rapture in music.

Although women provide impulse and inspiration, especially to artists, their influence on the work itself is by nature obscure and difficult to recognize. In a real sense the attempt to clarify it may violate the laws of discretion, which should always be respected. And yet, feminine sympathy stirs and releases the artistic process in such a decisive way that one must give special consideration to these relationships.

Vally Franck was a youthful adventure (1878–1882) for Hugo Wolf. It ended in grief, in keeping with the artist's nature, which drew its greatest vitality from melancnoly renunciation. One must characterize the encounter with Margarete Klinckerfuss as an episode and without serious significance. The attraction to Frieda Zerny, the singer of his songs (1894), was undoubtedly deeper. It was most likely love nourished by the hope that through this woman he might find again the inspiration that had long lain dormant.

The relationship with Melanie Köchert, however, belongs

to the innermost realm of his personality, embracing the person as well as the artist. The "communication through enchantment" (Ortega y Gasset) is accompanied by an intellectual understanding that reached to the depths of the creative regions. The "fulfillment," so to speak, of this spiritual union remained denied. For this very reason it developed its unique character. Once before, under very similar circumstances, an artist had met with the good fortune of such an understanding: Mathilde Wesendonck had led Richard Wagner out of a very critical period in his life and work and had given him new courage. Wagner described this relationship in a letter to his sister Klara: "Since there could never be any consideration of a union between us, our deep inclination has taken on a sad, melancholy character, which keeps everything that is commonplace and vulgar at a distance and acknowledges that its source of joy lies only in the well-being of the other. She has harbored the most untiring and sensitive concern for me since the time of our first acquaintance, and she has won most courageously from her husband everything that could make my life easier."

If such a candid letter had been possible from Hugo Wolf, he would probably have had to express himself similarly. However, there are no clear confessions of this nature, despite the comparatively large number of letters. Wolf was much too discreet as far as his personal life was concerned. One must also keep in mind that the letters written to Melanie Köchert were ultimately sorted by the recipient herself, and that in so doing she destroyed all that were too personal. We would know even more about Wolf had his diary, the existence of which now seems proven (letter 97), remained extant. Melanie burned it. In order to determine the significance of the encounter, therefore, it is necessary to draw some conclusions that go beyond the factual description in the available letters.

The letters to friends contain considerably more artistic substance, and yet the letters to Melanie are not love letters. Nevertheless, this woman occupied the key position in Hugo Wolf's life. Her influence unfolded in a personal relationship that lasted fifteen years (1882–1897). Although the letters link their otherwise separate lives, they were obviously written under the constraint of self-control and attest to the struggle against their feelings.

The companionship of this beautiful, intelligent woman opened a new world to the young composer. He was self-assured and confident, but inwardly ill at ease in the big city, despite a large circle of friends. Unsteady and plagued by unresolved creative problems, he was poor but proud. Happiness seemed to avoid his life as a matter of principle. Melanie Köchert was wealthy and belonged to the best social circles, yet retained an unspoiled sense of the true, simple life. Most important, this woman understood, and in fact discerned, Wolf's most secret poetic and musical thoughts. It was a particularly characteristic side of his nature that his tense, solitary planning and shaping needed to be shared, complemented by communication and animated with the understanding of another. This led him to seek friendship throughout his life. The serious exchange of ideas with a woman must naturally have gone beyond the bonds of friendship. Wolf was not just "bewitched" by feminine charm; he felt himself realized, sensed tendencies in his own personality within hers. Finally, this "transference" led him back to himself.

This power was generated by a married woman. As a result, new and complicated problems were imposed upon the young man's spirits. Conversely, since the relationship was not fully realized and sheltered from the commonplace by keeping transitory matters at a distance, it remained largely poetic in nature and served only the immortally poetic in Wolf's work. This higher region rested on a completely natural foundation: the protective care of a woman for Wolf's outward well-being. This would never have been possible without the truly noble attitude of her spouse, whose deep understanding of his wife's personality and of the extraordinary nature of genius played an important role in the beautiful and fateful aspects of this bond. Discipline and compassion ultimately transcended all tensions and made possible the continuance of a relationship that experienced the ideal but also had to endure human tragedy.

Coming from the southern part of the province of Styria, Wolf, as a young musician, quickly made many friends in Vienna who belonged to metropolitan society. In the years 1878–1879 he frequented the house of the composer Adalbert von Goldschmidt, where he got to know Vally Franck and became acquainted with the Langs, members of a very extensive Viennese family. Melanie Lang (b. 1858) had been married to Heinrich Köchert (b. 1854) since 1878. Heinrich Köchert was a co-owner of the Hofjuwelier jeweler A. E. Köchert business on the Neuer Markt. Melanie was descended from that branch of the family to which Wolf's best friends at the time, Edmund and Henriette Lang, belonged. Wolf became acquainted with Melanie Köchert in April 1879, but at first spent more time with other members of the family. On January 26, 1881, he could still write to Henriette Lang, "That I taught Frau Köchert piano did not seem to me to be worth mentioning. . . ." In April of that year, he severed his ties with Vally Franck.

Heinrich and Melanie Köchert lived on the fifth floor [*4. Stock*] of the Köchert house (Neuer Markt 15) with their children Ilse (b. 1879), Hilde (b. 1880), and Irmina (b. 1882). By 1882, Wolf was already seen frequently in this house. In December of the same year, the Köcherts made an attempt, for which Wolf was unprepared, to reconcile him with Vally Franck. Wolf withdrew from the situation by fleeing. In the summer of 1883, a year full of conflict due to his work on *Penthesilea*, Wolf spent seven weeks in Rinnbach, near Ebensee on the Traunsee in Upper Austria, the summer residence of the Köchert family. Heinrich Köchert wanted to put an end to the uncertainty of the young man's living conditions. He arranged and paid the salary for Wolf's position as critic at the *Wiener Salonblatt* newspaper. Without ever allowing Wolf to be told, he also helped in many other ways. In the next years (1884–1887), while Wolf's external boundaries were delineated by his activity as a music critic, certain undertakings were breaking the ground for the composer: the attempt and disappointment over *Penthesilea* [Wolf had hoped to have his tone poem, based on Kleist's poetic drama, performed by the Vienna Philharmonic in its regular season. The work was found unacceptable after a read-through] and the intense preoccupation with Mörike. Wolf was a familiar and frequent guest at the Neuer Markt residence and at the Köchert villas in Döbling and Rinnbach. These were his most important years, in all probability inwardly accompanied by Melanie. It has been shown that his affinity for Melanie reached its peak in their attuned experiencing of poetry, from which their mutual understanding took its point of departure. How a woman precipitates the turbulence in an artist's heart and in this way gives his fantasy the necessary measure of order and clarity, how she unravels creative problems by psychological confusion and helps give shape to his work, remains an impenetrable secret. Wolf had need of this influence more than any other. His personal development had been so agitated, tension-laden, and entangled that only the hand of a woman was truly able to loosen the knots.

One can therefore view Melanie Köchert's role in the creative illumination of 1888 as significant. The letters to her begin in 1887, already in a confiding tone, though with a dark undercurrent from the outset (2). Only two letters exist from this year. From the following year, in which the real Wolf emerged, letters are completely lacking, although Wolf was in Perchtoldsdorf, Bruck an der Mur, Bayreuth, and Unterach. There is no word either about the rich gift of songs from Perchtoldsdorf. Her strongest involvement would probably have been here. Not until near the end of the year 1888 do we find Wolf again a guest of the Köchert household. In November the young composer met the singer Ferdinand Jäger there and won him as an artistic herald who contributed a great deal to later successes. On December 27, Wolf composed "Epiphanias" in Döbling and in the first edition provided this acknowledgment of friendship to the whole family: "Composition written for the birthday celebration of Frau Melanie Köchert, sung and presented on the Day of Epiphany by her children Ilse, Hilde, and Irmina dressed in the costumes of the Three Holy Kings." Wolf also played with the children, spontaneously and with genuine understanding, within the routine of family activities. He was devoted to them, and the children loved him dearly. The year 1889 is represented by three letters. There are thirty-six from 1890 and twenty-two from 1891. In the following years Wolf relates in detail the cares and troubles of life, successes with his music, and the bliss of composing. Throughout, he remains irrevocably obligated and grateful to Melanie Köchert.

The remarkably conscientious daily reports doubtlessly respond to the request of his close friend and recipient in their detailed accuracy. They cover the years of the song cycles (1887–1891), the difficult time of his creative block (1892–1894), and, finally, the period of life dominated by *Der Corregidor* (1895–1897). One senses as a leitmotif Melanie's constant concern in making Wolf's life inwardly and outwardly tolerable. Complete mutual trust guides each step. Unfortunately not a single letter from Melanie remains.

Hidden personal ambiguity is often present (for example, 56, 82, 83, 107, 160). Wolf also becomes more articulate and rebels against the form of the letters requested by Melanie (48, 49, 118); the happiness over his work on *Der Corregidor* nearly causes him to forget his reserve altogether (163, 167, 168). The real core of the relationship is stated quite openly in letter 176.

Wolf did not have a light burden to bear as an artist (41, 82, 124). He was happiest when he lived in solitude (75, 124, 148). High society, even when it included him as an artist, was a constant nuisance to him (64, 91, 94). In the last analysis, he composed for his own pleasure (166), but always with the highest expectations and then only when he felt compelled (84). The particularly enlightening letter 233 arrives at the fundamental principles of musical creativity itself. The personal sides of the artist are represented very characteristically: his severity (77), a healthy ambition (98), and above all, his pride (110, 132). Their shared affinity for literature also assumes a prominent place in the letters.

Wolf's whole person seems to be deeply dependent upon nature. The sun, flowers, and changes of weather are constantly recurring themes. Struggle with the external world is recorded in lively detail: clothing that does not fit sends him into a "towering rage." Errands must be carried out immediately and exactly as instructed (he therefore states them in the form of a command). The hotel bed is regularly a dramatic concern. Sometimes Wolf also goes too far in his self-absorption, and Melanie's irritable response cannot fail to appear (99, 100).

As a whole, the letters revolve almost exclusively around personal matters. General occurrences and contemporary artists are mentioned only insofar as they touch the composer's own life.

The final years of this beautiful relationship are full of suffering and bitterness. As a young man Wolf had come to the big city, learned to know its pleasures, and presumably allowed himself to be ensnared by them soon after his arrival. Temperament and inexperience led him to take a step that must have been made in 1880. The young composer gambled everything for a fleeting hour of passion. Perhaps he could still have been saved if he had been given proper treatment at the onset. How much lonely agony must have accompanied him throughout his life. It was too late once the final phases of his illness became apparent. The medical opinion of the director of the Niederösterreichische Landesirrenanstalt [Lower Austrian State Insane Asylum] in Vienna on November 19, 1899, states, "Herr Hugo Wolf has been a patient here since October 4, 1898, treated in the first-class ward. He suffers from progressive paralysis. The illness is incurable. Its duration, given the normal course of events, is 2 to $2\frac{1}{2}$ years." The human aspect of this period of suffering is staggering. Hugo Wolf was overcome by a terrible feeling of abandonment before he became completely insane.

The Köchert family remained unswervingly faithful. When Wolf was released from Dr. Svetlin's clinic on January 24, 1898, after a stay of four months, Melanie Köchert and Wolf's sister Käthe took the patient on a trip to Italy. From May 21 on, Wolf stayed in Traunkirchen on the Traunsee where the Köchert family had kept a summer home, Puchschacher, since 1894. Barely a half hour's distance on foot from there, Mathilde Wesendonck lived in her Villa Traunblick that summer; she died there on August 31, 1902.

Arrangements were made for Wolf to stay in the vicinity of Puchschacher. After a suicide attempt in the Traunsee, he had to be committed to the Niederösterreichische Landesirrenanstalt on October 4. From there he wrote a last letter to his "dear friend" and no longer signed his name. Hugo Wolf passed away on February 22, 1903. Surrounded in life by a circle of friends, he died alone, in the arms of his attendant.

During this long period of suffering, Melanie made the difficult trip to the asylum three times a week. Three years after Wolf's death, she departed this life on March 21, 1906.

A truly great woman. For her, poetry and life were one

entity, just as they were in the creative sense for Hugo Wolf. He had given her all the manuscripts of his songs and confessed to her:

Of all those who deeply perceive the magic of music, no one has understood me as fully as you.

An Frau Melanie

Von Allen, die der Tonkunst Zauber lieb empfinden
Und Niemand mich so ganz wie die verstanden.

1887–1891

1

To Rinnbach
Arnfels, Sept. 11, 1887

Honored gracious lady!

With the help of the county court judge's wife in Arnfels I have ferreted out a very respectable colony of roosters. Now I just need to know whether I should send you a young specimen or one already fully grown (with two spurs). A good young rooster, six months old, costs only 40–50 kreuzer. Should I send you a half dozen right away? Hens of the best breeding, with excellent egg-laying qualifications, are also available for a trifle. Do you want some? Please write me at Leibnitz to let me know how I should proceed in this very critical matter and permit me to express the sincerest respect of your most devoted

Hugo Wolf.

2

To Rinnbach
Leibnitz, Oct. 22, 1887

Most honored gracious lady!

Today I gave myself the pleasure of sending you some fruit and hope that it has arrived undamaged. Unfortunately, the nicest, largest, and juiciest peaches were more or less past their prime, and I had to limit myself mostly to choosing the less ripe ones as being better suited for shipping, which, even though they won't decorate your dessert, will still enrich your compote supply. I hope this will not cost me the affection of Anna, that wanton stealer of hearts. Leibnitz has been a great disappointment to me, and I can hardly wait for the time when I can get back into harness to find the peace and quiet in the city that I longed for here in vain.

I have been living in the Gasthof zur Stadt Triest for a week and practicing patience and self-denial; have also become a complete dolt. My sole occupation centers on variations of the Seven Last Words of the Redeemer, during which it sometimes happens that I don't even get past the first "My God, my God, why has thou forsaken me."

When will I be able to say: it is—magnificent!?

The street noise from the confounded Schmiedgasse will certainly be the death of me before the first of October.

Will it be any better in Bruck?

When I get to Vienna—and of this I am certain—I'm going to take up residence in the catacombs. Yes, that's what I'm going to do.

But I'm beginning to bore you, so will quickly send my regards as your family's and your very devoted

Hugo Wolf.

3

To Vienna

Döbling, January 19, 1889

Honored gracious lady!

It occurs to me that our glutton Schalk is particularly fond of heavily seasoned and, above all, *strongly peppered* liver dumplings. Pretty Anna will know from this what she has to do. Now that I have cleared my conscience in this regard, I remain respectfully yours, etc., etc., etc.

Hugo Wolf.

P.S. A half dozen new songs have already been put to bed.
Most obedient servant!
Yes, indeed!

4

To Rinnbach [letter-card]

Vienna, June 7, 1889

Honored gracious lady!

Would you do me a special favor and let me know as soon as possible whether in my copy of Eichendorff poems, which you have at the moment, the passage " 's Schad' nur um's Pelzlein" is right, or whether it should read " 's ist Schad' nur um's Pelzlein." Please send the appropriate information to the address: I. Bartensteingasse 8, 5th floor.

With many, many greetings also to the children, Miss Park, and Heinrich

Your very devoted
Hugo Wolf.

5

To Vienna
Perchtoldsdorf, November 26, 1889

Honored gracious lady!
Until now (12 noon) have received no word from Materna; nor expect any. Actually all right with me. Am in good spirits. Composed "Blindes Schauen, dunkle Leuchte" this morning—not bad. Also hope to bang out something more this afternoon—Forgive the scratch paper—no stationery.
Very hurriedly   Devotedly yours

Hugo Wolf.

6

To Vienna [postcard]
Perchtoldsdorf, January 10, 1890

I intend to come to Vienna on Sunday. Please reserve a ticket for the "Philharmonic."

Most devotedly
Hugo Wolf.

7

To Vienna [letter-card]
[Perchtoldsdorf, January 15, 1890]

Most honored lady!
In my travel kit, which Ignaz has in his possession, there is a coffee sieve. Please direct Ignaz to give the aforesaid coffee sieve to a tinsmith, who should replace the damaged wire mesh with a new one. My tinsmith, who has often taken on this task, is located on Seilerstätte between Himmelpfortgasse and Weihburggasse, diagonally across from Ronacher. The request is to be carried out immediately and thanks most sincerely

Hugo Wolf.

8

To Vienna

Perchtoldsdorf, February 28, 1890

Honored gracious lady!

In case I should have the pleasure of welcoming you and your husband in Petersdorf Sunday—naturally only if the weather is good—please bring with you *everything* "Spanish" deposited in the "archive."

Please look up in the same whether measure 25 in "Er ist's" is written: or whether it's ⌣ ⌊ ⌉ or perhaps ⌣ ⌊ . The difference lies, as may be seen, in the division of the measure. Verbal news about this will be gratefully received by your most devoted

Hugo Wolf.

9

To Vienna

Perchtoldsdorf, March 31, [1890],

5:00 in the afternoon

Have just composed the crown jewel of all the Spanish. Am in a fantastically good mood. God!, if only no one comes to see me! The poem: "Eide, so die Liebe schwur"—the finest hidalgo. You'll be astounded!

Greetings.
Wölfing.

10

To Vienna

Perchtoldsdorf, April 30, 1890

Honored gracious lady!

Should I have the pleasure of welcoming you in Perchtoldsdorf next Sunday, please don't forget my three song volumes and kindly bring them with you.

With best regards

Your devoted
Hugo Wolf.

11

To Vienna

Perchtoldsdorf, May 13, 1890

Honored gracious lady!

If you give me the pleasure of coming to P. Thursday, please get my shoes from Ignaz and bring them with you. If you would be good enough to have about 50 Kr of eggs bought for me and also bring them with you, too, all my wishes would be fulfilled for the moment.

Now to something more pleasant!

I was tremendously happy yesterday. I succeeded in writing another new song, but good heavens, what [a piece]!!! When the German emperor hears it, he'll make me chancellor on the spot. It's titled after Reinick's "Dem Vaterland" and closes with the words "Heil dir, heil dir, du deutsches Land!" ["Hail, hail, thou Germanic land!"] Well, one can scream "Heil Dir" for a long time before it gets into the blood the way my music does. How I achieved this death-defying patriotic tone is a puzzle to me. By this time, I'm starting to think I can do just about anything. Jäger will turn cartwheels. It's really written just for him.—

I hope to see you in P. As always

Most devotedly your

Hugo Wolf.

12

To Rinnbach

Unterach, June 16, 1890

Honored gracious lady!

After one and a quarter hours of brisk walking I arrived in good shape at my lodgings. Awaiting me was: a case of baked goods from Rauchberg's "ladies"—superb goodies and not harmful to the tummy—, a letter written in cuneiform characters from Liliencron, the contents of which I'm still studying today and which I will never completely decipher, a charming letter from Grohe, a mailing from Eckstein (brochure on Sh[akespeare's] "Tempest"), as well as a letter from him in which he informs me that his people most certainly will not arrive in U[nterach] before the 25th of the m[onth]. And now at 11 in the morning I have just received word from Schur with an enclosed letter from Schott.

First of all, Sch[ott] passes over the proposal to share the profits without saying anything, apparently treating it as an inconsequential matter. He expands his first suggestion to the effect that after the sale of 300 copies of the twelve "Selected Songs," he would be willing to print the rest. I will answer him today that I *insist on sharing the profits* and that a complete volume must be printed if we are to come to terms. He may still print the twelve alone as single editions. Liliencron writes that he doesn't have the courage to adapt Sh[akespeare's] "Tempest." He's offering me a tragedy, which I'm refusing, naturally. He's full of admiration for my Mörike and Goethe songs. His attention was called to my things by Schalk's article in "Kunstwart," which he found to be highly interesting, and by an essay of Conrad's (contemporary German poet) in the newspaper "Die Gesellschaft." Moreover, he paid me the dubious compliment of including me immediately in the list of his favorites—Wagner and the "giants" of course—Schubert, Schumann, [Robert] Franz, and—Brahms.

The last [i.e., Brahms] has also set two of his poems, so L[iliencron] tells me. Otherwise what I still have to report from here is that I'm miserably cold. Last night I wrapped myself up in three blankets and a giant feather quilt and froze despite it all. My sincerest thanks for your cordial welcome and hospitality. I hope the bad weather will soon change and allow me the pleasure of welcoming all of you here.—Grohe is not in agreement with my Tempest idea: he sees too much "opera" in it. To counter it, he's urging me to set to music a "Buddha" by Heckel, which in all likelihood I'll leave alone.

Farewell and take care of yourself in the cold, damp weather. With greetings to all I remain, etc., etc., your most devoted
Hugo Wolf.

"Wandl' ich in dem Morgenthau" will—God willing—be finished yet today.

13

To Rinnbach
Unterach, June 23, 1890

Honored gracious lady!

As you requested, I'm letting you know that the negotiations with Schott have broken down. You will see from the enclosed letter that he was very serious about publishing my things. I hope Breitkopf or Peters will be more flexible and reasonable. My lodgings look dreadful. Every nook and cranny is being scrubbed, as the Ecksteins arrive on Wednesday.

This eternal, endless uproar is insufferable, and the worst part is that I'm doomed in this wretched weather to stay in my room. I would be very happy if there could be an outing to the Schafberg before my escape, for which the opportunity may not present itself again soon, if it doesn't happen in the next (beautiful?) days.

Please save the letter from Schott

In pleasant anticipation of being able to welcome all of you as soon as possible in Unterach, I remain in friendship and devotion

Hugo Wolf.

14

To Rinnbach
[Unterach], June 24, [1890]

Hurrah! The spell is broken!

Composed the confounded apple blossom wonderfully yesterday. St. Peter mends as much as can be. Also completed "Das trunkene Köhlerweib" [i.e., "Das Köhlerweib ist trunken"] from a sketch done on the 7th of the month. Sobbed horribly. Have finally, finally got all six together. Now come what may, my day's work is done. With greetings to all

Hugo Wolf.

15

To Rinnbach
Döbling, August 4, 1890

Honored gracious lady!

My move to Döbling was not auspicious. On the threshold of the vestibule I shattered one of the large windowpanes as I carried my suitcase in and discovered another misfortune shortly thereafter: the disappearance of my overcoat, which I had left in the carriage. With friend Schur, to whom I paid my first visit in Vienna, there was a visit to the police and from there to the dispatch area of the coach, the number of which I had noted, fortunately. For a 2-florin tip I got my overcoat back from the delighted coachman, after the miserable wretch had thoroughly plundered my cigar case. Well, thank God I have my cigar case and overcoat again! Now if only I still had that quiet room! But there doesn't seem to be much chance of that at the moment. Frau Fischer [the caretaker] informed me that Mama Köchert's apartment is absolutely not to be occupied, that it is not even available to Theodore. Marvelous! What am I supposed to do now? I'm already half out of my mind from the cackling and crowing of the hens and roosters and I curse Betty up and down. The only cool and tolerably quiet room would be Mama's. If you can persuade Mama K. to relinquish this room to me (the right side, on the street), then I could hope to stick it out here in Döbling. If Mama won't hear of it, then I absolutely have to leave Döbling.—Please put in a few good words for me. On top of this Frau Kraftl is also here with her daughter. "She's all I need!"—If Mama K. should let me have her room, what should be done with the provisions stored there? Should they stay there or be kept somewhere else? This question appears to be so important to Frau Fischer that I must kindly request information about it. Above all, however, I beg you for the *quickest* resolution to this most critically embarrassing situation. Please also let me know, by return post, how the Stadelmanns are reacting.

In the pleasant hope that you and your family find yourselves well, I remain with sincerest greetings to you and all

Your very devoted
Hugo Wolf.

Grohe sent me the enclosed card.

16

To Rinnbach
Ober Döbling, August 20, 1890

Most honored gracious lady!

Larisch paid me a visit today, and since he was not yet acquainted with my Keller songs, I played him two of Brahms' Keller settings as substitutes, which I'd just selected from [the publisher] Lacom's assorted collection. Oh, you would have taken

pleasure in that! What a master of the bagpipes and accordion
Brahms is! "You can't top this!" No one writes more authentic foot
stompers than he, and yet despite all the stompers, "let's be
merry" ditties and doodles, no one can be as melancholy as he.
"Wisst ihr, wie das ward? [Do you know how that was?]"———

I can't resist citing one remarkable passage here because of
its particularly original declamation.

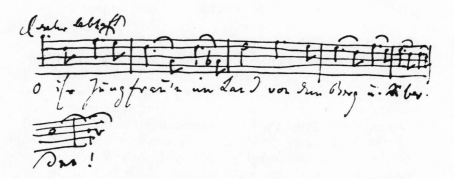

and so in this familiar, noble, popular vein it yodels away to the
end. Fortunately B[rahms] preserved only two Keller poems for
posterity under the titles "Therese" (Du milchjunger Knabe)
and "Salome" (Singt mein Schatz). In the first one the final
verse is even altered. It reads:

eine Meermuschel liegt	A seashell lies
auf dem Schrank meiner Bas':	on my aunt's cupboard:
da halte dein Ohr d'ran,	when put to your ear,
dann hörst du etwas!	then you'll hear something!

B[rahms] apparently used an old edition of K[eller] poems for
his criminal needs. By the way, I'm planning to retain the poems'
titles (entirely women's names in all probability).—Still haven't
had word from Schott, unfortunately. My inactivity is becoming
chronic and is causing me many painful hours as a result. The heat
is worse than ever and hardly bearable anymore. I'm looking forward to the autumn in Vienna with feverish longing.

You should be favored with the best weather in R[innbach]

now. May you drink it in to your heart's content. With this devout wish I send my most sincere grestings and remain as always
Your gratefully devoted Hugo Wolf.
Many greetings to Heinrich and the family, not forgetting Schalkus [Schalk].

17 To Rinnbach
Ober Döbling, August 27, 1890

Honored gracious lady!
Today I had a serious disagreement with Fischer. Having been away from Vienna for two days (Sunday and Monday) I found my apartment neither swept nor dusted as always, also unaired. Fischer could certainly have found time to clean my room and let in some fresh air, considering the cold weather. I was justifiably upset about this neglect and told her so in no uncertain terms. Also added how rudely she behaves toward me, that she never greets me, in short, that I don't wish to tolerate this nonsense any longer, whereupon she retorted that I should start looking for another servant; she said this in her usual impertinent manner. I replied that I wish to look not only for another servant but another caretaker altogether, to which she announced she was ready to leave immediately. Afterward I had a discussion with Frau Kraftl about Fischer, during which Frau Kraftl emphatically seconded my opinion. Well, "Fischer, the little one," eavesdropped on this conversation and, in the absence of her husband, sent her brother to me in my room. I explained to him that I wasn't at all "put up to this" (by Frau Kraftl, as he assumed), but that I simply require decent behavior and decent service from his sister, and I made it clear to him that I am not Fischer's servant, but that she is supposed to be mine and that, in any case, I have decided to *request* Frau Köchert to dismiss the Fischers from the apartment if his sister persists in her manner. He declared himself ready to move out. Now, rather than writing directly to Frau Köchert, since I can't assume definitely that the Fischers are inclined to move out and I don't want to upset Mama K. unnecessarily by a description of the above incident, I'm imploring you to inquire discreetly whether Fischer went directly to Mama and told her of our quar-

rel. If so, I would then write directly to Mama K. Of course, I would take it upon myself to find a replacement for Fischer, which, considering her unfitness, would be easy to do. Frau Kraftl would then remain in Döbling for a fortnight or three weeks. I think Mama K. could only be grateful to me for ridding her of this riffraff.

Yesterday you could practically feel snow in the air here, and in Rinnbach it probably did actually snow. Today the weather is pleasant and mild.

Today Liliencron sent me a periodical entitled "Deutschland," along with an accompanying and explanatory postcard. The magazine contains an article of Bahr's about the pantomime, an art form that is causing a great stir in Paris and that, in Bahr's judgment, corresponds most closely to the modernist taste in art. The conclusion of the article reads: "Nevertheless there are still long stretches to travel on this side of the Vosges [mountains] and on the other side toward the new art, about which there is so much talk and so little achievement. But meanwhile, during this long and already boring hiatus between the old theater, which is no longer tolerable, and the new, which is not yet invented, how would it be if we followed the Parisians' example by way of experiment and tried our luck once at pantomime too? *I'm thinking of something dreamed up by Liliencron, set to music by the highly gifted Hugo Wolf, and Böcklin would have to design the sets*—and after six weeks I'd wager the three would become fantastically huge millionaires, carried high above gazing admiration on golden stilts and transported from their Eiffel-Towered fame to sit among the blessed angels."—How do you feel about my being a fantastically huge millionaire? Of course, the pantomime composer would still be relegated to second place.

Liliencron, incidentally, takes all this very seriously and is suggesting his Indian horror-story "Pokahontas" to me for this purpose. But Böcklin? His eyes will pop out like one of his sea monsters! Damned fellow, this Bahr! By the way, Liliencron is completely charmed by Bahr's genius, as you will see from the enclosed card, which I have just received. Heaven knows why he is so infatuated with this hothead.—The "millions," incidentally, would be fine with me, even if I have to make "pantomimical" music with repeater rifles and canons. Everything's all right with me now.

I have fortunately eaten my way through to the middle of the 4th volume of "Brothers Karamazov," albeit after I threw up violently a number of times. But I have figured out that all the insane and entangled passages in this book are nothing more than the author's nasty teasing of the reader. In this sense as well, Dostoevsky is a "modern."

Went through the Keller songs with Fritzi Mayer. However, she understood "nothing about them at all." In the first song she made fun of the sausage [*Wurst*] and the filling [*Gefüll-sel*]—such a goose! Nonetheless, she sings well and her voice really sounds enchanting.

What's Schalkerl up to? I hope he's well and not running out of old jokes. I send him sincerest greetings, also to you and yours. Perhaps you will soon cheer, with a bit of news, your gratefully respectful

Hugo Wolf.

18

To Rinnbach

[Döbling, August 30, 1890]

Honored gracious lady!

It's very good to hear that Mama K[öchert] insists on observing a cease-fire for the moment, and I am happy to yield to this demand. Since I am now visiting my apartment only occasionally, the behavior of that gang is relatively unimportant to me. I can put up with it until Sept. 15th and then I go to Unterach, if the weather is halfway tolerable.

Today, after a warm, clear night with a full moon, it's cold, windy, and rainy—completely autumnlike.

Yesterday I was at Materna's. She was cordial and talkative, as always. To have a sensible conversation was impossible, every third word is Paris, Paris, Paris. She'll sing everything there, she promised me. When I spoke of Vienna with a sigh, she said softly: Paris. She's immovable on that subject.—

In expressing my most sincere thanks for your willing intervention in the matter in question, I remain in the usual manner Your very respectful   Hugo Wolf.

Please give *everyone* my greetings, including Mama, too, and Dlauhy and spouse.

19

To Rinnbach [postcard]
Ober Döbling, Sept. 9, 1890

Thanks very much for sending on Höfler's lines. Travel tomorrow with Schey to his estate in Hungary and then will go right on to Germany upon my return. I'm thinking of stopping in Unterach on my way back from Germany and spending all of October there. With best greetings to everyone most respectfully

Hugo Wolf.

20

To Rinnbach
[Vienna], Sept. 17, 1890

Honored gracious lady!

Day after tomorrow (Friday) I'm taking the express train in the morning to Unterach, where I'll be staying for an *extended* period of time. Should you by any chance be coming to Weissenbach, I ask you to please let me know.

Many greetings!

21

To Rinnbach [letter-card]
[Döbling], Sept. 18, 1890

Very honored gracious lady!

Would you be so good as to order me a case of light beer at the Eggenberg beer depot in Ebensee and have it delivered to me C.O.D. at the address: *H.W.* Villa Eckstein, Unterach. Please take care of this immediately and be explicitly clear in your directive that I be sent *light* beer. With many thanks, most respectfully

Hugo Wolf.

22

To Rinnbach
Unterach, September 24 [correctly 22], 1890

Honored gracious lady!

I hope that you arrived home safe and sound, in spite of the threatening weather, which fortunately blew over.

By 6:45 I was already in Unterach and and went to bed by 9:00. This morning I performed the chambermaid's duties: swept three rooms, dusted everything thoroughly, and arranged the piano room just the way I want it. Finally I have finished and am using this first free moment to write to you. The weather is not exactly pleasant, but mild and dry; I'll be content if it stays this way. The quietness all around me delights me, and if Lady Music would show her lovely face, I could almost consider myself happy. At the moment the steamship is traveling past my window, so I must hasten to finish. My warmest thanks again for your cordial welcome in Rinnbach. Maybe Heinrich will decide in favor of an outing to Weissenbach after all. And so, until then! Please give best greetings to Heinrich and the children.

Ever yours and as always your very respectful
Hugo Wolf.

How was the Dachstein excursion?

23

To Rinnbach
[Unterach], Sept. 24, 1890

Honored gracious lady!

I just met my celebrated competitor Brüll, all by himself on the lonely road to Stockwinkel. We both had hat in hand, although I cannot say whether the same things were in our heads.

I received the enclosed card today. Do read through the letter. If you don't like what I say about Grohe's songs, let me know and then don't send the letter. If you agree, however, then I ask you to mail the letter right away.

The weather continues to be good.

Beer arrived just now in time for the noonday meal.
Thanks very much. Best greetings to everyone and with the
hope of seeing you soon

Wölfing.

24

To Rinnbach [postcard]

[Unterach], Oct. 2, 1890

I just learned that the steamship doesn't run in the afternoon anymore, but at midday after 12:00 instead. I could come
to Weissenbach Saturday, then, on the steamship, where you
could meet me with the coach. That would be easier and we
could eat at your house at noon.

Please let me know.

Most respectfully
Hugo Wolf.

25

To Rinnbach

Munich, October 10, 1890

Honored gracious lady!

Since I don't know how long Heinrich will be staying in
Rinnbach, I'll get this note off to you right away. First of all,
thank you both from the bottom of my heart for so graciously
taking and accompanying me to the train station. I think back
on this ride with great pleasure.—The journey from Salzburg to
Munich, which is a pleasant enough trip in itself, was shortened
by the talkativeness of an old Benedictine—a handsome, virile
cardinal figure. There was a glorious sunset with alpenglow, as
we traveled from Rosenheim toward Munich. Since my Benedictine—parenthetically noted: a much-traveled, worldly man—
planned to stay at the "Deutschen Kaiser," I tagged along at his
heels, which was all right with him, as he was by himself and
had no companion. After we'd reserved our rooms, we took a
walk through the inner city and dined afterward—very, very
badly at the "Deutschen Kaiser." In addition to this, my room
was badly situated and was so miserable that during the night I

demanded a better room to keep from having bad dreams. This was given to me on payment of an additional 20 Pf and was not even comparable to the previous hole-in-the-wall.

Boller's letters of recommendation were already here by last evening. Today I'm having calling cards printed, so that I can begin making the rounds right away, the results of which you shall be informed of immediately. Please give my best greetings to Heinrich and the children; also Miss Park.

As always I am your gratefully respectful

Hugo Wolf.

26

To Rinnbach

Munich, Oct. 11, 1890

Honored gracious lady!

My chances here in Munich are looking better. Levi welcomed me in the most friendly way and immediately gave me a letter of introduction to Eugen Gura in order to interest the singer in my things. Gura was kindness itself. He informed me that he had ordered songs by Wolf, but received those of the wrong Wol*ff*. Gura is an intelligent, unassuming, industriously ambitious singer, and above all, he can sing; by that I mean very, very well; he has a *glorious* voice and sings *angelically*, which I had the best opportunity to hear for myself today. He gave a recital, to be specific, and ensured my attendance by sending me a ticket. The program was very shabby, as you will see from the enclosed. The Schumann [songs] were a complete failure. Applause was generally weak, despite Gura's great art, mainly because of the labored, long, slow, and boring compositions. The pauses between, thank God, passed without the piano thumpings customary in Vienna. I had the feeling that if Gura had sung a fiery piece, something like my Rattenfänger or even Fussreise or the like, the people would have gone mad with joy and happiness over a diversion of this sort. Gura was tremendously interested in my things. So tomorrow morning at 10 we're getting together with Levi, Porges, Merz, Liliencron, and Conrad; then he'll certainly become well-acquainted

enough with my things. Today I played my things for Conrad and Liliencron. The two of them were, in a word,
thunderstruck.
One wept and the other screamed. It was just insane.

Liliencron is determined to write something for me. Maybe I'll be the hero of the next novella he publishes. One of them cried, it's better than Wagner; the other roared, the devil couldn't have done it better; in short—the fellows went out of their minds. I hope tomorrow the others will too.

Despite all this, I long to get out of Munich and intend to spend tomorrow night in Ulm. A detailed report will follow about how our planned musical get-together went.

For today, as it's already 12:30 a.m., a *felice notte*. Many, many greetings to Heinrich and the children, also Miss Park. In constant faithfulness and devotion, I remain your

Hugo Wolf.

27

To Rinnbach
Munich, Oct. 12, 1890

Most honored gracious lady!

The production took place and everyone turned up but Merz. I performed the Goethe [songs] almost exclusively, but much of it was not understood at all, for example "Phänomen" and "Dies zu deuten." Also, the three holy kings ["Epiphanias"] did not have their usual effect; in short, it was rather humdrum.

Gura, who held out at my side the longest, sight-read my harper songs [*Harfenspieler Lieder*] for me in a really polished way, since only Liliencron was still there. He was most enthusiastic about them and thinks they are far better than Schumann's and Schubert's. He was quite delighted with "Auf einer Wanderung," which he wants to sing as it is written in the original.

Levi liked best the two Coptic songs, "Als ich auf dem Euphrat schiffte," and, strangely enough, "Wenn ich dein gedenke" and "Wie soll ich heiter bleiben." The Rattenfänger didn't catch hold, whereas everyone was thrilled with "Trunken müssen wir alle sein" and "Komm Liebchen, komm." Overall I got the impression that I was *not* understood, that they were preoccupied with the musical elements alone and forgot about what is new and original in my musical-poetic concept.

Always the same musicians' palaver! Oh, how differently you and even my Viennese friends understand me!

I'm leaving here in two hours and will stay tonight in Ulm. Tomorrow noon I'll be in Stuttgart, where I'll stay only a short time so that I can look around Heidelberg at leisure.

The weather is exceptionally fine and mild; it would be good for you too.

Many greetings to Heinrich and the children. As always, your

very devoted
Hugo Wolf.

28

To Rinnbach
Stuttgart, Oct. 13, 1890

Most honored gracious lady!

I wanted to write to you from Ulm, but there was no real opportunity. I arrived in Ulm after 10 p.m., and because I foolishly didn't take a room in the first hotel, but looked for a second-class one instead, I was bedded down badly in the worst sense of the word. I walked around the city until 1 a.m.—all by myself. It was an awesome sight, the immense old cathedral with its recently completed main spire, the white stone of which contrasted with the age-darkened walls of the building like a specter. Overhead, the heavens spread out in a canopy of sparkling stars and all around so still; and there I was, a complete stranger in an alien world, confronting this venerable witness to pious illusion. It was a powerful and exhilarating impression. The next morning I was up at 6 and wandered contentedly through the city, which is a lovely sight to see, especially along the Danube toward the Wilhelmshöhe. Here we have the beautiful Danube, albeit green, not blue, as clear and transparent as an Alpine stream.

The city has much in common with the streets of Bayreuth, only in Ulm there is a predominance of gables. An old town hall built in half-Gothic, half-Renaissance style has completely captivated me. It would also be to your liking.

I'm now in Stuttgart; a pretty city, but very philistine-looking. I'm living in Hotel Dirlamm, very close to the train station and am very well-accommodated. The cost of living seems to be low here, as I paid only 1 M 50 Pf for a "menu" consisting of soup, fish, roast beef, roast pork with vegetables, and fruit.

My first errand was immediately to Förstler, director of the local choral society. He was greatly pleased to meet me and will introduce me tonight at the local concert society, as it is ladies' evening, in order to give me the opportunity of appearing there in person. He spoke enthusiastically of the hymn "An das Vaterland," the performance of which is already arranged this season.

I'm also going to meet Speidel's brother, the composer, today. Tomorrow I'm going to Kauffmann in Tübingen, then back again to Stuttgart, and then to Heidelberg. The weather, if possible, is even more beautiful and mild. And so farewell. Best greetings to Heinrich and the children.

As always your gratefully devoted

Hugo Wolf.

Also conciliatory greetings from Stuttgart to the Jägers.

29

To Rinnbach

Tübingen, Oct. 14, 1890

Most honored gracious lady!

It is already after the witching hour as I write these lines to you. My bedchamber is not in the inn this time, but at Kauffmann's, who received me with open arms, also invited me immediately for the noonday meal and absolutely insisted that he take me in as a guest. I can't begin to tell you what lovely people the Kauffmanns are and I don't even know which of them I like best: him, his genuinely German wife, or his terrific sons. In addition, there is a son-in-law [Dr. Wilhelm Schmid], a philologist at the university here, who shows an understanding of my things more wonderful than I could ever imagine. This evening, in order to afford me the opportunity of making the acquaintance of a larger circle, Kauffmann invited a substantial number of ladies and gentlemen to the evening meal. Unfortunately I was seized with such a hoarseness after an outing to Bebenhausen (see "Bilder aus Bebenhausen" by Mörike), on which Kauffmann and his sons accompanied me, that I could only perform my things with the greatest effort. Despite this, everyone was enthusiastic, all [were] delighted and expressed their impressions in the kindest manner. This evening was truly a festive one for me. Bebenhausen, where Mörike sometimes spent the summer, reminds me very much of Heiligenkreuz [monastery on the outskirts of Vienna] near Baden. The convent with its cloisters and the various refectories etc. is beautiful.

A lady from the area also sang several of my songs, not badly, but without warmth and feeling; maybe she was too nervous. Tomorrow morning the Spanish and the Keller [songs] have their turn. In the afternoon I'm going to Stuttgart again, where I have a meeting with Förstler. The day after tomorrow I go to Heidelberg and will try to be in Mannheim on the 18th or 19th. I find it really difficult to have to leave old, lovely Tübingen so soon. The Kauffmanns really are such splendid people!

He looks exactly like I imagined he would.

Now good night and many, many sincere greetings from your grateful

Hugo Wolf.

30

To Rinnbach
Stuttgart, Oct. 15, 1890

Most honored gracious lady!

Although dead tired and having lain sleepless for two hours in bed, I realize that seizing my pen is the only escape to keep me from hanging or shooting myself. These damn hotels. I can't stand it any longer; they'll be the death of me. I must leave Stuttgart tomorrow, because I can't bear this torture chamber, this so-called "hotel," any longer. I'm starting to get a serious throat infection too, which is making the use of my voice virtually impossible; hence a stop here is useless. Oh, if I were only already in Vienna. This is my single, dearest wish. I left Tübingen with a heavy heart today. Kauffmann and his son-in-law,

Dr. Schmid, accompanied me on foot to Reutlingen (a 2½-hour walk), where we spent a stimulating hour of conversation over Bavarian beer in the "Schwarzen Bären." Then we parted, not without the thought of seeing each other again soon.—

This morning all we did was make music, and this time the Spanish and the Keller songs had their turn. Kauffmann and his enthusiastic son-in-law showed an understanding of these newest things of mine; this astonished and delighted me all over again.

The Keller ones, primarily the "Köhlerweib," were cheered outright. Both were also beside themselves over the Spanish ones. The devoted enthusiasm of these dear people could give me delusions of grandeur and so it was high time we parted.

At breakfast K[auffmann] read me the letters Mörike wrote to his father. Good heavens, what letters!!! They are almost better than his poems, such splendid things are revealed in them. We were all moved to tears. On our walk to the old castle, Kauffmann pointed out the castle wine cellar to me, which inspired Mörike's splendid poem:

In's alten Schlosswirth's Garten	In the castle keeper's garden
. . .	. . .
Kein Kegel fällt, kein' Karten,	No skittle falls, no cards,
Wächst aber schön lang Gras.	The grass has grown quite tall.

Today, on the way to Reutlingen, Kauffmann gave me amazing information about Mörike's relationship to Peregrina. According to him, her name was really Marie Mayer and she was found unconscious on the road to Ludwigsburg by a wagon driver. Revived and brought to Ludwigsburg by the driver, where she refused to give any information concerning her past and her homeland, she caused a big stir because of her fabulous beauty and especially her fascinating eyes. Mörike fell hopelessly in love with her. He was a student at that time in Tübingen. They wrote each other ardent love letters, since this object of his affections was well-educated and showed a particu-

lar understanding of Jean Paul. They were considered engaged
to be married.—One day M.M. disappeared from Ludwigsburg
without a trace. No one learned of her whereabouts for weeks.
Mörike was desperate. Then someone brought news from Carlsruhe that a certain M.M. was being held in jail for begging without a license and for flagrant indecency. This news came to
Kauffmann's parents, who had given the said M.M. a place to
stay in their home for a long time. Mörike was notified. He was
beside himself.—Then suddenly his lost love appeared early
one morning, encamped on the steps of the house where Mörike
was living. He turned her away, although he still loved her.
Thus, "an errant spirit came into the moonlit garden of a once
holy love" [Peregrina No. 3]. How clear his poems are becoming
to me now. Kauffmann then showed me the house Mörike lived
in at the time, and so I saw the steps on which Peregrina encountered the unfortunate poet for the last time.

Isn't that fascinating? Also, Mörike is said to have used the
mad Hölderlin, who lived and died in Tübingen, as model for
the Feuerreiter. But how much more I'll have to tell you in
person.

For today, since it's gotten very late, a good, good night.
Tomorrow I'm traveling to Heidelberg and hope to be in Mannheim on the 18th. You'll learn immediately of my address from
there. Your telegram deeply pleased and delighted me. May you
soon, by a letter, delight your gratefully devoted

Hugo Wolf

Many greetings to Heinrich and the children.
Finally it's become quiet enough at 1:30 a.m. to risk trying to
get to sleep.
Good night!
Oct. 16. Good morning! This morning it's raining horrendously.
I'm leaving immediately.

31

To Vienna

Heidelberg. Oct. 16, 1890

Most honored gracious lady!

I'm now in Heidelberg, that "exquisite, quaint city," and
still so filled with impressions that it's impossible to describe

them to you in an orderly way. My first move, after going to the hotel, was to visit Domaszewski, who received me kindly and cordially and immediately prevailed upon me to give up the hotel room I had not yet moved into and to rent a vacant room in his building. Now we live next door to each other and I have a view of a wonderful old garden with magnificent terraces and old stone steps, immediately adjacent to the blooming ruins of the splendid Heidelberg castle.

My room is as quiet as a tomb. Nothing stirs; you could hear a pin drop. The furnishings are all antique except for the bed, which, thank God, in every way shows a tendency toward the modern. It even has a horsehair pillow. I'm filled with joy to have finally found a room that is to my liking. The stillness delights me and the lullaby that the rustling and bustling wind [*Sause- und Brausewind*] in the arbor sings to me makes my stay here even homier. Of course, for tomorrow I would wish myself better company than clouds and wind, since we intend to make an outing to the Königsstuhl. I've already taken a tour of the castle today, and Domaszewski most graciously played the cicerone. I'm enclosing an ivy leaf, which I took from the "ivy wall" [*Epheuwand*] in the castle courtyard. Oh, I'm as if in a dream "from the old fairy tales a white hand beckons" [*aus alten Märchen winkt es hervor mit weisser Hand*]—if you were only here! If only you could enjoy all of it with me. It's too much all at once.

– – – – – – – – – –

In Stuttgart nothing ever actually got played, for a number of reasons that I'll tell you about in person. Tonight I was supposed to perform my things at a private party arranged by Förstler, except it was an impossibility with pharyngitis, which has now turned into a terrible head cold. So I had to cancel and, in order not to waste time in Stuttgart, went immediately to Heidelberg, where I can finally snore away with complete peace of mind. Sunday is "Tristan" in Mannheim. Grohe has been advised of my arrival. Should you really want to give me the pleasure of a few lines, address me at Karlstrasse c/o Dr. Alfred v. Domaszewski. More tomorrow. Domaszewski is already waiting impatiently for me and I, too, am getting a bit hungry. And so good night. To all, all sincerest greetings as always your grateful

Hugo Wolf.

N.B. Shortly before my departure from Stuttgart, Göschen

(publisher's bookstore) sent me a volume of Mörike poems with the inscription: To the tone poet in respect and admiration,

the publisher.

This piece of mail was all the more surprising because I hadn't even been in Göschen's bookshop. Some nice fellows in Stuttgart too, aren't there?

O my head cold!

my head cold!

Oct.17 morning.

Since I forgot to mail this letter yesterday, I'll take the opportunity to provide it with your Vienna address; the bad weather—today it's raining and storming—will also hasten your departure from Rinnbach. If this bad weather situation continues, I won't go to Cologne and will then arrive in Vienna a few days earlier.

Please address: *Mannheim, poste restante* [general delivery].

My head cold still rages.

32

To Vienna

Mannheim, Oct. 19, 1890

Honored gracious lady!

I have now met Weingartner and Grohe face to face and like them immensely. Weingartner is nothing short of an ideally handsome person and Grohe a figure of almost superhuman height. I'm being put up at the latter's, in fact as well as one could ever imagine. Yesterday we stayed up until 1 a.m., during which I bore the responsibility for the musical entertainment. Both were full of admiration for my Spanish and Keller songs; Weingartner was particularly taken with the sacred "Die ihr schwebet etc.," which I had to play over and over again. Unfortunately, Weingartner also composes and I will have the dubious pleasure of hearing his newest opera, "Genesius," played today at Grohe's. I'm quite dismayed about this, because from what I've seen here of Weingartner's talent for composing, I don't think much of it. How hard it will be for me to be hypocritical and feign enthusiasm when my duty should be to be honest and candid. However, "truth is a dog, which must [crawl] into a hole" and then

—*Kakarakamuschin* [untranslatable onomatopoeia]!—

The weather here is terrible. Constant rain. I haven't even seen the Rhine yet, which is really a scandal. But who would dare to go out in such foul weather and with the sniffles? Tomorrow morning I'm going to Schott (an hour's trip to Mainz), returning by evening to Mannheim again, where I'll be staying for a few more days.—Please write me c/o *poste restante* in Mannheim.—

My Christnacht cannot be performed here, even though Weingartner admires it, for reasons with which I must concur. On the other hand, Prometheus is still on. I'll end up having to go to Cologne after all, to saddle Wüllner with my Christnacht. Aggravating enough.—

I must hurry, since I have to pay visits with Grohe. Farewell and please give my best greetings to Heinrich and the children. Greetings also to Schalk when you see him. Always your gratefully respectful

Hugo Wolf.

Tannhäuser will be performed today instead of Tristan.

33

To Vienna

Mannheim, Oct. 22 [correctly 21], 1890

Most honored gracious lady!

Since I have just a quarter of an hour remaining before the iron horse abducts me to Mainz, I'll shorten my time in the train station in this pleasant way. First of all, heartfelt thanks for your cordial lines, which I read more than once, since they were barely decipherable and at this moment still contain several illegible words to me.

A letter also came from Schey, according to which I have good prospects for getting the position in Graz.

Yesterday we were all together again. Weingartner played his opera Genesius. A quite fiendishly barren and noisy thing, devoid of inner strength and warmth, all just theatrical fluff put together only for effect. I was very cautious, however, about expressing this aloud, though I was probably pretty bad at pretending. But "can a novice be perfect"? It's the most beautiful, fine weather today. The Rhine trip will be delightful.—Oh my, the train is pulling out right now.

Many, many greetings in all haste from your grateful

Hugo Wolf.

34

To Vienna

Mainz, Oct. 22, 1890

Honored gracious lady!

Now I'm finally in Mainz, the final destination of my trip, as I prefer to believe, because traveling to Cologne (10 hours by steamer) is not particularly inviting. Also the weather, while beautiful to be sure, is still very cold and I don't want to get chilled again, as I'm still suffering from my head cold anyway. I'm staying at the Stadt Coblenz Hotel. The Rhine is flowing in front of me and there appear to be something like mountains in the background; I think they're the Vosges. The city is fairly large and imposing, but not at all interesting. I wish I were already gone. I can't see Schott for another half hour, because he is unavailable to everyone from 12:00 to 3:00. I'll let you know immediately about my visit with Schott. My Mannheim friends made me promise to be in Mannheim again on Sunday or even on Saturday. It's a shame that Grohe's grandmother had to die just now, which means that I can no longer stay at his place; living in a hotel is very expensive. Fortunately I've been invited to Schuster the concertmaster's at noon and in the evenings, so I can at least dine in pleasant company. Schuster is one of the most entertaining, droll, and charming fellows on God's earth. We are also the best of friends. His wife, a beauty *non plus ultra*, contributes in no small way to the enhancement of our merry mealtime group. You would surely find these people delightful. Only here have I gotten to know what true congeniality [*Gemütlichkeit*] is. If it weren't for several things in Vienna holding me back, I would immediately go to Mannheim forever.

Christnacht is going to happen in January *after all*, performed along with Bruckner's Eighth Symphony and Richard Strauss' symphonic tone poem "Don Juan." Yesterday I went through Prometheus with Livermann. He is completely enthralled with the piece and swears there is nothing better than my Prometheus. But then I, too, am very satisfied with his performance. I'm to convey many greetings to Jäger from a tenor, Mittelhauser, who works in Mainz and stayed with Jäger in America. Now I have to go to Schott.

– – – – – – – – –

1 a.m.

Hurrah! Hurrah! Hurrah!!!

Schott and I are now in agreement. He received me like an old friend, immediately invited me to supper, just the two of us, and the champagne flowed. I played him a lot of things, and he entered in enthusiastically, although he is fairly conservative on some points. Today we argued into the night over the Keller songs—amicably naturally—without a resolution. He is *against* the poems. But I have his wife on my side, a very nice little woman. Dr. Strecker (Schott's actual name) is a young and exquisitely educated man with the mostmostmostmost ingratiating manners. I have a standing invitation to dine there, and his board is a princely one. Above all, he now wants to publish Christnacht. I have the impression that he will comply with all my demands. A truly marvelous fellow through and through. Can't stand Brahms either. In short, a terrific fellow!

Most of the Spanish songs are already printed, and very splendidly indeed. I have them in my possession to proofread. Good night, for now.

Good morning.

It's already close to 10:00, so I ought to be wishing you good day. Schott expects me to be in Biberach on the Rhine this morning, where I had intended to go. However, I overslept the steamboat['s departure], and since the cold weather has already taken on a wintry character, I'll not have missed much by it. It's also ice-cold in my room; the sky, though, is completely cloudless.—

Please, write to me in detail c/o the Mannheim *poste restante* how you and your family are faring and what else is going on in Vienna. I'll be attending a performance of Walküre in Mannheim on Sunday and shall begin my return trip Monday. Oh, I'm already overjoyed at being able to be in Vienna again, despite how much I like it here too.

And now many sincere greetings to Heinrich as well and the children.

Entirely yours
Hugo Wolf.

35

To Vienna
Mainz, Oct. 22, 1890

Worthiest, honored gracious lady!

It's 9:00 in the evening and I'm sitting in front of the lighted stove in my small but very cozy, comfortable little room and I want to chat with you now and tell you what you like to hear. Above all, I must share my successes, because if anyone can take heartfelt pleasure in them, it is most surely you. Today I had a big success at Schott's with my Christnacht. He was very excited about this piece and only wants to wait for the performance in Mannheim before starting negotiations on it with me. Weingartner, too, said the most marvelous things to me about my Christnacht. I'm glad that Heinrich also liked it, since all the wise "doubting Thomases" thought otherwise. Meanwhile, at least I have a conductor and a publisher who will stand up for my work and that's really worth something too.

Dr. Strecker (Schott) is showing me attentive kindness that truly defies every description. This afternoon he directed me through the workrooms of his establishment. My, what a lot to see! I became acquainted with all kinds of things about which I'd never had the faintest idea. For the first time, I saw the zinc plates on which the notes will be engraved and the stone that absorbs the impression from the zinc plate. What a tedious job, murderous on the eyes! And yet how nimbly these people handle everything, how one cog meshes with the next, how each thing has its place, everything runs like clockwork. There is no noticeable difference between man and machine. Here strong determination appears to govern everything, wherein each stands at his post, each is important, and yet no one excels, but only forms a link in the powerful chain. Such a collective accomplishment is truly impressive. This unceasing hustle and bustle made me quite dizzy, and I only began to catch my breath when I got out into the fresh air again. I wouldn't be the supervisor of such an establishment for all the money in the world; it would make me utterly miserable.—

After I had somewhat recovered over a Munich beer, we went to the concert, which offered as its first number a symphony by a certain Bischoff. A pathetic hackwork, completely stereotypical, without flair or spirit, without the least bit of originality. The audience also responded very coolly to the work and when the composer (an old pedant) appeared at the end of the last movement, there was only a smattering of applause; nor had they forgotten a laurel wreath. But this hocus-pocus was over quickly enough. I listened to only two more numbers: Mendelssohn's Violin Concerto, very beautifully played by Ysaÿe (or something like that), and a highly interesting piece by Borodin, "In the Steppes of Central Asia" for orchestra. Incidentally this piece fell flat—undeservedly. Today Dr. Strecker also showed me, among other rarities, the complete Meistersinger book in the original handwriting, in which Walter's verses to the Preislied are completely different from those we know; likewise, those of Beckmesser's bungling differ from those familiar to us. I've copied them out as a curiosity. Oddly enough the spelling error, with which I believed only myself to be infected, happened with Wagner too: he wrote Augen*lie*der [instead of Augen*li*der]. Strecker showed me, in addition, the first sketch of the Meistersinger from the '50's. In this there is talk of a Konrad [instead of Walther] von Stolzing and — *Veit Hanslick*, city scribe. Instead of Bogner [Pogner] it was Boglar, etc., etc. And so good-night. Humperdinck is coming tomorrow from Frankfurt to hear my things. The day after tomorrow I go to Cologne, then back through Mainz to Mannheim, where I hope to find a letter from you.

Many, many greetings, Heinrich and the children included. Always and everywhere

Your grateful
Hugo Wolf.

36

To Vienna [picture postcard]
Cologne, Oct. 24, 1890

Honored gracious lady!

I've become so ill that I'm not going back to Mannheim, but am traveling tomorrow to Frankfurt, where I might spend two days together with Humperdinck. I'm already longing so horribly for Vienna, although I've had a kind and warm reception everywhere. Tuesday or Wednesday at the latest I hope to set foot on home soil again. The weather here is horrible.

Many, many greetings, your
Hugo Wolf.

37

To Vienna
Cologne, Oct. 24, 1890

Dear, gracious lady!

I've arrived at my hotel, Cologne's best, late at night from Dr. Wette's, a friend of Humperdinck's to whom the latter recommended me. If only I had always stayed at the best hotels. Hotel Disch is really fabulous. I live like a prince, and for the price of 3.5 M.—So, Dr. Wette was already acquainted with my Mörike songs and was absolutely delighted to get to know me. I played my songs at his place late into the night, and the reciter Strakosch, who was also there, was enthusiastic too, beyond all measure, about my things. Strakosch knows Brahms, Hanslick, and Speidel very well, particularly the last two: he's going to put in a good word for me to both of them.

Dr. Wette is the most delightful, charming person, no less so his brother-in-law Humperdinck, who traveled to Mainz solely on my account and whose favorites among my things are *Sänger* and Mignon [Goethe songs]. Bravo!

Neitzel is going to write an article in the Cologne [newspaper] in two weeks. Tomorrow Neitzel will be worked over again. Wüllner was very reticent. He couldn't make any commitment for the present. I'll look up Le Simple tomorrow. Good night for now.

All is quiet; finally I shall sleep well.

Morning

Slept exceptionally well. Only too long. Have to hurry. Haven't seen the cathedral yet, besides looking up Lesimple, Neitzel, etc. Must hurry!

Many, many greetings
Wolf

38   To Vienna [picture postcard]

[Rüdesheim], National Monument, the 25 of Oct. 1890

Honored gracious lady!

I want to shout here: "Hail to thee, Germany, from the
bottom of my heart!" Dr. Wette, whom I have to thank for the
view of this splendid area, is my traveling companion. Even
though the weather is rather dreary and cool, I am satisfied beyond all measure with all this beauty. The Rhine wine plays its
part in creating utmost pleasure. Many, many greetings.
Wednesday, God willing, we meet again.

Always your grateful
Hugo Wolf.

39   To Vienna

Mainz, Oct. 26, 1890

Most honored gracious lady!

After a dreadful trip back from Rüdesheim to Mainz I'm
literally drawing a deep breath at the thought of finding myself
on the return trip at last. Imagine: several drunken fellows be-
longing to the blue-collar class entered my second-class compartment in Rüdesheim and started to snore right away in the most
barbaric intervals. Unfortunately, this racket was interrupted
shortly afterward by a far worse one, accompanied by a nauseat-
ing wine odor spreading through the compartment. The fellows
lay there on the floor and vomited in the most scandalous manner. As I thrust my head out the window, in spite of the pouring
rain, I saw heads hanging out low in the adjoining compartments
on either side throwing up great loads. I think the whole train
was drunk except for me and the locomotive. And they call it
Rhine revelry here! Some revelry!

My ride from Cologne to Rüdesheim, on the other hand,
was very pleasant. Dr. Wette, Humperdinck's brother-in-law,
made every effort to acquaint me with the beauties of the Rhine
region, and particularly with the romantic banks of this river.
Among other good qualities such as, for example, that he is full

of enthusiasm for my songs—(hear, hear!), I also discovered in him a genuine and true poet whose lyric verse will someday rouse attention. We quickly formed a friendship that I hope will bear good fruit. Wasn't it nice of him to accompany me from Cologne to Rüdesheim and leave his patients stranded in order to—tolerate, and it was only for this reason—my companionship longer? Don't you like him!?

Dear God, that I can go to Frankfurt as early as tomorrow makes me very happy. I hope that by Wednesday I'll be in Vienna, although it appears not out of the question that my arrival will be delayed until Thursday.

Tomorrow I make my farewell visit to Schott. Today I received a second installment of proofs. Letters that might have been sent to me in Mannheim will be forwarded to me at the Brüsseler-Hof [hotel] in Frankfurt. And now good night; it's already late and it's also cold ['s *wird schon spät u. 's ist auch kalt: Liederkreis*, No. 3 (Eichendorff), by Schumann]. Good night.

Many greetings to Heinrich and the children. As always your grateful

Hugo Wolf.

40

To Vienna

Döbling, Nov. 13, 1890

Honored gracious lady!

Today during the noon and afternoon hours I had the good idea of letting two "Italian" songs occur to me: "Wer rief dich denn?" and "Der Mond hat eine schwere Klag' erhoben." If it continues like this, maybe by Saturday I can oblige with half a dozen. The solitude and lack of human company is rejuvenating me. I'm full of joy and in exceptionally good spirits.

If you wish to pay me the honor of a visit on Saturday, don't forget to bring my coffee grinder. The other thing that I could use has slipped my mind for the moment. Surely you'll remember it.

Until soon.

Hurriedly, your
Hugo Wolf

41

To Vienna

Ober-Döbling, Nov. 21, 1890

Honored gracious lady, would you be so kind as to send "An das Vaterland," the hymn that is in your possession, to Herr Lacom and request that he forward it to Prof. W. Förstler, conductor of the Stuttgart Liederkranz. Förstler has just let me know that he is willing to perform the piece this season. I'm at a standstill again with the music for Fest auf Solhaug. I'm beginning to despair over it. If only everything, everything were nearing an end. I'm yearning intensely for a better existence, even if it's only in hell. It can't be any worse for a person than on earth. Farewell.

Hugo Wolf.

42

To Vienna [postcard]

[Döbling], February 6, 1891

Received 12 copies of the "Keller" songs from Schott. *Everything corrected*. My collected songs are advertised on the back pages. Looks quite impressive. I'm extremely pleased. Many greetings. Wölfing.

Your telegram didn't arrive until 8:00 in the evening.

43

To Vienna

Mannheim, April 8, 1891

Most honored gracious lady!

Arrived in Mannheim quite exhausted from lack of sleep. Am staying at the Pfälzerhof; a tiny little room—cold and quite cheerless. Saw a lot of snow on the trip. Conversed pleasantly with my two other fellow travelers until Munich. There two Americans got on board, one of whom whistled the Siciliana from *Cavalleria Rusticana* incessantly through his teeth and drove me crazy with his off-key whistling.—Have just undertaken a thorough washing-up, brushing, and ironing and will now go to see Weingartner. Naturally, a sore throat, which unfortunately is growing worse, began on the trip; the left tonsil completely inflamed, despite my not smoking at all. Am very out of sorts over this, will try treating it with lozenges; maybe it'll get better. Going now to Weingartner. More tomorrow.

Many many greetings!
Hugo Wolf.

44   To Vienna
〰〰   Mannheim, April 10, 1891

Well, I managed to get through yesterday! Christnacht has already made me richer by two laurel wreaths. But that's all, or wait, so I don't lie—I'm also richer by one experience, which counts for something too. Yes, the finest April weather prevailed in the orchestra. Occasionally the sun shone, then a threatening cloud appeared, then a few rain showers thoroughly capable of annoying, suddenly a ray of streaming sun again, and again shadow upon shadow, alternating without pause, keeping me constantly between fear and hope. Oh, it was absolutely agonizing. After the initial impression at the dress rehearsal I decided not even to wait for the evening and to depart immediately. I was so unhappy. The instruments all seemed to have become monsters and ghouls wanting to devour me. I felt like Richard III, threatened by the ghosts of the murdered. Trombones and double basses literally bared their teeth at me while the oboes, flutes, and clarinets howled and squawked away, creating a real horror. I wanted to scream for help. Weingartner was very upset about it because he assured me the empty hall was solely responsible for all this imagined abomination. He tried to tell me that in the evening the whole thing would take on a more human form. As I said, I was completely shattered. Humperdinck, who was sitting next to me, kept talking to me like a priest trying to console me and in the kindest way attempting to revive my sunken courage. I spent the time until evening in real fear of death. Finally, the dreaded moment drew near. Dr. Strecker and Humperdinck took me between them and I must have looked like a man condemned. Because of my agitation I barely heard Beethoven's Second Symphony, which opened the concert. Finally, Christnacht. The introduction, which is certainly the best-orchestrated, sounded very beautiful. The woodwinds had again become themselves, and the answering horn sounded so tender and pleasant that I actually felt the cramp in me loosening. The buildup to the entrance of the full orchestra with the main motives sounded absolutely beautiful. It was like the sunrise. Weingartner threw me a beaming glance at that point. The entrance of the angel at the annunciation was also splendid and the sound of the trumpets and trombones created a truly solemn mood. So for a short stretch everything went along fairly well. But during the course of the narration of the angel's annunciation I noticed that I had miscalculated the tonal effect or that perhaps the orchestra was unequal to its task. Only a performance by our Vienna Orchestra could tell me this for sure. I must leave this unresolved for the time being. But I feel quite certain that I did not economize enough with the use of the violins in the highest register, justifying the reproach that it seems overladen and that in this way I myself have contributed to limiting the work's success. Nevertheless, its success was not negligible, thanks to the truly magnificent-sounding entrance "Preis dem Geborenen [Glory to the Newborn]," which made up for some of the earlier faults. Unfortunately, there were places later on where I must have deceived myself about the effect, so that the "Preis dem Geborenen" theme had to jump in helpfully again at the conclusion to garner at least the barest honors for my poor composer's head. Forcibly dragged to the podium by Grohe and Weingartner and threatened with two laurel wreaths, I thanked the audience for their kind response by bowing three times. In the evening we got together at Hotel Metropole, where, thank God, there were no official speeches and replies. We were pleasantly and cheerfully regaled with amusing anecdotes until about 2 a.m., particularly by Kapellmeister Langer and friend Schuster. Strecker came only to the performance, so unfortunately I couldn't talk with him about the publication of Christnacht. I don't know, therefore, if he'll buy it from me. Maybe I'll visit him in Mainz though, which he emphatically urged me to do. He also doesn't seem to want to get to know the Fest auf Solhaug, despite Humperdinck's urging him to do so. Today I'm going to play my latest opus for Weingartner. Tomorrow I'm traveling to Grohe in Philippsburg, near Carlsruhe, where I'll spend several days. Please write to me there.

Since Weingartner will knock at any moment, I'll bring this scribbling to a close and send you very best greetings as your most devoted

Hugo Wolf.

Enclosed a literary prelude, written by Grohe.

45

To Vienna

[Philippsburg, April 12, 1891]

Honored gracious lady!

Yesterday afternoon I arrived in Philippsburg and was met at the station by Grohe. Unfortunately, his wife is indisposed, so I still haven't seen her, although 24 hours have already elapsed since I've been here. Your dear letter was given to me at breakfast today; it sweetened breakfast for me in a very real sense, as the coffee was beneath contempt. The surroundings here are rather boring and the weather very cool. How glad I am to have my winter coat!—I hope you received my second letter and the various reviews of Christnacht. I'm only waiting for word from Förstler, in order to go as soon as possible to Tübingen and then, via Lake Constance, to Vienna. Grohe is a very obliging, attentive host, who entertains me constantly, for which I'm not always grateful, by the way. Last evening I read a little book by Karl Stieler, "Winter-idyll." I thought of you often and imagined what you would particularly like about it. Do get it for yourself. You should have Peter Cornelius' poems, too. They are really poetic effusions and supported by the most elegant feeling for form; inspired insights.—

Right now I'm reading a notice by Humperdinck in the Frankfurter-Zeitung [newspaper]. I'm enclosing it with this request: instruct friend Larisch (living in the Johanneshof) to have this printed in the Fremdenblatt [newspaper] and Deutsche Zeitung. I'll wire at the same time as I mail this letter at the post office so that you have news of me soon. Please write me a few more lines here. Greetings to all, I am, as always, your very devoted

Hugo Wolf.

Another letter will come tomorrow.

46

To Vienna
Philippsburg, April 13, 1891

Honored gracious lady!

My departure for Vienna may be delayed a week, as the prospect has come up for me to arrange a Liederabend in Mannheim. Grohe has recommended to me an excellent, so he says, lieder singer (tenor) from Berlin, who is to be engaged to sing my songs at the expense of the Mannheim Wagner Society. A female singer (light, high soprano) has also already been obtained for this. Should no cancellation from Berlin be forthcoming, the concert will take place next Sunday. If the project falls through, I'll travel to Tübingen the day after tomorrow in order to spend two days at the Kauffmanns'. There is still no news from Stuttgart.

I have now finally met Frau Grohe. A shockingly ugly woman with intelligent eyes. She talks very little, behaves very awkwardly and is, generally speaking, somewhat brusque in her manner, but she is a great admirer of my muse and displays a considerable understanding of it. She is very enthusiastic about Christnacht, even though she was present only at the dress rehearsal.

The area here is downright dismal, and added to that, the weather is horribly raw; I'm freezing like a yellow butterfly in April [*Citronenfalter im April*]. Grohe is delighted with my Fest auf Solhaug; he says the Mannheimers shouldn't pass it up. The divining talent of Frau Grohe was evidenced by the fact that the first soup set before me was Ulm barley and the second course was roast mutton that brought me painfully in mind of our good Josepha's glorious art. Took a walk yesterday along the old Rhine; reminded me vividly of the Wagthale (Hungary) region. Tomorrow we are going *by skiff* downstream to Speyer, where the German emperors are buried. It's only an hour's trip. When the wind's right we've heard the famous bells of Speyer all the way over here in Philippsburg.

Please, dear gracious lady, write me sometime whether you are receiving all my letters. Address: Philippsburg c/o Dr. Grohe. Should I leave the day after tomorrow, letters will be forwarded. Is everyone there well? What are the dear children up to?

Greetings also to Öhn and Schalk.

As always your
Hugo Wolf.

47

To Vienna
Philippsburg, April 14, 1891

Honored gracious lady!

I will probably stay in Philippsburg until Monday or Tuesday, as Mottl and Chelius may come from Karlsruhe on Sunday. We're not counting for certain on Mottl's appearance, since he apparently still hasn't completely gotten over a grudge he's been nursing against me for some time, although Jäger (so I've been told) has tried to bring him around to a more favorable opinion of me. In any case, I won't seek him out. If he comes, it's fine with me; if not, that's all right with me too. On the other hand, a renewed acquaintance with Chelius, whose brother in Berlin is *persona gratissima* with the emperor, could be of great advantage, which is why I'm making the sacrifice of waiting around for another week in Philippsburg. The time is passing here in a pleasant do-nothing fashion; a little music-making here, a little critiquing there, taking walks, dining, supping, and thus we cheat the Lord God of his time in the most respectable of endeavors.—Once again: get yourself the poems of Peter Cornelius. I can't read enough of them. He is one of the truest poets the Germans have—and fail to recognize. His music, however, of which Grohe has a fairly good selection, I like considerably less; everything is intention, but nothing is realized. Great desire, but little ability. I wish I'd been given one hundredth of Cornelius' poetic gift, and operas would come into being out of nowhere, one after the other. Nothing more beautiful than poet and musician; that alone is the consummate human being and artist.

The boat excursion on the Rhine has been postponed until tomorrow because of cloudy weather. I'm looking forward to it.

Hermann Götz (the composer of "Widerspenstigen") has also "written and composed" an opera. Yesterday I played through this concoction, "Francesca da Rimini," whereupon I felt a great sense of relief. I think I certainly received indulgence beginning from that moment for the next 20 years of my sinful life. This lack of talent is indescribable.—Compared to this, "Widerspenstige" is admittedly an inspired work.

I am obliged to play my songs over and over again. Grohe and wife are absolutely enthralled. And now *do write* to me, too, sometimes.

Telegraphed messages, like today's, are just too skimpy. With best greetings to all, as always your

Hugo Wolf.

48

To Vienna

Philippsburg, April 1, 1891

Honored gracious lady!

Many thanks for the letter delivered to me today. Unfortunately, I totally forgot to report about the rapid progress of my sore throat. It was already gone by the day after my arrival in Mannheim, thanks to my vigorous use of lozenges. *Please* write me first of all somewhat *more clearly* and always acknowledge the receipt of my letters. Also I still don't know whether you received the various reviews from the Mannheim papers. I sent them to you the day after the performance. As one Mannheim paper writes, the Fest auf Solhaug will soon end up being performed in the castle. Please enlighten me about this in detail. Today is the first fine day here in Philippsburg. Unfortunately, nothing will come of the Rhine trip, as the boat is not available. I'm very put out about it.—

Afternoon.

The Rhine trip has been postponed until Saturday.—I've just received your second dear letter. Two letters from you in *one* day—what an event!!! My very best thanks for them. I'm enclosing a letter from Humperdinck. Tomorrow I'm going to see Schott in Mainz, but will be back in Philippsburg by evening. I'm enclosing the reviews by Humperdinck, since you gave the others to Larisch. Please God that Schott will bite.— The date of the performance of my hymn [*Dem Vaterland*] in Stuttgart vacillates between the 24th and 29th. I'm planning to be in attendance if the performance takes place on the 24th, since I have to stay in Philippsburg until the 20th to make the acquaintance of Chelius, who can be of great use to me. Otherwise, I will hasten my departure.

There is still no news from Berlin. Presumably the singer is unavailable, in which case the projected concert will not take place. *Don't forget to mention whether you received the Mannheim reviews.* Rauchberg sent me Boller's recommendation letter to Schön in Worms. But what should I do with Schön? What can he do for me? I really can't borrow money from him and I won't get fatter from his praise. It's quite a silly story.—I'd have a lot more to tell you, but you alone are to blame when you get dry notes from me. I'll probably linger until Tuesday in Philippsburg. Please still write to me here. Best greetings to all, as always your

Hugo Wolf.

49

To Vienna

Philippsburg, April 17, 1891

Most honored gracious lady!

The cancellation of the prospective singer from Berlin has now arrived. The concert, therefore, will not take place. I also gave up the trip to Mainz because of such bad train connections from here. Since I'll probably leave here Tuesday, I'll pay a visit to Schott on the way to Stuttgart, and as I have to stay overnight in Stuttgart anyway, in order to attend one rehearsal, I'll do everything at the same time. If the performance of the hymn [*Dem Vaterland*] is to take place on the 24th, which is Friday, I won't leave here until Wednesday. But if the performance is postponed to the 29th, I won't wait around for it, but will leave here as early as Monday. I'll stay two days at the most in Tübingen, one day in Constance. Unfortunately, I can probably not make it to Vienna in less than a week. Today Grohe is gone for the whole day on business. So I'm all alone here with his seductive better half. We've just picked our way on the piano through Richard Strauss' symphonic poem "Don Juan" after Lenau. This dreary sterility of invention and these affected harmonic spasms defy every description. It's the sort of thing considered to be original and daring here in Germany, however. But I'd rather be an untalented poltroon than a "revolutionary" like that.

The weather continues to be cold and unpleasant, stormy and rainy besides. But thank God I'm vigorous and healthy. The noonday meal today was excellent. Exceptionally good sago (tapioca) soup and excellent filets. Frau Grohe is a very attentive housewife as well, even though I can't always adjust entirely to her way of doing things. The *two* Bechstein grand pianos, which are absolutely unique, give me great pleasure. I've never heard my songs [sound] so beautiful as on these instruments. No matter how pleasant it is here, my thoughts still drift off into the distance to a subject that I cannot mention to you, but that possesses my entire being. And now adieu! Greetings to all, also Schalk and Öhn. Always your

Hugo Wolf.

50

To Vienna

Philippsburg, April 18, 1891

Honored gracious lady!

I must implore you to write *more clearly*, as I cannot decipher your letters any more, even with Grohe's help. For example, what does this passage about Mottl say? I can't figure out from this whether Mottl likes or doesn't like my things. Even Grohe, who can otherwise make out every chicken-scratching, was at his wit's end when I requested his assistance. So write me once more what opinion Mottl has of my things.

The weather continues to be of the vilest order, and since the wind incessantly persists, we've had to postpone our boat excursion from one day to the next.

Yesterday we went by coach on an outing into the area

around Philippsburg. The surroundings, as I've already mentioned, are fairly monotonous and remind me of the Hungarian plains. We returned to Philippsburg half-frozen. Yesterday a magnificent sunset was granted us. But that's also all that Philippsburg can offer in the way of nature's dramas. Tomorrow Boné and Chelius are coming from Carlsruhe for a visit. Both are intimate friends of Mottl. Am very eager to find out whether the two can be won over to my things. Please answer in *clear handwriting* soon.

Always yours,
Hugo Wolf.

51

To Vienna
Philippsburg, April 22, 1891

Honored gracious lady!

Upon my arrival in Philippsburg (8:00 in the evening) I found a message from Förstler that said that the performance of the hymn [*Dem Vaterland*] will take place on Saturday the 25th of the m[onth]. So I'll leave Philippsburg on the 25th and hope to arrive in Vienna during the last days of the month of April. My journey to Frankfurt, Mainz, and Mannheim has made me 20 marks poorer rather than a thousand marks richer. Schott [Strecker] wants to print Christnacht under the same conditions as the songs, but he won't pay and that's what is most important to me now. He was very cordial, very entertainingly witty and talkative, also went with me to the train and broke open a bottle of Rhine wine, which we emptied together to my good health; in short, he was as nice as a man can be who doesn't, of course, have to worry about money. But from that point on, unfortunately, Strecker's niceness stops completely, and he appears insufferable and actually hateful, totally loathsome and insane. He also promised to come to Stuttgart to the performance. Am eager to see if he keeps his word. In spite of Humperdinck, at whose place I spent the night, having accompanied me to Mainz the other day to stand by me in my misery, or as he says: "with the two of us I can torment you better"—it still didn't help. Strecker slithered around like an eel; he was everywhere and nowhere to grab hold of, and so the sly fox slipped out of the sling, the scum. The sneaky, slick, slippery sheen personified.—

The d[evil] take him. I've also had unpleasant experiences with Frank, Weingartner's successor in the Choirmaster School at Mannheim. The fellow appears to imagine himself God knows who, as he hardly acknowledges me on the street. Such a worm! Tomorrow I'm going to Carlsruhe to Mottl, who's expecting me. This pleases me.—

April 22. Morning.

The weather has changed markedly. Sunshine everywhere and warm air. Praise God. Saturday I'll be in Stuttgart, Hotel Royal, hope to find Kauffmann there, with whom I shall then go to Tübingen for one or two days. Write to me here until Saturday, then Stuttgart and then Tübingen. Letters will be held. With very best greetings to you and all

Your very devoted
Hugo Wolf.

Förstler just wired me that the hymn cannot be performed until May 10.

I am furious.—10:00 a.m.

[pencil P.S.] Greetings from Carlsruhe, where I've just arrived.

52

To Vienna
Carlsruhe, April 22, 1891

Honored gracious lady!

I finally met Mottl at the tavern and was welcomed by him in the most cordial manner. I'm writing these lines to you in Mottl's apartment; during the entire time he was taking a nap after returning from a trip to Munich I held in my hands—just think—the original score of [Wagner's] Rienzi and devoured the cherished handwriting with astonished eyes. The score encompasses four volumes, and the notes are so precise and clean that you think you have an engraving in front of you. I'm staying in Carlsruhe today because I've been invited for the evening by the leading female singer of Carlsruhe, who will also sing a few things of mine.

Tomorrow I'm going to Philippsburg, returning here again

the day after tomorrow to attend the performance of Götterdämmerung on Sunday. Mottl expressed himself very enthusiastically about many of my songs and cannot understand at all how
I can consider him an antagonist. Naturally I'm very glad that
the situation is in such good order.—With regard to Stuttgart,
it really seems that nothing can be done. Nor will there be a
performance on May 10th, I'm afraid. The devil take these
thick-headed Swabians.—

Unfortunately, I must close as we're on our way to a party.
Please write to Philippsburg

Your very devoted
Hugo Wolf.

53

To Rinnbach [letter-card]
Unterach, May 5, 1891

Honored gracious lady!

I'm writing in great haste from the post office to say that I
reached the coach just in time and rode all alone to Weissenbach. It was absolutely splendid. I walked to the post office and
am already looking forward to coming home. Please look around
a bit; there might be a nest someplace where I could be comfortable. I'll take the flat in Roith in any case, if nothing better turns
up. And now sincerest and best greetings to you and all

from your faithfully devoted
Hugo Wolf.

54

To Rinnbach
[Unterach, June 6, 1891]

Honored gracious lady!

Upon arrival home I found quite a respectable number of
letters, among them an especially endearing one from Mama
Köchert. The presence of the case of beer was a pleasant surprise as well. On the other hand, I was annoyed by a letter from
Thornton, that crazy musician who sends his dream fantasies to

everybody in the entire world. He was inane enough to address me as "most honored master" and to expect me to obtain the favor of a patron for him, someone who would help him with varying sums of money to get through the lost lesson time in the summer. Could anything crazier be demanded of me?

Grohe wrote a friendly note and thanked me for my nasty inscription. My mother and sister Kathi are really besieging me to spend this summer at home [in Windischgraz]. You know very well, however, how alluring home is to me. Hence, it won't be too difficult for me to stand firm.

In any case, please take a look in and around Rinnbach and as a *last* resort secure the flat in Roith. Also, the detailed conditions have yet to be more accurately nailed down, especially with regard to cleaning, laundry, board, etc.—Schmidt is still waiting to receive my repaired coat. Would you be so kind as to ask Ignaz in writing to attend to this mailing *as soon as possible?*

The weather today is horrible; the mists are hanging so low that one can hardly see the other side of the lake; moreover, the lake is very rough and there is a biting wind. I think back with much pleasure on the three lovely, if also occasionally stormy days spent in Rinnbach; may I be granted many such more!

With sincere greetings I am as always you very devoted
                              Hugo Wolf.
Many greetings to Heinrich and the girls.
The weather has suddenly turned beautiful. The fog has lifted and a cloudless blue sky rules the firmament. It's probably no different where you are.
A letter from Frau Grohe was just given to me, which I'm enclosing.

55

To Rinnbach
Unterach, June 12, 1891

Once more! What is going on with my coat? Please respond. Honored gracious lady!

It's impossible for me to come to Rinnbach tomorrow (Saturday), as I'm not at all ready to travel. Also, the weather is not especially good for moving, and although my stay here is more bothersome from day to day, I plan to stick it out for a few more days. An addition is being built onto the Pötzleithner house, which causes a maddening noise all day long. There are also some finches, irritating to the utmost with their monotonous, banal, beastly twittering, so that I don't have a moment's peace. From Eckstein, whom I asked to get me an india-rubber atomizer, I've heard absolutely nothing and have been sent nothing either. My condition is highly variable, good today, bad tomorrow; I've already gotten quite desperate about it. Schott sent me the Lessmann newspaper today with the enclosed card. Now I've absolutely decided to keep the flat in Roith. Please take care of the necessary arrangements, if that is possible without too much effort. My landlady will surely be able to give me bed linen? In addition, I'd like to request only a small horsehair pillow, the rest is unimportant.

Write me, please, as to when you think my living arrangements will be completed, since the sooner I can say adieu to Unterach the better.

The weather has been really awful for several days and there is no prospect of improvement. Naturally, I'm not working *at all*. That will be the constant refrain of my reports from now on.

And now God be with you. Sincerest greetings to you and all as always

Your very devoted
Hugo Wolf.

56

To Rinnbach [postcard]
[Unter-Gaisbach, July 18, 1891]

Just arrived in Wels. Am very well accommodated. Have an entire compartment for myself. Saw the sculptor Benk in Attnang, but didn't speak. Read and sleep intermittently or stroll through the corridor. Am enjoying it very much; glad I didn't go until today. Rochefoucauld utterly remarkable—fine mind. Will not eat the ham until Linz—not hungry yet.—Thinking about this and that—however, *silentium!—Linz*. Connection very easy. Weather very beautiful. Am together with the gang. Sincerest greetings, hurriedly

Wolf

57

To Rinnbach [postcard]
[Budweis train station, July 18, 1891]

Am just sitting here comfortably in the restaurant with a beer from Budweis and have realized to my horror that I forgot to lock the suitcase I left behind. As an afterthought, I ask you to please take care of this personally and keep the key.

Sincerest greetings from your

Hugo Wolf

58

To Rinnbach
Bayreuth, July 19, 1891

Most honored gracious lady!

Here we are at last in Bayreuth after a long and boring trip. As I feared, my flat, which Humperdinck got for me (a few houses away from his), is unusable. I have spent quite a sleepless night. The bed, above all, defies every description. I'll have to find myself another flat today. Humperdinck was waiting for me at the train station and went with me to the flat. Franz Schalk was at the station too. Josef Schalk and Höfler had the misfortune to miss the train in Marienbad, which gave us much to laugh about. Schalk didn't even have a hat with him. It was hilarious how the two of them watched the train speeding off, as disheartened as they were dumbfounded. Boller almost met with the same fate. I'm writing these lines in Franz Schalk and Löwe's flat, both of whom are lodged across from me. Löwe is in possession of Christnacht and it's at the Pfeiffers' in Gmunden. Yesterday we were at Samet's. Theodor led the discussion—as always—and Wolzogen listened with the true patience of a sheep. I also renewed my old acquaintance with Winkelmann, which he initiated, to be sure. Please write to me here c/o *poste*

restante (main post office). Wette has written to me here. Wüllner wants to perform Christnacht. Also the Holländer Quartet in
Cologne wants to engage me for concert tours. Neitzel is going
to come out with a long article in the Cologne paper soon.—
Grohe wrote here too. God only grant that I get a quiet flat. In
any case, I'll already be in Rinnbach by Friday. I'll make the
return trip with Löwe.

    And now farewell. I'm continuously bothered by the con-
versation of the other two. I hope I'll write better tomorrow.

    With sincere, heartfelt greetings, your very devoted
                                            Hugo Wolf.
Many greetings to the children.

59   To Rinnbach [postcard]
                       Bayreuth, July 19, 1891

    I've decided to keep my old flat after all, since I've been
given the prospect of a mattress. It's pouring rain at the moment,
and the wind is blowing from all sides. The performance of Parsifal begins in an hour. I was alone practically the whole morning. My so-called friends (except for Humperdinck) just don't
pay much attention to me. I'm writing these lines at Humperdinck's. I got together with Porges and Merz at Samet's today.
They were very pleasant and communicative. I also paid a visit
to Wolzogen accompanied by Ferd. Jäger. More soon.

    Many, many sincere greetings from your most devoted
                                            Hugo Wolf

60   To Rinnbach
                       Bayreuth, July 20, 1891

Honored gracious lady!
    Happily, the first performance is over; I also dozed from
time to time in Acts 1 and 3 and am only glad that I was still
somewhat able to take in the better part of the work. Bayreuth
has put me into the worst of moods and I will hardly sacrifice
myself again to the local conditions, which are terrible beyond

all measure. I scarcely eat anything anymore and even the beer tastes bad. As to what sleep is, I no longer have a clear idea. One can't get to sleep before 2:00 in the morning and at 4 or 4:30 one is startled by the most diverse noises. I'm really a complete wreck and wish for nothing more fervently than that this Bayreuth pilgrimage may come to a quick and peaceful end for me. The people here *all* disgust me (with the possible exception of Humperdinck, who, as I'm writing this, is brooding over a review for the Frankfurter-Zeitung and from time to time encourages me to hurry). My round-trip ticket makes me fume with anger. What stupidity to set out on the trip via Nuremberg, when you can make the trip easily in *one* day via Weiden. Now I'll actually have to stay overnight in Nuremberg if I'm not allowed to travel the other route. If I'm permitted to travel via Weiden, I'll be in Ebensee by Thursday evening, otherwise not until Friday unfortunately.

I can't report much about the Parsifal performance, as I only took part with half-open ears and ditto eyes. People said it was very beautiful and so it probably was.

Today is Tristan. May God keep me awake.—Have been together with Levi, Porges, and Merz:—they were very nice. Haven't seen Mottl yet. Paumgartner avoids me—fine with me. Now you should thank God you're not in Bayreuth. Soon I'll be able to be human again too and enjoy eating, drinking, and sleeping—ah, sleeping!—Hang all these spiritual enjoyments when the body is a wreck.

Many, many sincere greetings from your grateful

Hugo Wolf.

61

To Rinnbach

Bayreuth, July 21, 1891

Honored gracious lady!

It was really the voice of a kind spirit that urgently whispered to me *not* to go to Bayreuth. If only I had heeded this warning; how many irritations and misfortunes I would have been spared. For example, I got into an almost dangerous situation today because of the bungling of Humperdinck, who procured me the flat. It was after Tristan; the performance, which I attended in full possession of my mental and physical powers (I had had a good sleep in Joseph's flat beforehand), was of the highest caliber almost throughout. Sucher and especially Plank as Kurwenal peerless and incomparable. After the performance we stayed together in the "zur Sonne" restaurant—"o this sun!" ["*O diese Sonne!*"]—until 1:30 in the morning—all of us Viennese and good friends. As I made my way back home with Franz Schalk and Löwe, there was still light and a fairly lively commotion in the beer hall on the ground floor. Naturally, I had to wait for the departure of the night owls before I could even think of sleeping. After about 30 minutes of impatient waiting, it seemed to be quieting down. But I had hardly gotten into bed when below me on the second floor an infant began to wail dreadfully. It finally went on so long that I had to get up; I got dressed and wanted to await the dawn taking a walk. But just to get outside, one has to unlock two doors of the house and I only had the key to one of them. No amount of ringing, calling, and screaming for the people of the house helped. So I went directly to the family on the second floor, which resulted in a heated argument, interspersed with curses and threats of all sorts. Finally, the furious people unlocked the door for me and I rushed out. But since the weather was cool and I, on the other hand, hadn't the best protection, I decided to wake up Löwe and Schalk living across from me, which I managed to do with considerable effort. I told them the whole story, over which they almost laughed themselves to death and I finally had to laugh along with them. Nevertheless, the night, which I spent at their place on a miserable sofa, counts as one of my worst memories. I hardly need to mention that I barely slept at all. It is still very early as I write these lines, Löwe and Schalk are sleeping peacefully as my pen runs scratching across the paper. May God let the cup of suffering the joys of Bayreuth pass most quickly from me. This is my only wish. I will arrive *Thursday*, the 23rd of the m[onth] around 6:00 or 5:30 in the afternoon in Ebensee, i.e., Traunsee, and would be very happy if you could meet me with a boat, weather permitting. If I don't wire to the contrary, I'll be in Traunsee at the designated time.

Humperdinck delivered your lines to me during the intermission between the first and second acts of Tristan. I'll check today to see whether there are any messages to be picked up at the main post office. Tristan moved me tremendously. It is most certainly the crowning achievement of all Wagner's creations. What a shame that you couldn't hear it. You would only have basked in this magical, enchanting orchestra. I won't write again, as I'll be in Traunsee by Thursday. Sincerest greetings from your

Hugo Wolf.

62

To Vienna

[Döbling], Dec. 2, 1891

I believe, most honored gracious lady, that there is no better way to consecrate this lovely stationery than by conveying the wonderful news that I have succeeded in writing two Italian songs. "Ein süsser Schrecken geht durch mein Gebein" ["A sweet tremor goes through my being"]. I am as if in Elysium.— The count is 33! God willing, I'll still write a third one today. Who would have thought such a thing!

To a happy reunion!

Hugo Wolf.

63

[small card in letter envelope]

[Vienna, December 31, 1891]

Zum neuen Jahr	For the new year
. . .	. . .
. . .	. . .
In ihm sei's begonnen,	In him it was begun
Der Monde u. Sonnen	Of moons and suns
An blauen Gezelten	To the blue tents
Des Himmels bewegt.	Of the heavens moved.
Du, Vater, du rathe!	You, Father, you advise!
Lenke du u. wende!	You guide and turn!
Herr, dir in die Hände	Lord, in your hands
Sei Anfang u. Ende,	May beginning and end
Sei Alles gelegt!	May all be laid!

1892–1894

Dear and honored gracious lady!

I'm finally finding time to write. If I'd written these lines two hours ago, I wouldn't be in such an embarrassed state now. And this is how it all came about. From 4:00 on, I was at Weingartner's, where I was greeted most cordially—he even kissed me. His wife, a stately beauty, received me no less warmly, although without a kiss. Enough. We had a lot to talk about and passed the time very pleasantly. At 8:30 he drove with his wife to the opera, where he's conducting "Cavalleria." So I packed myself off back to the hotel so that I could finally dispatch a sign of life from me. That's where Fate caught up with me. A message from a Herr vom Rath awaited me. In Grohe's Bädecker, Frau vom Rath is described as an aristocratic, charming lady who has "money to burn." Now listen. Since it was already a quarter past 9:00 when I arrived at the hotel, I dashed out of the hotel to the Viktoriagasse immediately upon receiving the card, only taking time first to wash my hands. But oh dear! Starting right at the entrance I was taken aback. I was surrounded by an army of servants. This made me suspicious. Despite this, I was stupid enough to give them my card instead of turning around right on the spot. The master of the house, a kind old gentleman, received me most graciously. Also the lady of the house. But oh horror! Everyone was in white tie and tails, and I, lowly worm, not even in a fresh collar, let alone white tie and tails. Meanwhile, I was being introduced to a swarm of beribboned and decorated gentlemen and ladies arrayed in formal attire. I didn't know where I could hide and I sensed only too well the uselessness of my apologies. I asked for permission to withdraw. They tried to put me at ease. In order to completely tranquilize me, the lady of the house requested that I sing something, because she was under the impression that I *sing* my songs *myself* in concert. I clarified the unreasonableness of such a request to her in the most persuasive words possible. Finally, a man at the party offered to sing some things and asked me to play for him. This I did. He sang "Flutenreicher Ebro" and "An die Leyer" and, with it, bored the crowd visibly. After this a pencil-slim, flaxen-haired girl in the group with a thin little voice sang the famous yodeler duet of Brahms "So lasst uns rüstig wandern" with a handsomely groomed man, which elicited general delight. After that, I made my exit quietly and quickly. That was my first debut. Unfortunately, I got totally lost going home and wandered about looking for the way for the longest time. It was 10:30, and yet far and wide there wasn't a soul to be seen. And it's said there is an exciting night life in Berlin! Finally, a policeman's directions got me on the right track. I only realized then that I'd been walking around and around. By the way, I'm getting along very well, armed with the Bädecker. I used a cab only for the drive to Wolff in his office and back. The few calls I made during the noon hours [i.e., to leave a calling card] I made on foot, in order not to meet anyone. What I've gotten to know of Berlin, I don't like at all. The streets of the city remind me vividly of Mannheim's uninteresting squareness. I'd say it's just a larger version of Mannheim. How many thousand times more beautiful is our dear old Vienna! How incomparably more beautiful!! I could never feel any warmth here, being stared at so soberly and bleakly by the uniformity of these masses of gray stone. Heavens, who could feel any coziness here! "Oh you, my Austria" I want to cry out at the top of my voice, not "Hello, Germany," etc.

My trip on the train wasn't exactly the most pleasant. From Dresden on, there were eight of us in the compartment. Saxon Switzerland [mountainous region of Saxony] reminded me of botched-up theatrical scenery. It's supposed to be something, but really isn't; a cheap edition of the Hinterbrühl. The dinner in the dining car, table d'hôte, was scandalous, the price no less: 2.10 [marks], not including beverage. One bottle of beer, filling two water glasses, cost 30 Pf. You can well imagine that I didn't eat anything at night. And so I went to bed hungry at the Sans-souci [hotel]. Not until the next day at 2 in the afternoon was I revived by a rather bad meal and good drink in the Kurfürsten-keller: dinner a la carte 1.50 M. My room at the hotel is quite decent and fairly quiet. I don't yet have a piano. (Didn't eat supper again today.)

My first trip this morning was of course to Wolff, who was not in his office because he was at home indisposed. He advised me decisively against postponing the concert, since the undertaking has already cost so much. After some looking around, a replacement, to the extent Jäger can ever be replaced, was found in Herr Grahl, a concert singer. Herr Grahl has a good reputation, along with a lovely, pleasant-sounding voice, sight-reads extremely well, and has an affinity for the music. He's also a thoroughly modest, unassuming, undemanding, and highly intelligent man, a great exception among tenors, who will carry out his assignment well, if anyone will. So the program will remain for the most part as planned.

Tomorrow I'll get on with the visits. And since it's already 12:45 a.m., I'll wish you a lovely good-night and remain with many sincere greetings to Heinrich and the naughty children, your always devoted

Hugo Wolf.

Address: Hotel Sanssouci, Linkstrasse
I'm in despair over my new collars, which have turned out to be much too tight. Will have to have something made here. Scoundrels, these Viennese businessmen.

65

To Vienna

Berlin, Feb, 21, 1892

Most gracious, honored lady!

Last night I went to Meistersinger, which was performed uncut under Weingartner's truly consummate baton. Betz, particularly, sang especially beautifully. Also, the Walter of Herr Rothmühl (a pupil of Gänsbacher) proved an entirely acceptable performance, especially from the vocal standpoint. The Evchen [young Eva] of Fräulein Leisinger left much to be desired because of the inadequacies of her talent. On the whole, it was a magnificent performance. Following the performance we couldn't find room in the various restaurants, which we always had to leave because of overcrowding. Finally, after considerable effort, we commandeered an unlaid table in a Bavarian restau-

rant where excellent Westphalian ham was served, and we
talked until the wee hours of the morning. Monday is Carmen.
Weingartner offered me a seat for it next to his wife.

Herr Grahl will sing eight songs. Gärtner, Rattenfänger,
Anakreon, Tambour, Musikant, Verschwiegene Liebe, Heimweh, Wer sein holdes Weib verloren. How's Jäger? Couldn't he
still come and sing on the 24th? That would be something else
again. Give him my greetings. Genée and his interesting daughter, Frau Laske, received me most cordially. I dined with them
yesterday and am invited there this evening. The visiting never
stops. Am already completely numbed by it all.

Over and above this, Boller offered me visits to Sternfeld
and Seckendorff. An invitation arrived just now from Frau
Schmid-Lafourcade to the noonday meal at 2:00. At 12:00 I must
be at Frau Lipperheide's for breakfast, as you can see from the
enclosed card.

Genée is going to go with me to Bote & Bock. I hope this
will be my new publisher. Haven't found out yet whether
Sudermann's here. Enough for today. One more thing: you
cannot possibly imagine the fabulous style of living here. At the
Schmid-Lafourcades' as well as at the Lipperheides' (especially
at the latter) sheer Asian splendor dominates. One is literally
struck dumb and rendered senseless by the elegance of the furnishings. The lavish, luxurious, ostentatious character reigns in
all fashionable homes. What a contrast to what the *back* premises
must be!!

And now to conclude.

Many, many sincerest greetings to you and the family from
your very devoted

Hugo Wolf.

66

To Vienna

Berlin, Feb. 22, 1892

Dear gracious lady!

I feel more at home in my hotel room from day to day,
even as the socializing becomes more loathsome day by day. My
room, which faces east, offers a very lovely view—the chimneys

of the neighboring buildings. But as compensation, the sun peeps in through the window first thing in the morning. And right now it's bathing the entire room in gold, and also my disposition, which is struggling to vent itself against my tailor in several unutterable expressions. It is unspeakable what a blockhead a tailor can be. Now my vest is driving me mad. And he'll regret it!—

Breakfast at Frau Lipperheide's was colossal. Oysters and champagne sank in value when compared to the delicacies that graced the table in every conceivable variation. In spite of this, it was deadly boring. Frau Begas, a painter—not the famed Begas beauty—was the only one who paid me any notice. She is familiar with the circumstances in Vienna and so we had a topic of conversation. In the afternoon I had a rehearsal at Grahl's. He'll do his things quite well, but is singing only eight songs. Last evening passed very pleasantly at Genée's, who listened to my songs with the greatest interest and understanding. We were alone with Frau Laske and her husband and we talked and chattered away to our hearts' content. Genée is a splendid fellow and his daughter no less so! Today he escorted me to Bote & Bock and a few critics. I'm at Weingartner's at noontime—Carmen this evening—gala performance, must go in tails and white tie.—Fräulein Mayer has probably already arrived and checked into my hotel.

The devil take her—I'm not going to do much about that.

I still haven't been to Unter den Linden [avenue]. Nor have I become at all acquainted with Berlin. If only there were no social affairs. They rob me of all my time.—Greetings to Heinrich and the children. Always your most devoted

Hugo Wolf.

67

To Vienna
Berlin, Feb. 23, 1892

Dear honored, gracious lady!

Today only in utmost brevity, to say that the concert will take place on the 24th. Frl. Mayer has already rehearsed with me; it's going pretty well, in any case quite decently. The male singer will do his best. Today will cost me a lot of money, as I have to take a coach in order to finish up a number of calls I still have to make. I'm not having a single peaceful hour in this infernal Berlin. The Helmholtzes have invited me to a soirée this evening—I shudder at the prospect. Am going to cancel. I can't take it anymore. Yesterday I was at Carmen. Gala performance. Frl. Rothauser fabulous as Carmen. Was a good performance.

Hope to be in Vienna again soon. I'm very much looking forward to it.

Many greetings to everyone.

In greatest haste your
Hugo Wolf.

68

To Vienna
Berlin, Feb. 23, 1892

Received telegram. Thanks. Program enclosed. Made a tremendous number of calls today. Mostly to critics; Eichberg (Börsencourier [financial newspaper]) very nice fellow. Easygoing chap—also had respect for me. Lessmann—boring chatterbox, not much underneath it all. Am half dead. Tonight at Genée's; we'll play tarok all by ourselves. Genée a charming fellow who is very helpful to me. Invited to Helmholtzes today, but sent my regrets, as large parties do me in.

Haven't yet seen a pretty face on the street or in the theater. Horrible fashion styles. Common taste.

Must close, as in terrible hurry. A thousand greetings to everyone. Longing for Vienna. Don't like the Berliners. Disgusting people. A thousand greetings!

Hugo Wolf.

69

To Vienna
Berlin, Feb. 24 1892

Honored gracious lady!

As you were already informed by my telegram, I'm now confirming by letter the cancellation of my concert. Frl. Fin-

kenstein announced at the last minute (presumably out of fear)
that she doesn't feel well enough to appear in public. You can
imagine what my feelings were when I received the news. My
first thought was simply to leave for Vienna. But Wolff advised
me to arrange a concert on March 5th. I've also wired Schur to
see if the necessary funds can be raised. I'd like best to be off
and away. I may still leave tomorrow or the day after.

Among other things that happened to me today was an encounter with—Schönaich at Wolff's, fortunately on the stairway.
We looked at each other in astonishment, without further collision. Wolff told me later that Schönaich has been here for eight
days on business.

Today I noticed—how strange—a letter in the post office
addressed to M. Gaigg. I guess there are upright mountain folk
[*jibts biedere Jebirgsbewohner;* written in Berlin dialect] in Berlin
too. What do you think?

I've just learned that Frl. Mayer, in response to my message, intends to stay here until March 5th. That's all I need. I'd
rather leave tomorrow. By the way, she's laid up in bed.

O God, if only I were already away from Berlin. I will bless
that moment. Weingartner and wife sent me the enclosed telegram from Mannheim. These good people have no idea of my
misfortune. I'm so furious! But calm down, calm down! Screaming doesn't help. Many, many greetings to Heinrich and the
children.

Always your
Hugo Wolf.

70

To Vienna
[Berlin], Feb. 25, 1892

Most honored gracious lady!

Jäger is an unbelievable fellow. Wired him this morning at
11:00 and requested telegraphed reply whether he could perform on March 5th, since the concert was postponed. Now it's
6:30 in the evening and still no answer.

It's enough to drive me mad. The definitive decision has

to be made tomorrow whether the concert will take place or not. I announced that I won't agree to March 5th without Jäger's commitment. Since Jäger continues to shroud himself in proud silence, I don't know what to do. The smartest move would be to forget him. His behavior is just plain abominable.—

When will this man finally come to his senses.

I'm so furious about Jäger, because I'd like to see him here if only to spite Schur and Mayer.

But this angry bull still sees only the red flag of his imaginary spooks and goes charging after them. The devil take him. I do what I can here to promote him and wrestle with all those who have objections to him—and he abandons me so disgracefully and doesn't answer. These tenors!!!

Today I paid a call on Sternfeld who lives on Schill-, not Schillerstrasse, as I had been told. He was very surprised that this whole enterprise is being undertaken by Wolff and was not put into the hands of the Berlin Wagner Society, which would have cost me much less. Among other things, he is an intimate friend of Sudermann's. I learned through him that Sudermann will be coming to Berlin on March 1st on the occasion of the engagement or wedding of his publisher, Lehmann. He would be very happy to introduce me to Sudermann, who is said to be a very fine man. He also recommended me to Dr. Welti (author), whose wife (Herzog) sings leading roles at the opera and is reportedly interested in my music. Her voice is a high, light soprano, for which I've always sought in vain.

Frau Mayer was just here and strongly urged me to hold the concert on March 5th. Since Genée is also for a postponement and something is being done in the Wagner Society as well, I've decided to remain here and wait it out until March 6th. This time, too, shall pass; but then it will all be over for Mayer for all eternity, even if Schur hangs himself over it.

Now good night. I'm extremely tired and overwrought. I only eat once a day. About 4:00 I have a dinner in a restaurant for 1 M 25, which serves as breakfast, noonday meal, and supper.

Finally the telegram from Jäger. 8:00. He can't come before the 11th or 12th of March. Good grief. There will hardly be a day available then. Will inquire of Wolff immediately.

More tomorrow. A thousand greetings!

[no signature]

71

To Vienna
Berlin, Feb. 26, 1892

Honored gracious lady!
    Well, the concert is scheduled for March 5th. Jäger appeased me with the 11th or 12th. I cannot, and will not, wait until then and besides the hall is not available until April except for March 5th. Please tell Jäger that I regret having to forgo his participation. Today I took a somewhat closer look at Berlin and am passably gratified. There are splendid parks and squares here, the streets are very busy, and the pavements clean as a whistle. Everything is grand, but rigid. I bought a photograph of Sudermann for 75 Pfg. He has to write me a few words at the bottom, then I'll send you the picture. You won't believe your eyes though, because Sudermann looks like anything but a poet. The income from the canceled concert was 160 M. Weingartner just now sent me a ticket for Meistersinger. I have to hurry. Sincere greetings from your
Hugo Wolf.

72

To Vienna [postcard]
Berlin, Feb. 27, 1892

Most honored gracious lady!
    Please send me *by return mail* Schalk's first article in the Münchener Allgemeine [newspaper] and if possible Kauffmann's review of the Goethe and Spanish songs too. I'm writing these lines at Gumprecht's (critic), who is taking the most active interest in my things.
    Sincerest greetings from your devoted
Hugo Wolf.

73

To Vienna
Berlin, Feb. 28, 1892

Most honored gracious lady!
    Enclosed a clipping from the Vossische Zeitung (one of the leading Berlin papers). Yesterday and today I waited in vain for a sign of life from you. You would make me very happy with

frequent news. Also, you don't appear to read through my letters very well, because you don't answer my questions. What's going on with Jäger? I've been in touch with the Wagner Society here. There's going to be a matinee for them Thursday. Sternfeld is championing my things with enthusiasm. Please say hello to Boller. Most devotedly

Hugo Wolf.

74

To Vienna
Berlin, March 3, 1892

Honored gracious lady!

I've just come from the Lipperheides'—one of the richest homes in Berlin. I was invited [there] to dinner with Shakespeare-Genée, where, as far as food and drink go, the sky was the limit. Afterward I played and sang a few of my things and all those present were electrified. They won't let me leave town. I'm supposed to stay a few additional days. As the Lipperheides want to arrange a large *festino* on Sunday in my honor, I'll have to stay over Sunday. Wildenbruch also wants to meet me. I'm being talked about in all circles here. Dr. Sternfeld is picking me up in a quarter of an hour to go to the Wagner Society. Everyone who has anything to do with art and literature will be gathering there today.

The Lipperheides have invited me to their castle near Brixlegg in Tyrol. Both husband and wife are charming people. Enclosed is a letter from Major v. Vigneau, who is one of the leading people here and hosts the most elegant social gatherings. Sternfeld is coming, I have to close. Sincerest, sincerest greetings to you and all. Your very devoted

Hugo Wolf

75

To Vienna
Berlin, March 3, 1892

Honored gracious lady!

The dinner at Meyerheim the painter's went pathetically enough for me. The preceding production for the Wagner Society also turned into a wretched affair. There were about fifteen people there in all, among them Fritz Mauthner, who took special interest in my things. But neither Wolzogen nor Seckendorff, nor for that matter anyone else of note, was present. Neither did Mayer appear.

Now to the dinner at Meyerheim's. Sudermann was present. Since I was late in arriving at the dinner because of the production in the Duysen Hall, I was seated between a very disdainful Jewess and an empty chair, which was later occupied by a decidedly inferior creature. Next to said Jewess and flanked on the other side by the Countess Osten-Prokesch (Gossmann) sat Sudermann, the handsome man, who talked about French literature, about marriage, women, children, death, and the devil. Since I was sitting two seats away from him with the Jewess in between, we couldn't talk to each other. Nor did he seem to want to, because he addressed his comments only to the ladies. Moreover, he already knew about me beforehand from Meyerheim the painter, and Sternfeld spoke with him about an opera libretto, which Sudermann flatly refused as being something totally foreign to him. Our greetings to each other were very friendly, by the way. Sudermann said a few courteous words to me, which I of course returned with even more courteous ones. That was all that was spoken between us. As I found the party to be terribly boring, I sneaked out the door after dinner in such a clever way that not even a servant noticed my escape. Now I'm sitting in my room at 7:30, reporting. Dr. Welti is expecting me around 10:00 at the Leipzigerhof, the hotel where Sudermann is staying. Sudermann is in Berlin for four weeks. I haven't yet decided whether I should pursue my connection with Sudermann; maybe I'll just let it drop. He can't, or doesn't, want to help me. Was at Siegfried Ochs's this morning. A terrific fellow: young, fiery, enterprising, charming, and—sincere. A prince! He received me with open arms, raved about my songs, and is very eager for my choral and orchestral things. Tomorrow evening we're getting together to make music. He's certain to perform something of mine. By comparison, Weingartner keeps his distance. He didn't come to my production today, in spite of an invitation. A two-faced brute!

Ah me, I'm becoming so clever and blasé about the world's ways. My heart takes no part in it; I just keep laughing scornfully and outwitting them and thinking how foolish it all is. Good night. Good night.

Hugo Wolf.

Dr. Welti is waiting.
I'm planning to leave Sunday, Monday at the latest.

76

To Vienna
Berlin, March 4, 1892

Honored gracious lady!

Many thanks for your dear lines. I'll be arriving on *Tuesday* morning around 10:00 at the Nordbahnhof in Vienna. I have to stay here through Sunday. Am invited at noon on Sunday to Siegfried Ochs's, who wants to perform my Christnacht, and in the evening to Lipperheides'. At 8:00 Monday morning I'm leaving Berlin. Am staying in Dresden until evening and traveling through to Vienna overnight. Enclosed is a concert program that has just been sent to me for perusal. I hope to God it all goes well. Everyone is very anxious. If a big success, will wire. Sincerest greetings from

Hugo Wolf.

77

To Vienna
Berlin, March 6, 1892

Dear, honored gracious lady!

Yesterday's success has earned me a position here, according to the assurances of experienced people. In fact, the audience's participation was so kind, open, and warm, the applause so clearly meant for the composer, that I dare to truly believe my art will find a sympathetic response in the hearts of the Berliners from now on. Of course, they don't clap here the way they do in Vienna, but the audience warmed up noticeably toward the middle of the program, and after Gärtner and Tambour there was a general ripple through the hall. Also, I could have repeated Rattenfänger, "Wenn du zu den Blumen gehst," etc., if I had chosen to do so. I had a little set-to with Frl. Mayer. At the rehearsals I called her attention to the wrong interpretation of the final repeat of "Ach nein"! ["In dem Schatten meiner Locken"] and informed her how she should do it. She promised to follow my instructions. But at the concert it was different. She obviously thought, when I'm on the platform I can sing it as I like, then no one can interrupt me.

So to my anger and the horror of all those who understand music (including Siegfried Ochs, Weingartner, Genée) I had to listen to the ending done in the tasteless, obtrusive, affected way Frl. Mayer sang it in Vienna. You can imagine my delight over this. But punishment was immediate. The *composition* made such a hit that there was a stormy request for a repeat. Mayer asked me to repeat. I refused her. And when I finally appeared on the platform without the singer, tumultuous applause for me broke out, to the greatest annoyance of the goose, who wanted to ruin the piece all over again. As a result, Mayer didn't get to repeat anything, whereas Grahl was able to participate in the applause, which was really meant just for my things. Thank God I'm rid of the goose. Let's hope forever. Weingartner and wife congratulated me, and a crowd of other people offered best wishes, including complete strangers who only came back because of the evening's success. Kauffmann's son and several Tübingen friends also came around. Fortunately, the concert didn't last long, from 8–9:15 p.m. That meant no one left before the end of the program. This morning, or rather at noon, I'm going to breakfast at Begas, the woman painter's, at 4:00 to Ochs's for dinner, in the evening at Schmid-Lafourcade's and, if possible, should also go to Vigneau's. Tomorrow, Monday noon, breakfast at Lipperheides', evening at Fritz Mauthner's, author of the pamphlet "Nach berühmten Mustern" [*According to Famous Models*]. Mauthner is crazy about my things. Incidentally, he's a very sought-after personality here because of his genial and witty nature. You would like him very much. Day after tomorrow (Tuesday) I leave here at 8 a.m., stay in Dresden until about 9, and will arrive Wednesday about 9:30 in the morning at Neuer Markt. Greetings to Heinrich and the children. As always, your very devoted

Hugo Wolf.

78

To Rinnbach

Döbling, June, 10, 1892

Most honored gracious lady!

I would have answered your cordial lines long before this, had I not been told that postal service between Rinnbach and Ebensee was cut off for the time being because of the continuous rainfall. Today Heinrich wrote me that the Ronners will be staying in their own villa this time and that the priest is expecting me to put in an appearance. So I'll ask you to notify the priest that I'll be arriving in Traunkirchen on the 17th of the m[onth] and that he should have the piano put in my room. As to whether Schalk can be persuaded to rent the room next to mine, I have my doubts.—

I'm having bad luck with the soloists. Kaulich has canceled and Kraus positively will only sing Gudmund's 2nd song, "Ich fuhr wohl übers Wasser," transposed, in which case I'd rather forgo his participation. Forstén will probably replace him. No one has any idea at the moment who should sing the role of Margit.

It must look dreadful in Rinnbach. Who could have imagined this! Let's hope the deluge lets up soon; regard this little letter as the dove with the olive branch. A few lines in your hand would greatly cheer your always devoted

Hugo Wolf.

Many greetings to the children.

79

To Rinnbach [letter-card]

[Vienna], June 10, 1892

Most honored gracious lady!

I just had a verbal conference with Heinrich from which I was given to understand that the priest is asking 15 Fl for the flat only—*without* use of the piano. Now you are writing me that the priest will let me have the flat *with* piano for 15 Fl. What's going on here? Please talk with the holy man yourself and write me what you find out *immediately*.

Sincere greetings!

80

To Rinnbach

Traunkirchen, August 5, 1892

Most honored gracious lady!

Schalk's sister can return no earlier than Saturday evening, so we're going to visit the Pfeiffers today instead of Sunday. If it's all right with you, Schalk (alone) and I will spend Sunday with you.

Greetings to all, your very devoted

Hugo Wolf.

81

To Salzburg

Traunkirchen, May 23, 1983

Most honored gracious lady!

Today I'm having the most beautiful day since I've been here in Traunkirchen: my piano is finally here. My delight over this is simply indescribable. I keep staring at this yellow, old-fashioned piece of furniture like a lovesick monkey and asking myself, unbelieving, whether this thing really belongs to me or if I'm only dreaming about it. Heavens, if I don't compose this time, I'm definitely over and done with. My trunk, for which I've likewise pined so long, also arrived with the piano. Today, after a long period of time, I wanted to drink my usual "Schwarzer" [black coffee] once again, and as I was fixing myself the best Virginia tobacco to go with it and already savoring in advance this precious moment, all of a sudden there was an explosion and the pieces of my coffee machine were lying on the floor. In my joy over the piano I forgot to fill the machine with water, and hence this surprise. Fortunately, an itinerant tinker was here in town just by chance and he repaired the damage, or I'd have had to send the machine to Gmunden.

While I'm writing these lines there is a great commotion again in the church next door. It's been driving me mad. On Pentecost Monday there were *four* masses. Sunday I was at the Pfeiffers' and traveled back again in the evening to Traunkirchen. I see Spitzl [a dog] frequently. We're good friends in spite of his meanness.

I've given up my intention of getting a flatboat, since the people here are asking 15 Fl for a space in their boat house and I just paid out 15 Fl to have the piano delivered.

How's Irmi? And you and all the others? Best regards to you and all. A few lines would really please your

Hugo Wolf.

82

To Salzburg

Traunkirchen, May 26, 1893

Honored gracious lady!

It's been downright dismal here these last few days. The whole region is shrouded in fog and the rain just won't stop. To be sure, everyone says the barometer points to good weather, while the sky seems to have opened all its floodgates, intent on drowning man and mouse. The steamship pier is already in the greatest danger of being swept away, and if this stormy weather doesn't end soon, Traunkirchen will presently be transformed into a Little Venice. Today I'd have liked to go over to Ebensee to have myself measured by a well-renowned shoemaker there for climbing boots, as the Schnurch ones are absolutely unusable. But in such weather even the attractions of a train ride— "yes, his heart beats for joy, who rides in the coach"—are gladly forgone. Since I couldn't squabble with a shoemaker, I settled for a local tailor. (Dear God, my head always filled with shoemakers and tailors—and one is still supposed to compose!)

Aforementioned tailor—the phantom of my dreams—has also, how many times now?, just been to my place, with my God-knows-how-often-already metamorphosed knickers and spats, which have finally begun to take on a halfway human shape. I'd really given up all thought of his ever completing such a work of art; I even rewarded him with two shiny guldens. So, insofar as my problems with the tailor have been resolved, I actually could get on with the composing—don't you think? Good Lord! That's where my misery just begins!

Actually I've managed to write down four measures, but the instantaneous realization that a "wanting to" rather than a "having to" brought about this venture made me blush with shame and—so I gave it up again and was even happy about the fact that I'd caught myself in an act of deception. Yet it almost breaks my heart when I realize how one day after the other slips away, idly slips away, and this beautiful solitude, perfectly created for concentration and contemplation, does not mean more to me than to the casual summer vacationer: a *dolce far niente* with more or less boredom or amusement, whichever comes. And yet the others are, as a rule, tormented people who need vacations, who have every right to be lazy, to graze like cattle, and to take leisurely siestas—but I—I, who according to the calendar am always on vacation, who can only be counted as superfluous among the thousands, he who is nothing, can do nothing, and worst of all *does* nothing—dear God, where will it all end?

Siegfried Ochs wrote me recently and dispelled my fears over his long silence with the remark "Everything's in good order," and promised me a more detailed letter.

God knows, I can't work up enthusiasm anymore for the Berlin propaganda. There's really very little for me to get excited about on this demented planet; it would be just fine with me if a wayward comet gave it a smart rap on the nose, so that it broke into a thousand pieces. And then the fun is all over. And you're not particularly happy either in that little corner of the world, Salzburg? For that matter, where would it be sufferable at all? But where the body is at least healthy, the soul grieves less. O my poor soul!

Good that you're in Salzburg and not in Rinnbach. It must be a horrible sight there today. Nothing but clouds and fog and fog and clouds. Over toward Gmunden it looks somewhat more pleasant. The philistines—I'm thinking of acquaintances—always have a private little heaven shining down on them. The devil take them! Recently I fetched Musje Spitzl so that he could chase away the cats, which are behaving quite indecently at night. But my valiant Spitzl took to his heels when he saw the whole pack of cats—our hero! Just like certain braggarts; first talking big, acting quite huffy and puffy, yapping furiously and making a terrible racket, and when it comes to getting his man—drifting away. O man! o dog!

Have I forgotten to write you about anything else unimportant? Right. Physically I'm in good shape. The kitchen has improved markedly, compared with its concoctions last summer. The topfenstrudel [an Austrain pastry] served to me today was truly excellent. Karobats bow to the ground to me in greeting. Why? Because they're naive enough to believe that I will support their shameless requests for recommendations to Schey. What stupid and common and—polite folk. My fingers are getting stiff with cold. Herewith *ad finem*. Greetings to beautiful Salzburg and may you and your family also be greeted most warmly from your unwaveringly devoted

Hugo Wolf.

83

To Salzburg
Traunkirchen, May 28, 1893

The gracious lady is not much charmed by hearing laments, rather by dancing for her! *Eh bien!* We'll attempt to dance! What one won't do to please someone! Dancing really will be somewhat easier for me now, since my sad face displeases you so much. True, I'm still not quite in a dancing mood, yet if you wish it so, I will be polite enough to honor your wish as my command.

After all, if even the most cantankerous bears have learned to dance, should a mere grumbling little Wolf be prevented from doing so? So dance! If there were only someone here who could whistle me a happy tune; but as it is, I feel like that wedding party in the Spiegelgasse, which went through the motions of dancing but didn't actually dance, because the soul of the dance, the music for it, was missing, which amounts to about the same thing were I to try now to appear cheerful and carefree, when my soul is walking among the graves in sackcloth and ashes. But dancing it shall be, by all means. Shall I play a dance for you? perhaps as scarecrow [*Schreckenberger:* title of Wolf's setting of Eichendorff's poem] or—oh irony!—as fortune-hunter [*Glücksritter:* Eichendorff setting], or even as—desperate swain [*verzweifelte Liebhaber:* Eichendorff setting]? Confound it, I *can't* dance, and I don't want to dance either, any more than I am able to compose or do anything at all unless a strong inner need compels me. At the moment, Satan has me in his raven-black claws and there's nothing to do but wait, wait, and wait some more. Therefore, there will be *no* dancing, honored gracious lady, not even the tiniest little dance—to what purpose then? Besides, the world plays one for enough of a fool—can one, should one make a fool of himself as well?

I think a little change of scenery might do me good. Would you have any objection if I were to surprise you soon with an unscheduled visit? I want to enjoy a beautiful view, a great open expanse again and the Gaisberg [mountain] is said to offer this, which, nota bene, can be reached in an easy manner. Maybe you'd like to come along? Write me when I could come at a convenient time for you and *whether* at all. The sky is clearing a bit, thank God. When the first faint rays of sunshine peeped out of the clouds this morning, I knew of no other way to express myself for joy and happiness than Ibsen-like and to call out: Sun! Sun! Sun! But you mustn't prematurely conclude on that account that I've already gone mad. There is still plenty of time until that happens to your truly devoted

Hugo Wolf.

84

To Salzburg
Traunkirchen, May 30, 1893

Honored gracious lady!

Many and kind thanks for both your letters. If it should be as acceptably pleasant tomorrow as it is today, I'm coming to Salzburg tomorrow, in which case I'll arrive right at 12 noon at the train station there. But as I said, I'm coming only if the weather is halfway decent, otherwise not. I will be immensely pleased, of course, if you wish to meet me at the station. Announce my arrival officially in any case; in the event that I don't come, the surprise will be that much greater. If only tomorrow doesn't take a backseat to today, as far as the weather is concerned! For today the air is actually mild and the sun more generous with "light and warmth" than all the recent days together. And so this morning, despite the fact that I found myself on a downward slant (on a slanted plank from the steamship pier across from the church, to be specific), I was able to bask in the pleasure of the sun's hot rays, really luxuriating, lost for hours in the view of the lake and its romantic shore, and now and then casting a glance at Stirner [i.e., Stirner's book] lying nearby, contemplating his wondrous world of ideas. At such times and hours I really cannot comprehend why I'm not at all in a mood to compose. Today, for instance, everything is so still and solemn around me; even the chirpy finches, which I hate, have become quieter. Only the flies buzz their lulling melodies—otherwise, the deepest silence and solitude. Truly, life is beautiful after all! I'm counting on these lines reaching you by tomorrow morning, so that you can then be at the train station at 12 noon. Herewith, until we see each other soon. Always your

Hugo Wolf.

85

To Rinnbach
Salzburg, Sept. 1, 1893

Honored gracious lady!

Here I am sitting at a really terrible breakfast in the Cafe Bazar and waiting for a telegram from Grohe, who left for Bruck-Fusch an hour ago. Depending on how his telegram reads, I'll either travel tomorrow to Matzen or tonight to Vienna, i.e., Döbling. It's raining torrents today and a stopover in Bruck-Fusch would be pointless under such conditions, which is why I preferred to spend today still in Salzburg and to wait for the telegraphed message from Grohe, as to whether the Lipper-heides definitely plan to remain in Fusch. I don't want to go back to Traunkirchen, mainly because of the unusually insolent behavior of my sweet Marie. Since the priest was away on a trip, she imperiously demanded the sum of 50 Fl rent from me and maintained that I had committed myself through the end of Sept. to pay 60 Fl. She gave me not one word of thanks for the 5 Fl tip. I finally learned that the priest was of a mind to rent the flat in the future only to *one* family; thus, I would have no prospect of ever being able to live there again.

The consequence of this revelation was that I decided immediately to have the piano moved to Vienna. For this purpose, I handed over 5 Fl to Marie. I ask you now to arrange that Natzl have the railway personnel at the Traunkirchen station undertake the moving of the piano along with my trunk as soon as possible. Marie will pay their fee with the above-mentioned 5 Fl. I would be very pleased if Natzl would oversee the packing of the piano so that nothing improper happens to it. The piano should be sent to Bösendorfer, the trunk to my Döbling address.

Yesterday Grohe, Schickinger, and I were up on the Mönchsberg all afternoon and had very good weather for it. By contrast, it's horrible out today. My overnight lodging at Stein's was terrible. Didn't sleep the whole night. Tomorrow you'll learn whether I'm staying in Vienna or Matzen. For today the most cordial greetings from your thankful, devoted

Hugo Wolf.

Many greetings to Heinrich and the children.

86

To Traunkirchen

Windischgraz, October 1, 1893

Dear honored lady!

I arrived in Windischgraz at noon today completely unannounced, to the great surprise of my mother and my sister Kathi. The rainy weather in Klagenfurt caused me to hasten my trip home and so, in a manner of speaking, I've gone from the frying pan into the fire, because here, too, there is no end to the rain. From this, it would seem that the magnificent days of autumn are over. In Klagenfurt I landed miserably enough, incidentally. Is that ever a wretched hole! I still shudder when I think of my overnight lodging at the Kärtnerhof. It was just my misfortune that a club of song-happy brothers held choral practice on that evening in a hall of the hotel that was just within hearing range of my quarters. From that, you can judge what kind of a mood I was in. About 1 a.m. the wild goings-on came to an end and I threw myself on the bed, my ears stuffed full of cotton wadding. But oh, this bed! It might have suited a beer guzzler, but I got goose pimples at the feel of the damp sheets and pillows. I could have been put to bed just as well over a snake's nest. How I managed to fall asleep for a short time is completely incomprehensible to me. Waking up was horrible though, as still in the half-light, the gentlest goo-roo, goo-roo [sound of pigeons] brought me to the full realization of my sorry plight.

Furious, I threw on my clothes and departed with a curse that consigned the Kärtnerhof and all of Klagenfurt to Orcus.

Now I'm on home ground again and am particularly happy about the heartiness and good appearance of my mother, who, as she confessed to me, no longer has a head for anything but—politics. "Farewell, then, art and music of the masters"—now only a political song is worth anything—well, that could be rather nice. How did the cornerstone ceremony go? May a good spirit have ruled over it—to the health and happiness of all its inhabitants. These heartfelt wishes greet you, Heinrich, and the children from your always devoted

Hugo Wolf.

Best greetings to Frl. Hermine.

87

To Traunkirchen

Windischgraz, Oct. 6, 1893

Honored gracious lady!

The rainy weather that has kept me imprisoned in the house until now has finally had to give way to the force of a furiously oncoming sirocco, and so I've once again been allowed to calm my badly irritated nerves in some measure on solitary walks. What I have to endure at home with regard to our unfortunate neighborhood defies every description. Each day I resolve to leave W[indischgraz], but I'm still sitting in this cursed hole. It's highly unlikely that I'll get away before the 12th of the m[onth].

My days here drift by, empty and boring. Out of sheer boredom I've become a secret tippler. My mother keeps an "excellent" Tyrolian in the cellar that, I maintain, tastes like Russian leather. On the principle that one can get used to anything, however, thanks to my ceaseless attempts to get used to everything, I have already gotten to the point of finding this hellish brew to be "excellent" indeed. Only in the case of the moralist novellas of Heyse have I been unable to accustom my particular taste, to which my sister Kathi also had to take exception. I much prefer the "red" to this insipid Heyse-lemonade.

Siegfried Ochs wrote me recently. Elfenlied will be done— Mendelssohn will be set aside. On the other hand, Ochs writes me that he has not received the Feuerreiter score and requests it be forwarded as soon as possible. You can imagine my horror over this news, as I must assume that the mailing was lost, because I did send it, you can swear to that yourself. I'm still hoping that the score will turn up in Ochs's possession, as I bade him first to look around thoroughly among his papers and scores.

On the 12th of the m[onth] I'm planning to go to Graz and spend a few days there. I am anxious to make connections again through Gottinger with Frl. Wiesner, who is not going to get rid of me so easily this time. I wish you the most pleasant weather for these interim days in Winkel and send greetings to you and your family most sincerely as your always devoted

Hugo Wolf

88

To Vienna

Graz, Nov. 27, 1893

Honored gracious lady!

I'm writing these lines late in the afternoon in Baron Schey's flat. The master and mistress of the house left shortly before my arrival, and in order to while away the time in the least unpleasant way until their return, I'm deciding on this epistle. The trip here passed pleasantly. At the Semmering everything looked wonderful, and there was a truly springlike temperature. (Excuse my shaky handwriting; just before this I took it upon myself to do gymnastic exercises on Schey's piano.) I neither saw nor heard anything at the remaining stops from there on because of my happy absorption in Stinde's peat-bog story, a very witty and sarcastic thing, which you'll enjoy a lot too.

When I arrived in Graz, Potpeschnigg with wife and *Purgleitner* were already awaiting my arrival. A reserved two-horse carriage brought us first to the pharmacist's flat, where I was given an extremely comfortable room; a large salon adjoins it, which is adorned by a rather good instrument, along with other very comfortable furniture. Purgleitner is full of respect and veneration and speaks *only* when I speak to him; he is a colossal figure with a huge black beard and, in any event, a fellow with a heart of gold.

Dined with Potpeschnigg and Purgleitner at the Thonethof [café] and had the pleasure of seeing the "famous" balladeer Plüddemann there, who was feeding at the nearby table. Looks quite disreputable and seedy, just exactly like a ballad-phantom in Plüddemannic garb.

The concert is posted in huge print in every nook and cranny. My photograph, exhibited in Tendler's music store, appears to be tremendous publicity for me; there is much milling about there.— I've already made a new acquaintance too, i.e., with a very intelligent provincial court counselor, well-informed about music and especially fond of my things, whose name escapes me for the moment and who is a close acquaintance of Schey's.

I've also met Frau Prey, Hermine's mother—at Schey's of course—a very elegant lady, whom no one would ever suspect of being the mother of our good Hermine.

Am going to Pagliacci by Leoncavallo this evening. At Widl's after the performance to go through the things, and then together with Potpeschnigg and Purgleitner. Tomorrow Hausegger will be visited. Despite my already waiting about two hours for Schey, not a soul has come. So I have to leave without having seen him, as curtain time is approaching.

Address: c/o Herr Purgleitner, Spohrgasse, Graz.

In all haste and with the very very best greetings—including Heinrich and my tormentors, your always devoted

Hugo Wolf

89

To Vienna [postcard]

Graz, Nov. 27, 1893

Honored gracious lady!

Please send me Peter Cornelius' Headache Verse [*Kopfwehsprüchlein*] immediately care of Josef Purgleitner, Apotheke [pharmacy], Graz. Most devotedly

Hugo Wolf.

90

To Vienna

Graz, Nov. 30, 1893

Honored gracious lady!

I'm using an already late night hour to give you a sign of life, as my daytime activities allow me no time to write.

Today was the dress rehearsal. Aside from the critic, who was most favorably disposed toward me, there were only a few friends present, among them also Hofmann with family, Schey with wife, etc., etc. The rehearsal went very well for the most part and from all appearances, tomorrow evening will be an eventful one for Graz. You would take great joy in Frau Widl's performance, although Herr Krämer is doing a most respectable job also.

I couldn't ask for better interpreters, for no one could show more understanding, cooperation, zeal, and enthusiasm than these two people do. May God reward them.

This noon I dined at Hansi's. Hermine was also invited on my account, naturally, since I insisted upon it. I got to know—and value highly—the infamous Frau Ludovici today. She sang Gesang Weyla's [Weylas], Zur Ruh, Wächterlied, and Wiegenlied No. 1 [Wiegenlied im Sommer] with a still full-sounding, ringing voice and proved herself to be an artist of the first rank in their execution. Of my family, only Kathi will be coming here. Jenny and mother are staying at home. Also, I've already been to my sister Modesta's several times. She's quite a pathetic fool and beside herself with joy over my concert. Alfonsa—*vulgo* [nicknamed] Funzen—has turned into a delightful young girl with a roguish face, the artful likes of which you won't find anywhere. I'm cordial to my brother-in-law, but reserved—very reserved—and also prefer to avoid him. However, I invited him to the dress rehearsal and honored him with a ticket to the concert. A damnable fellow, the cad.

I received the Cornelius song and thanks very much.

Maybe I'll stay here a few more days than I originally planned. They don't want to let me leave and would like to just keep me here.

— — — — — — — — — —

Tomorrow is a very strenuous day for me; I still have a lot of visits to make and preparations to attend to for the concert.

Business is not doing badly, Tendler says. Let's hope so. And now, good night, I can't keep my eyes open; hardly slept at all yesterday. More tomorrow! Sincerest greetings! Always your most very devoted

Hugo Wolf.

91

To Vienna

Graz, Dec. 2, 1893

Honored gracious lady!

It wasn't possible anymore yesterday to report on how the concert went; I'll make it up today. First, let mention be made of a laurel wreath that was given me in the midst of lively acclaim following Frau Widl's performance of "Hochbeglückt in deiner Liebe." The applause, in my judgment, was in no way comparable to what was accorded me that time in Vienna. Even the "cool" Berliners gave me a more energetic acknowledgment than these "hot-blooded" Styrians. Nevertheless, general opinion reflects an unprecedented success and an unheard-of enthusiasm in Graz. Only "Er ist's," "Der Soldat," and "Heimweh" had to be repeated, the rest [were] more or less applauded. The singers acquitted themselves very well indeed, although their performances were better at the dress rehearsal. Krämer even became totally confused a few times and it was only because of my presence of mind that a complete accident was avoided. The laurel wreath bore Joseph and Hansi Schey's card. We stayed together after the concert until after 2 a.m. and it was very congenial.

I probably will not return to Vienna until Tuesday. Many thanks for your cordial lines.

For today then, as I still have a lot of visits to make, sincerest greetings from your very devoted

Hugo Wolf.

92

To Vienna

Graz, Dec. 2, 1893

Most honored gracious lady!

The evening papers just came out and I'm sending you two of them.

You'll be happy over the Hausegger article. The people here don't want to let me leave. Tomorrow (Sunday) I'm going to the country with the Krämer-Widl couple, where they manage a farm. The day after tomorrow I'm invited to Countess Attems', who is giving a party for me. There is such a "big fuss" over me here that I hardly know what I'm doing. The devil take all this fame.

Schalk has made a loge available to me tonight. Heilmar der Narr by Kienzl, who was "frightfully" enthusiastic about my songs, by the way, is being performed. I invited Potpeschnigg and Schey with wife to the loge.—Meanwhile, I'm planning to depart Tuesday; it's possible, though, that I won't come until Wednesday. Word has it that my concert brought in about 300 gulden. Well, one may certainly be content with that.

Sincerest greetings to all, as always your very devoted
Hugo Wolf.
Hansi and Schey send greetings.

93

To Vienna [letter-card]
Graz, Dec. 4, 1893

Honored gracious lady!
I'll arrive tomorrow *Tuesday*, the 5th of the m[onth] at 9:30 in the evening in Vienna and would be very indebted to you if I could spend the night at your house. With very sincerest greetings to you and your dear family, your very devoted
Hugo Wolf.

94

To Vienna
Graz, Dec. 5, 1893

Honored gracious lady!
I'm writing these lines in Café Thonethof, where I'm waiting for Schey, with whom we're going to the theater tonight. They're giving a parody of Pagliacci, which is supposed to be just terrific.

Schey is the one responsible for my not leaving for Vienna this afternoon as I'd originally intended, since he's determined to have me spend an evening at his place. He's coming to Vienna with me on Thursday, but is going on immediately to his estates in Hungary. I'm very annoyed about this recent delay in my departure, particularly since my brother-in-law Strasser is causing some unpleasantness here. If only I were already in my quiet cell in Döbling; this endless traveling around is becoming unbearable by this time.

Walküre was canceled in the final hour, or rather the final quarter hour (at 6:45). I had invited my sister Modesta and brother Max to join me in a loge that Schalk had made available to me. When nothing came of the performance because of Frl. Wiesner's sudden hoarseness, I invited them both to my apartment and played and sang Walküre for them on the piano, which satisfied them completely.

I'm looking forward immensely to seeing you all again soon. I hope I'll get to see your dear girls as well Thursday evening (10 p.m.). The letter Heinrich forwarded was from Eckstein; it contained an invitation from Princess Liechtenstein. Tomorrow I'll pay Hofmann a visit. Hausegger must also still be visited. I'm continuously on the lookout. If only tomorrow evening with Schey were over. I'm horribly disgusted at being paraded mawkishly like a well-trained horse. Oh well, it will all end eventually. So to a joyous reunion on Thursday at 10 p.m. With sincere greetings to Heinrich and the children, your always devoted

Hugo Wolf.

95

To Vienna
Berlin, on the day of Epiphany, 1894

Most honored gracious lady!

My trip went very well. For a while I even traveled all by myself in the compartment, then with a military officer and, finally, from Dresden on, with an elderly lady. I arrived in Berlin punctually at 1:45 p.m., took a first-class carriage to Potsdamerstrasse 38, where I was received most cordially by the housekeeper. The cold weather is considerably worse here than in Vienna. One freezes miserably here. The Lipperheides aren't coming to Berlin until the end of January. I've been given a very attractive bedroom and an elegant salon. After a thorough freshening-up, I went off to visit Ochs. He lives a few hundred steps away from my lodging on the opposite side of the street. Ochs wasn't at home, but had just gone to the rehearsal of the Philharmonic. I took a carriage immediately, rode back to my flat, picked up my scores of the Feuerreiter and Elfenlied and told the coachman to drive to the Philharmonic. I arrived there just as d'Albert was conducting his "trash." I hadn't sat long as a listener in the concert hall before Ochs came over to me. Our greeting was extremely cordial. He was overjoyed at my appearance. Frl. Corver was also present; I conveyed greetings from you and the girls, which she cordially returns. Sternfeld was there, too, and extremely pleased to see me. Ochs really is charming. He himself is inconsolable about the omission of Mignon, but thinks I'll still hear the piece here anyway, i.e., with orchestra.

Then the time came for my things, first the Feuerreiter and then the Elfenlied. Sternfeld, who was following the original score with me, was truly stricken with St. Vitus' dance in his delight over the effect of the [orchestral] sounds. Although the pieces were only being rehearsed for the first time, it went quite marvelously. I was congratulated from all sides. The chorus is exceptionally well prepared and the orchestra plays extremely well. The colorful instrumentation and the originality of my sonorities received praise from all around me. The Elfenlied, too, which simply sparkles and flashes in its instrumental garb, had an electrifying effect.

In short, I'm happy about the enthusiastic cooperation on the part of the conductor as well as the chorus and orchestra personnel. Both pieces were played through a number of times. Incidentally, there will still be rehearsals on Sunday and Monday morning. Gesang Margit and Anakreon were not played through, due to lack of time. Tomorrow I'll go through Margit with Frl. Corver, who also lives on Potsdamerstrasse; a tenor is singing Anakreon. Frl. de Jong sings *absolutely delightfully*; you can't imagine the solo in Elfenlied performed any better. After the rehearsal, around 6:00 p.m., I was invited to supper by Ochs, together with Bruckner, the royal travel companion Karageorgievich, and unfortunately also the agent Lessmann (a colossal idiot!). Stayed together in amiable conversation until 10:00 p.m., at which time we all took leave and I went home to write this letter. For tomorrow evening I'm invited to Lehmann's, who publishes Sudermann, Hauptmann, etc. A lot of literary people are coming. There's a concert at the opera house beforehand, at which Bruckner's 7th Symphony will be performed. I'll attend this concert.

For today, good, good night. As I've just seen with my own eyes, it was indeed possible to get hold of a horsehair pillow for me. It's gotten to be 11:00 p.m. And so to bed. Good night.

9:00 in the morning. After a well-spent night, except that I dreamed of arguing emphatically with van Dyck and spitting continuously in his face, I got up early and got dressed. My breakfast table, already splendidly set, awaited me in the salon, an old Indian teapot containing a marvelous tea, butter, eggs, whipped cream, as I ordered. Second breakfast at 12 noon, which I canceled for today, however, on account of my rehearsal with Frl. Corver. Had a stroll through all the rooms of the Lipperheides' home; felt all the while as though bewitched. Such magnificence and such luxury defies every description. And these splendid paintings! I can justifiably save myself the visit to an art gallery, since what one is given to see in this house alone can bring on enough of a headache.

Now I have to close. Ochs is expecting me; we're going to Frl. Corver's together. Every drop of Rhine wine and champagne that passes my lips tonight shall be a reminder to me that you are celebrating your birthday today. This will be my private pleasure at Lehmann's festive table. And now many, many sincerest greetings to *all* from your grateful

Hugo Wolf.

96

To Vienna
Berlin, January 8, 1894

Honored gracious lady!

The cold weather has eased up here and one dares to go out on the streets again. Nevertheless, I still haven't gotten beyond the lindens [the avenue Unter den Linden]; in the next few days, however, I'm going to venture all the way out to Grunewald, where Fritz Mauthner lives and plants his cabbages, poetical and botanical cabbages. Mauthner has become a home-owner and farmer and the whole escapade hasn't cost him more than 20,000 M. From his description his property also offers scenic charm, to which people like us must first grow accustomed.

The evening before last at Lehmann's I also met Herr Grahl, who sang a few songs of mine that I was told were purportedly of special interest to Spielhagen, who was present. Sudermann, too, with whom I spoke only a few fleeting words, had listened attentively and asked me for an encore, whereupon Tambour was sung. Actually, I conversed only with Mauthner and his refreshing, vivacious wife, who worships her husband like a god, which I can very well understand.

Now I have to see to it that his poem is set to music; it would give him a great deal of pleasure because, as he says, there would be something special about it.

I've just been interrupted by the visit of a man who wants to play his songs for me at all costs. Consequently, I have to stop.—

After a lapse of three quarters of an hour I'm writing further in a mood of deepest dejection. The man, Nodnagel by name, an enthusiastic admirer of my songs (so he thinks), carried out his horrible mission and massacred me with a dozen of his songs. You know, gracious lady, what I'm able to suffer when it comes to listening and playing the most miserable music, but what I had to hear from Nodnagel really "goes too far" [*geht über die Hutschnur*], as they like to say here in Berlin. Bawdy love songs, like the ones that adorn the contemporary Viennese almanac, performed by a raucous baritone voice with that madly affected ardor and passion typical of all those who imagine themselves to be geniuses—I was reminded of Goldschmidt—along with the merciless flogging strokes on the poor hostage instrument, which creaked in every joint, not even to mention the musical composition, this embodiment of cretinism and bestiality . . . Oh, it was maddening. And to top it off, as he ingenuously maintained, he was inspired by acquaintance with my "fabulous" songs, albeit without, as he candidly added, his "originality" having been encroached upon, with which concluding statement I could agree from the bottom of my heart. "How nice," one wants to say along with Ilse, Hilde, and Irmina. In one volume of his debauched compositions is the dedication: to Hugo Wolf, the great, the would-be-great; in the other: to the highly gifted poet of sound Hugo Wolf in respectful admiration. To think that an honest man must put up with such abuse!

Yesterday I renewed my acquaintance with Capellmeister Muck. We greeted each other most cordially and feel the strongest sympathy for each other. He's acquainted with most of my things and recognizes their value. The performance of Bruckner's 7th Symphony was a masterful accomplishment of Muck. The first two movements rather fell by the wayside. Bruckner was only called after the Scherzo and Finale and then appeared on the podium at the conclusion as well. Bruckner was very happy about his success. We were invited to Muck's at noontime yesterday—bad feed but good conversation. In the evening Bruckner, the prince [Karageorgievich], and I went to Fliegender Holländer, the 50th anniversary of the first performance. Muck got the seats. The performance was excellent, but the scenery was extraordinary, incomparably more beautiful and effective than in Vienna.

Tonight is the concert. Margits Gesang went very badly at yesterday's rehearsal. Frl. Corver sang uncertainly and also recited very badly. The piece will fall short. Anakreon's Grab won't have any effect either. But Ochs concerned himself too little with the orchestra. The attacks are sloppy and the detail is blurred. I'm very dissatisfied. Not to mention the tenor, who screams out the tender song to the audience like a bullfighter. Elfenlied and Feuerreiter still went the best. I was so depressed at yesterday's rehearsal of Margits Gesang and Anakreon that I wanted to leave Berlin on the spot. Bruckner and Muck had their hands full to calm me down and convince me to set foot in the concert hall again. God knows how it will go tonight.

I hope to prevail upon Lilli Lehmann for a Liederabend here. Lehmann is a better drawing card for Berlin than Herzog is. This is the general view. I would be guaranteed a full, completely packed hall if Lehmann participates, i.e., Lehmann by herself. Mauthner is supposed to convince Lehmann to do this. It will be decided in the next few days. Baroness Lipperheide wrote me such a kind, heartfelt letter from Matzen today that I shed tears over it. Write one like this once too to him who sends sincerest greetings

Hugo Wolf.

Best greetings to Heinrich and the children.

97

To Vienna

Berlin, January 8 evening, 1894

Most honored gracious lady!

I've come into my flat sad and depressed from an ear doctor and found your cordial lines and a letter from Selzam, the first lieutenant. The cause of my distress was an ear doctor Ochs recommended to me, whom I consulted and who, for a consultation of five minutes, made me about 20 M, let's say twenty marks lighter. Such a scoundrel! Twenty marks to clean out my ears three times with warm water! Have you ever heard of such a thing? But I have to tell you the whole story from beginning to end. The direct railway coach Vienna-Berlin must have been a particularly ailing one. There was a squeaking and grinding and sawing that simply became unbearable after a while, at least for me. To my horror, I discovered too late that I'd forgotten to bring along cotton wads. Unfortunately (although at the time I considered it fortunate), it occurred to me that I could use the [bakery] rolls I'd been given as a substitute for the missing cotton wads and I cheerfully stuffed the soft dough of the rolls into my ears. It helped. But the dough in my left ear, on which side I slept, pushed in somewhat too deeply, so that it could no longer be gotten out with my finger. Meanwhile, since it seemed not to affect my hearing in the least, I consoled myself with the assumption that the remaining little piece wouldn't create any further disturbances, when suddenly today the thing caused me some discomfort. I told Ochs about it and he recommended an ear doctor by the name of Schwabach. This *filou* [rogue] examined the situation, said it wasn't anything serious, blew water three times through a little tube, and impudently demanded 20 marks. The shock over this left me completely speechless, and sighing, I handed the ear extortionist what he asked for, secretly wishing him to all the devils. That damnable roll has cost me a pretty penny.

I won't tell Ochs the story until after the concert, since I'm not going to see him beforehand. The concert begins in an hour. I've invited the Lipperheides' housekeeper (an elderly but very good-hearted spinster) to make use of my second seat. We're also going together to the concert. In the evening after the concert there's a big party at Ochs's. Bruckner and the prince are going too, of course. Ochs is really a nice fellow. This morning he told me that he hadn't been able to sleep the whole night because he had learned of my dissatisfaction and had greatly reproached himself. We're again on the best of terms. I visited Frau Herzog today, but spoke only with her husband. She would have liked to participate, but the implacable theater manager would not allow it. A shame, just a shame. But must close now. I have to dress and write in the diary. With warmth and affection from your very best greeting

Hugo Wolf.

98

To Vienna
Berlin, January 9, 1894

Honored gracious lady!

My head is still reeling at the moment from the excitement of last evening. I can definitely say that I had a significant success and that the audience received me warmly without any doubt. But compared to the homage given Bruckner—apart from the orchestral fanfare and laurel wreaths—I can hardly claim a noteworthy success. The words of the Old Testament kept ringing in my ears: Saul slew 1,000, but David more than 10,000. As I had correctly suspected from the beginning, I was only there to act as a foil for Bruckner. I'm really too good for that, with all due respect and admiration for Bruckner. Not that I envy Bruckner his success—let him be worshipped like a *Vitzli-putzli*—but to saw away forever on second fiddle *ad majorem Bruckneri gloriam* [to the greater glory of Bruckner] when I'm used to playing first violin in my own way, I've had enough of that forever.

But I owe you a report on the actual concert. So here goes. Margits Gesang and Anakreons Grab got practically no applause. Performances of both pieces were extremely flawed in terms of the orchestra and soloists. The rhythmic accents in Margits Gesang were executed in a really alarmingly sloppy and wishy-washy manner, making the already mist-enshrouded mood in the character of the piece even more nebulous. Anakreons Grab was simply hurried through, especially by the singer who couldn't wait for it to be over. The situation changed abruptly, however, during the performance of Elfenlied. Orchestra, soloist (de Jong), and chorus performed at their peak. The effect of the sound was even more crystalline than at the dress rehearsal, a moonlit kind of atmosphere seemed to hover over everything, and it was easy to imagine hearing the little silver bells of the elves, their dainty laughter, their comical leaps . . . in short, it was really wonderful. *The piece had to be repeated.* The phantasmagoria of the Feuerreiter had an even greater effect on the audience. Everyone followed the story in breathless anticipation and broke out in stormy applause at the end. They wanted the piece played over again, but since Ochs had left the podium to look for me in the house, there was no repetition. Meanwhile, the applause went on and on, stopped, then began again with increased vigor, because they wanted to see the composer above all. But I had entrenched myself unnoticed in the standing-room section and didn't budge an inch. After the applause had died down, I reappeared at my seat, which Ochs had assigned to me in a balcony loge. I had hardly come into view when the orchestra and chorus began applauding madly. The entire audience stood up en masse and applauded me in the loge. I was completely dumbfounded, but I collected myself and bowed from my loge about a dozen times. And so the eventful evening came to an end. This morning I received the following note from the publishing house Ries & Erler: "Should the Elfenlied performed last night not yet be published, and should you be inclined to have our publishing house do so, we ask that you pay us a visit during the morning hours between 10:00 and 1:00." Finally a publisher who is inviting me! Of course, I'm prepared to sell him the piece, given the offer of a suitable honorarium. I haven't seen any reviews yet. As soon as I get around to it I'll

send you a few. This evening I'm going to Tristan with Sternfeld. Muck is conducting an uncut performance. Tomorrow I'm
going to Mauthner's in Grunewald with Sternfeld.

Sternfeld is my most ardent admirer. He says, "hinterm
Berg, hinterm Berg brennt es in der Mühle" [*Der Feuerreiter*] will
become a byword in Berlin. Ochs has assured me he's going to
incorporate the Elfenlied and Feuerreiter into his repertoire.

A visitor's coming and I have to break off. I'll write again
soon. With very best and sincerest wishes to you, Heinrich, and
the children. Forever your grateful

Hugo Wolf.

99

To Vienna

Berlin, January 11, 1894

Most honored gracious lady!

Many thanks for your second dear letter. Today I'm send-
ing you a review of the most feared of all the Berlin critics, Wil-
h[elm] Tappert. I'll send the others together in a bunch soon.
This evening I'm going to hear Shakespeare's Midsummer
Night's Dream at the theater. I had to postpone the visit to
Mauthner's, as Lilli Lehmann just came back today from a trip.
Sternfeld and I are going to Mauthner's tomorrow. I hope we can
win Lehmann over. Went with Ochs to the museums yesterday;
unfortunately the arsenal was closed by the time we got there.
I'll look at it another time. I received a charming letter from the
Lipperheides again. Both of them wrote to me. They insist on
seeing me. I should wait for them until the end of January, but
I'm not to take off immediately then either, the longer I stay
around the better, as far as they're concerned. Everything's going wonderfully for me here. I've become so immodest that I'll
soon be asking for the moon. What I enjoy most is wandering
through the ostentatious elegance of the Lipperheides' home
by electric light at night. It all looks so magical and dreamlike.
Every piece of furniture here is a Renaissance masterpiece, the
most valuable embroidery, splendid Gobelins [tapestries] hang
on the walls, not to mention the paintings. And each of these
magnificent things is arranged in its appropriate place with such

impeccable taste. God, when I recall my barren room in Döbling! It will be hard for me to get used to it again.

Sternfeld pawned off a few of his songs on me today. Insipid stuff. Of course I praised them. Nothing can be done about these people. *Mundus vult decepi, ergo decipiatur* [The world wants to be deceived, therefore it should be]. Old story. And Sternfeld is a kind, nice fellow, but one can't speak honestly with him beyond a certain point. He must *also* compose. But who doesn't compose these days? 'pon my soul, I'm the only one today who doesn't. A thousand greetings. More next time.

[no signature]

100

To Vienna
Berlin, January 15, 1894

Dear honored and gracious lady!

Please save the enclosed reviews after reading and send them back to me in Berlin in case I should need them. For the most part they're just lukewarm twaddle, such as one is accustomed to hearing from critics.

Have I already reported to you about the performance of Midsummer Night's Dream at the royal theater? If not, let it be said just between the two of us that there is nothing far and wide so pitiful as the histrionics at the Berlin royal theater.

With the exception of Frau Conrad as Puck, the performances of the remaining ensemble were of such philistine coarseness that they would not be tolerated on our provincial stages. But the biggest indignity to the bombastic world of comedians was committed by Herr Vollmer in the role of Zettel [Bottom]. Oh you kind good devil-of-a-Zettel! You simple, harmless lad! What a mish-mash of imbecility and monstrosity they made of you! You are supposed to turn into a donkey, to be sure, but you appeared only in the bespangled jacket of a trained monkey, brazen, shameless, brutal as only a monkey can be. At the conclusion this simian Zettel even turned completely into a dog, because the final words: now dead, dead, dead, dead, dead were a hoarse bark: haw, haw, haw, haw, haw, haw. The theater program should have announced: "Midsummer Night's

Dream, dog and monkey comedy, freely adapted from Shakespeare"—then it would have been correct.—

The day before yesterday Sternfeld and I were at Mauthner's, who received us most cordially. Mauthner is a marvelous fellow and chatting with him a real pleasure. We also talked about an opera libretto and he thinks he can help me find a good subject, but I have to be patient until summer. He was very secretive and I suspect he'll have a hand in it himself. Unfortunately, Frau Lilli Lehmann was out of sight for me. Mauthner, who had conferred with her in the meantime, did not come up with a favorable outcome. She is too busy with her affairs abroad and is unable at this time to occupy herself in any way with my things. What to do now? We positively cannot get Frau Herzog, as much as she'd like to participate. I'd like best to return to Vienna, if this damned Darmstadt thing weren't standing in the way. Today I'm going with my Dutch friend van Santen Kolff, a charming fellow, close friend of Emile Zola, to visit three Dutch women. They are giving a concert in the Singakademie February 7th and it occurred to me to have the Holy Three Kings [setting of Goethe's "Epiphanias"] sung by this "charming" trio on the condition that Julie Asten will agree to accompany at the piano, which, of course, is still very questionable.

Since the weather is now mild and clear, Sternfeld, van Santen Kolff and I want to go to Potsdam tomorrow morning and visit the royal palace Sanssouci there, the famous summer residence of Friedrich II. Meistersinger's being given on Wednesday. Muck is conducting. He's promised me two orchestra seats for the performance, which again, like Tristan, will be performed without cuts. Many thanks for your last letter, which I just received. It cost me considerable effort to decipher the hasty, irregular penstrokes, but it was a pleasant effort. I will not, however, follow your well-meant advice to stay in Berlin and settle here permanently, and for very valid reasons, which we can discuss better in person at another time.

The Lipperheides wired best wishes to me from Matzen. They will arrive here the end of January. The celebrated, sacrosanct Wagner Society of Vienna, as I learned through Sternfeld, is now going to perform several Wagner [songs] with orchestra (orchestrated by Mottl) instead of my songs. One just has to know how to get ahead.—Ries & Erler, these two Dogson and Fogg from the Pickwickians, wanted to offer me 200 M for the Elfenlied, specifically 100 M only after covering the printing costs. I, however, demanded immediate payment of 300 M. The publishers asked for time to consider this, which I granted. They're certain to bite. They also want to undertake the publication of songs. I replied: I would always be at their service for a good fee. Must close now. Many greetings to Heinrich and the girls. Always your grateful

Hugo Wolf.

101

To Vienna

Berlin, January 17, 1894

Most honored gracious lady!

I can breathe easy again after the last few days. A big load is off my mind: the Liederabend will *not* take place. The only annoying thing is the affair in Darmstadt, which is keeping me in Berlin one more week. If only the 29th of January were over with! Then quickly via Mannheim, Stuttgart, and Tübingen, where I won't stay longer than 24 hours, back to Vienna.

Today I paid visits to Erich Schmidt and Frau Ida Becker. The latter, a sentimental old biddy but quite good-hearted, very wealthy, and uncommonly music-loving, welcomed me as a lost son. Again she sang "Auf ein altes Bild" for me, once again she drove me to despair in doing so, and once again I paid her my most obliging compliments. On Saturday she is inviting a large group of people over to honor me—better said, to torment me. The renowned Jul[ius] Schulhoff, among others, is also coming—in God's name! This cup of suffering too shall pass. Ochs, the tireless one and always eager to please, has found another publisher for Elfenlied. It's this Fürstner in Dresden, who is in Berlin at the moment. Fürstner has the publishing house for Rienzi, Holländer, and Tannhäuser, which is to say, not an unimportant establishment. He offered me what I asked for Elfenlied (score and piano reduction): 300 M. Negotiations over the publication of the Feuerreiter score are already in progress between Ochs and Fürstner. I hope this attempt also leads to a happy conclusion. The visit to Potsdam has been postponed until tomorrow. Van Santen Kolff and his fun-loving young wife are going to play cicerone. Muck has given me two orchestra seats for this evening to Meistersinger (uncut!). Saturday Medici will be given in the presence of Leoncavallo for the first time. Muck will probably conduct, has already promised me an orchestra seat for this too. I visited the violinist Saize yesterday, but didn't get to see him as he was out of town. His wife greeted me most graciously, however, and invited me to the noonday meal Sunday so that I might have the opportunity to get acquainted with her husband. Unfortunately, I'll no longer be able to welcome the Lipperheides here, as they aren't intending to come until February 3rd. What a shame! The devil take this absurd arrangement with Darmstadt. *Never again* will I be lured into such a mousetrap. The Lipperheide cutlets and beefsteaks are immensely tasty. If this were to go on much longer, I would soon be ready for a fattened cattle exhibition, it agrees with me so well. During an attack of extravagance I bought myself 100 cigarettes for 7 marks, which are the *non plus ultra* of all Turkish cigarettes: small, but excellent. They bear the dynastic title Prince Heinrich, and it appears to me quite rightly so, since upon smoking them, one feels quite princely (not to be confused with prickly).

Bruckner left all alone yesterday for Vienna, Ochs told me today. Reportedly no one accompanied him to the station. By the way, you'll soon hear tell of wondrous things about Bruckner,—but don't give it away—the prospective husband (sh! sh!). But as I said *Silentium!* I'm telling this to you alone. Don't talk about it with another soul—understand? It's a deep secret, or is supposed to be, until it's announced. So, seal your lips and keep it under cover.

Recently, as I was wandering absentmindedly through the streets, my gaze was suddenly arrested by the sign of a flower shop in whose display windows wonderful lilies of the valley peeped out. I bought a small bunch, as such decoration is much less expensive in Berlin than in Vienna. And since I liked the flower-shop girl, I inquired after the name of the business. You can well imagine my astonishment when the sign announced to me a name one only gets to hear in the Salzkammergut, but particularly in Rinnbach. Shall I give it away? But you'll guess it yourself and name it in your next letter.

Until then with sincere greetings (including Heinrich and the dear children) your always devoted

Hugo Wolf.

102

To Vienna

Berlin, January 22, 1894

Most honored gracious lady!

I've become a very lazy correspondent in the last few days. Don't be angry on this account, but I had no desire to write at all. It's better today, although my head is pounding badly. Yesterday was the tenth commemoration of the "Liberated Ones" [*Zwanglosen*] and there were lively goings-on here beginning at 9:00 p.m. and lasting until 5:00 in the morning. I have a lot to report about that, such as how animatedly, wittily, and spiritedly everyone toasted, rhymed and joked, even danced at the end; then there were choral rounds [sung] over coffee by all the ladies and gentlemen (in tails and ball gowns, of course); and what huge quantities of beer were quaffed by Paul Schlenther, the "winebag," along with lots of other things. And then the wild comedy, presented by the Liberated Ones, written by a Liberated One. Despite the fact that Gerhart Hauptmann is very respected by the Liberated Ones, that didn't prevent them from doing a parody of Hannele [Hauptmann's play *Hanneles Himmelfahrt*], and a highly amusing and farcical one at that. Around 4:00 in the morning, in order to avoid a threatened toast to my health instigated by Mauthner, I had to sit down at the piano and sing something of mine. Had an immense success, too, with Cophtisches Lied I and—"Abschied." Didn't get to bed until 5:30 in the morning. Now the splendors will soon come to an end. Thursday I'm leaving Berlin with Fritz Mauthner. First I'm traveling to Mainz and will make my way from there on Friday to Mannheim. I'll be living there at Grohe's, L 14 No. 7. On the 24th I'll be in Darmstadt. From there again to Mannheim, where I'm going to accompany my songs in a quartet soirée given by Schuster. On Feb. 5th there will be a concert, i.e., Liederabend in Stuttgart. Faisst thinks I can earn 400–500 M for this. Well, we'll see. On the 4th or 3rd of Feb. I'll spend a day in Tübingen at Kauffmann's. On Feb. 6th I'm definitely departing, will stop one day in Munich, however, to discuss an opera libretto with a "poetess" and at the same time also meet with Porges to make arrangements for a performance of Elfenlied and Feuerreiter. So I hope to arrive safely in Vienna on the 8th. Things just can't be moved ahead with any more steam.

Today I was at Fürstner's and signed the contract, whereupon he paid out 300 M to me. Fürstner is also eager to get his hands on other things of mine. I'll try to maintain his appetite, in any event.

The weather has been warm and muggy for some time now. But once again I'm not going to get to Potsdam—it wasn't meant to be. Arrange it so that I find a letter from you Saturday in Mannheim. This would make immensely happy your most sincerely greeting

Hugo Wolf.

Best wishes to Heinrich and the children.

103

To Vienna

Berlin, January 24, 1894

A letter just came from Faisst. The concert in Stuttgart won't take place until the 7th. A postponement again! The devil take it!

Honored gracious lady!

Having just returned from Potsdam and Wannsee [Berlin suburb surrounding the lake of the same name] I discovered your last letter, for which I most kindly thank you. Tomorrow noon I'm leaving, i.e., with Mauthner and possibly also Siegfried Ochs.

I'll get to Mannheim tomorrow night around 1:00 a.m., where you may also write to me. Today was a splendid day. Not a cloud in the sky and the sun shone more pleasantly than ever before. We (Sternfeld and I) started off about 2:00. We traveled first to Potsdam, had a look at the city, the mausoleum of Friedrich III by Begas, went up to Sanssouci and looked at the inside of the palace. Wonderful Watteaus adorn the walls and everything is so delicate, artful, and droll, witty as if the spirit of Voltaire spoke to one from every corner. An entirely different picture was presented at a place on the Wannsee, where we made a stop on the way back. It's the place where our Kleist lies buried. A large grave fenced in by wrought iron, at the base of which grows a fairly large tree. The grave itself is entirely overgrown with ivy. There was a splendid atmosphere at 5:30: the sinking, blood-red sun through the sparsely planted firs shimmering over the Havel [river], which widens to a lake here, and all around solitude, deep silence. Not even a visible path leads to the grave. Yet the gravesite is well kept. You can well imagine my feelings in the presence of this hallowed site. I was deeply shaken.

Schott wrote. He would have liked to have published Elfenlied and wants to take on the publication of Feuerreiter for 300 M.

On Feb. 5th there is a Liederabend in Stuttgart. On Feb. 1st in Mannheim (Schuster soirée). I hope I will already be in Vienna by Feb. 7th. Sincerest greetings from your

Hugo Wolf.

104

To Vienna

Mannheim, January 26, 1894

Most honored gracious lady!

I've been in Mannheim since yesterday, or rather today at 1:00 a.m. in the morning. Grohe was waiting for me at the station and lodged me with one of his countless aunts, whom I've not yet, as of this moment, had the pleasure of meeting. I'm writing this note in the morning, still before breakfast, so that it reaches you promptly. The trip from Berlin to Nordhausen, where the famous Nordhauser (Schnaps) comes from, was considerably shortened for me by means of Mauthner's social talents. The journey to Frankfurt was all the more boring in the company of a Jewish banker from Hamburg with wife and daughter. From Frankfurt on, I rode alone again to Mannheim, where I have just now arrived at 1:00 a.m. in the morning.

I must mention that a letter from Faisst in Stuttgart arrived shortly before I left with the news that the concert in Stuttgart will take place on the 5th *after all*, not the 7th. So I will certainly arrive in Vienna on Feb. 7th. Please send me all the reviews of the Berlin papers *immediately*, Mannheim, L. 14 No. 7, Dr. Grohe. I need these for Schott, who will be at the Liederabend in Darmstadt. I haven't seen anything of Mannheim yet, other than the few houses where I'm staying near the railway. Am wondering what impression the city will make on me this time. I'm getting together today with Schuster. From Berlin I took an express train that covered the distance between Berlin and Frankfurt in $8\frac{1}{2}$ hours. It only made three stops the entire trip. It was as if we had wings. Apropos! Has Kosak, the cabinet-maker, gotten around to fixing my bookshelves in Döbling? If not, please arrange to have it done before my arrival.

How's everything at home? Everyone well? I'm fine, except for a head cold. Grohe says I look like a chubby-cheeked apple. He's exaggerating. Best greetings to Heinrich and the children as always, your faithfully devoted

Hugo Wolf.

105

To Vienna
Darmstadt, January 29, 1894

Most honored gracious lady!

First of all, my kindest thanks for both your letters, which Grohe delivered to me. (I'm not staying with Grohe himself, as you know, but with one of his many aunts.) I received the second letter this morning shortly before my departure for Darmstadt, to which I traveled in the company of Faisst, the lawyer from Stuttgart. I'm writing this note in a so-called coffeehouse, better called coffee dive so as not to insult a Viennese café. Darmstadt is a rather pitiful small town. Here and there one comes across a blue poster with the heading Hugo-Wolf-Evening. I'm being presented to the Darmstadters as a *Berliner*, to which my Austrian heart reacts fairly painfully. The rehearsal in the concert hall took place at noon today, right after my arrival. It went quite peaceably. Frl. Zimmer, a pretty, delicate creature, sings quite well, with much understanding and pleasant voice. The baritone Senff is less satisfying, but his performance is nevertheless acceptable. The Blüthner grand piano makes me very happy; it is a splendid instrument. Selzam has assured me of 50 M travel expenses. Dr. Strecker, who, I hope, will pay me the 300 M in cash for the Feuerreiter score, is also coming this evening from Mainz. In Faisst I've found not only a warm friend but also an excellent interpreter of my things. He came to Mannheim yesterday in order to get to know me personally. We made music almost the entire day and he sang a countless number of my songs for me with unusual perception.

(The pen is of such quality that I can only scratch out these hieroglyphics with the greatest of effort.)

The concert in Stuttgart will take place on Feb. 7th, as a result of Faisst's intercession. He hopes that it will bring me 300–400 M. On the 8th I'm going from Stuttgart back to Mannheim to take part in the Schuster Quartet. The quartet evening is on Feb. 8th. Frl. Zimmer and Herr Faisst are taking part and will sing 12 or 14 songs of mine. Meanwhile, I'll go to Kauffmann in Tübingen, where I plan to stay two days. I'm also going to look up Rich[ard] Voss, who lives in Stuttgart. Frau Begas-Parmentier recommended me to him. I'll stay with Faisst in Stuttgart. On Friday I go to Stuttgart, Saturday and Sunday I'm at Kauffmann's. Monday I'll go again to Stuttgart, where I'll stay until Wednesday, which is also the day the concert takes place. Thursday, the 8th, in Mannheim. Friday, the 9th, in Munich. And God willing, Saturday evening in Vienna.

More soon; I have another letter yet to write, therefore I'll close.

Sincere greetings to Heinrich and the children. Always your devoted

Hugo Wolf.

106

To Vienna

Mannheim, January 30, 1894

Honored gracious lady!

Yesterday's concert in Darmstadt went off very well. I was told that *such* a success is completely unheard of for Darmstadt. You see, the people there are truly not enthusiastic by nature.

It even appeared at the beginning as if the things might be a flop. "Klinge mein Pandero," "In dem Schatten" etc. and "Geh Geliebter" faded away almost without a ripple. But gradually these amphibians were made warmer by my music, and when Elfenlied [Mörike setting], as 13th, came up, the ice was broken and its repetition stormily demanded. I specifically was called out by name twice. They told me that such a thing was unheard of here, had never happened. We traveled to Mannheim again after the concert. Dr. Strecker was there too. He was beside himself for joy over the fine success. He was sweet as sugar, completely melting, in short, charming. He also brought the contract with him and wanted me to sign it immediately. He wanted to put money in my hand right away too. However, since I'm traveling to see him in Mainz tomorrow anyway, the matter can be settled there. Humperdinck is also coming to Mainz, at Strecker's bidding. Steinbach and Volbach were also mentioned by Strecker, and if I'm not mistaken, Frl. Zimmer as well, who sang the things really very beautifully. Unfortunately she's not a soprano. She had to sing transposed even things like "Auf ein altes Bild." It's a shame, because she could otherwise be very useful. On Friday I'm going to Stuttgart to talk over the concert in more detail with Faisst. If only this event were over. Perhaps I'll stay just one day at Kauffmann's. In any case, I'll expect a letter in Stuttgart c/o *poste restante.* Grohe, who has just come by, is scolding me for all my writing and can't wait until I'm finished. So, his will be done. For today then, ever so quickly, sincerest greetings from your most devoted

Hugo Wolf.

107

To Vienna

Mannheim, Feb. 1, 1894

Most honored gracious lady!

I'm not going to Stuttgart until Sunday and will go on the same day to Tübingen, where I'll spend Monday. Tuesday I'll be back again in Stuttgart to rehearse, Wednesday is the concert. Thursday I'll be in Mannheim again to take part in the Schuster Quartet (Frl. Zimmer sings 12 songs, Herr Faisst 6, i.e., 18 altogether). Dr. Strecker, whom I visited yesterday in Mainz, was kindness personified. He picked me up at the train station and accompanied me to the station again for the trip home. We talked about everything imaginable, including business. I think he really means well toward me and most definitely wants the best for me.

Unfortunately, Humperdinck was prevented from coming. On the other hand, I made the acquaintance there of Capellmeister Steinbach and of the musician Volbach. Both really terrific fellows. I've been coughing wretchedly for several days and my head cold won't go away.

Grohe recently gave me two quite remarkable books by Maupassant. Little stories. But what stories! You must definitely read them! My only pleasure at the moment is derived from the Gypsy Dance in La Jolie Fille de Perth (Bizet). It's the same piece that was played on the occasion of the Berlin production of Carmen as a ballet interlude and delighted me no end at the time. Now I can play it whenever the mood strikes me, and I revel so in this wildly graceful music. You, too, will never get enough of these piquant rhythms and unusual harmonies. How I already look forward to acquainting you with them. I've also formed a close attachment to a charming minuet and a very willowy serenade from the opera. Nothing much goes on in the rest of it, unfortunately. But it's musically well crafted, if not always ingenious. Nothing much else to report here. Grohe's mother-in-law, with whom I am staying, mothers me in the most touching way. She's a kind, educated, highly sensitive, yet amusing and sometimes even high-spirited lady. Naturally, I want for nothing, and yet that which I'd like, no one here can give me. And now I must close. Many greetings to the children and Heinrich. [I'll] write you again soon; your ever faithful

Hugo Wolf.

Have received the reviews. Thanks.

108

To Vienna

[Stuttgart, February 5, 1894]

Most honored gracious lady!

I've been in Stuttgart since last evening and am staying with Faisst the lawyer, where I'm provided for most comfortably. Yesterday a musical evening was held in my honor by the champagne manufacturer Engelmann, who also fancies himself a poet in addition. It was dreadful enough to blow one's brains out. Frau Engelmann and her daughter tried to outchirp each other and did everything to make my things as unrecognizable as possible. I cannot comprehend the audacity of such people. And moreover, they want to be praised for it as well.

On the other hand, Faisst sang my harper songs [*Harfenspieler*, Nos. 1–3] and the two Coptic ones [*Cophtische Lieder*, Nos. 1–2] quite uniquely. We didn't break up until late at night. I was so horribly tired, as I've been suffering from terrible insomnia ever since my stopover in Mannheim, that I no longer had the strength in me to reply in the most ordinary prose to the speech composed for me by Herr Engelmann, one in verse—hexameter. As for the rest, the party bored me to such an extent that mustering up a halfway animated mood was totally out of the question.

It's going to be decided today at noon whether Frl. Merk will sing in the concert on the 7th or not. She is completely hoarse at the moment. Presumably she'll cancel.

In this eventuality I have already advised Frl. Zimmer, who recently studied my things with me and which she now performs enchantingly well, to substitute for the indisposed Frl. Merk. The concert in Mannheim is on the 8th. On the 12th— imagine, there's actually going to be a concert in Tübingen. I'll hardly arrive before the 15th of the m[onth] with all of this, in which case I must also take into account my train ticket, which I believe is good only through Feb. 15th.

At noon I've been invited as a guest to a very wealthy and eminent home here. Perhaps I'll meet Rich[ard] Voss there, whom I'll seek out in his hotel in any case. God grant that this cursed trip finally comes to an end. I can hardly hold out much longer. We have clear, sunny weather at last. The gloomy, rainy sky up until now made me quite melancholy.

I received letter to Stuttgart. Kindest thanks for it. *Thursday* and *Friday* I'll be in Mannheim again. Please send a few lines there to your most sincerely greeting

Hugo Wolf.

Many greetings to Heinrich and the children.

109

To Vienna

Stuttgart, Feb. 8, 1894

Most honored gracious lady!

I'm reporting in all haste on the success of yesterday's Lie-derabend. Stupendous reception. Laurel wreath. Everything went splendidly. Rich[ard] Voss, who was also at the concert, embraced and kissed me after it. We formed a close friendship. He's quite a wonderful person.

Am going to Mannheim today, where [there's a] concert. Am in Tübingen on the 12th, where [there's a] concert. Must close, unfortunately. No time. Heavily in demand—have already fallen apart completely. Sincerest greetings!

[no signature]

110

To Vienna

Mannheim, Feb. 11, 1894

Most honored gracious lady!

The concert in Tübingen has had to be postponed until Sunday the 18th of the m[onth] because of Frl. Zerny's laryngitis. Meanwhile, we're planning to give a concert in Heilbronn or Frankfurt. On Friday I'm going to Stuttgart to talk over my opera project with Voss in detail. Saturday I'll be in Tübingen. The concert on Sunday takes place 11–12:30 in the morning. The evening in Mannheim on Feb. 8th passed without particular enthusiasm. I wasn't called until the very end; the invitation, however, brought no result.

Incidentally I've been sleeping somewhat better the past few days and my cough bothers me less.

The weather is completely unbearable. Almost always rain and wind, accompanied by mist, which settles like lead over the dirty city.

If only I were gone from this square, boring Mannheim! How are you? What's going on in Vienna? I learned about Bill-roth's death several days after the fact from the newspapers. Now friend Hanslick should come through as well [i.e., die].

Today Meistersinger will be given (uncut). The theater manager has placed a ticket for the visitors' loge at my disposal.

Am very eager to hear the tenor Herr Kraus, over whom there is a great deal of fuss here. He's supposed to sing lieder very beautifully as well. Perhaps the man can be useful.

The performance of Meistersinger begins at 5:00. And since the afternoon is already almost over, ever so quickly the sincerest greetings (including Heinrich and the children) from your very devoted

Hugo Wolf.

111

To Vienna
Mannheim, Feb. 14, 1894

Honored gracious lady!

From your last letter, which has just been delivered to me, you appear not to have received the letter postmarked from Mannheim. I informed you in this that a matinee will be arranged on Feb. 18th in Tübingen. Yesterday's telegram was forwarded to me from Tübingen to Mannheim, where I plan to stay until Saturday. Faisst from Stuttgart recently suggested to me arranging a concert in Heilbronn. Should this materialize I'll stay in Stuttgart until the 15th of the m[onth]. My train ticket is good until March 2nd, as is noted on it in black and white. In my next letter I'll be able to fix the day of my arrival, as I must first wait to see whether the concert in Heilbronn materializes. I would have returned to Vienna long ago, if Kauffmann hadn't insisted on concertizing in Tübingen no matter what. But now Feb. 12th must be postponed to the 18th— so there's nothing to do but wait it out. It doesn't make me very happy either; nevertheless it's advantageous and useful to proceed along a path already traveled. As soon as I learn more about Heilbronn, I'll write again. Sincerest greetings to you, Heinrich and the children. Always your gratefully devoted

Hugo Wolf.

112

To Vienna
Mannheim, Feb. 17, 1894

Most honored gracious lady!

I'm writing these lines in the early dawn, since I'm traveling this morning to Tübingen. I'll spend Sunday at Kauffmann's. Monday and Tuesday in Stuttgart with Rich[ard] Voss. Wednesday I'll travel directly to Vienna, without stopping in Munich, so that I'll arrive on Wednesday evening or Thursday morning.

Incidentally, I'll wire my arrival. For now, suffice it to say that I'm fine and that I'm facing my future filled with good cheer. To a happy, warm, and speedy reunion. With greetings to all, the finest good morning, honored gracious lady, wishes you your always devoted

Hugo Wolf.

113

To Vienna
Stuttgart, Feb. 20, 1894

Most honored gracious lady!

I'm finally getting around to reporting on the concert in Tübingen. It went brilliantly. The enclosed report says the rest. It was really splendid. Kauffmann was warmer and more ardent than ever and dear old Tübingen in the moonlight awakened wonderful old memories in me. I stayed at Kauffmann's, who didn't want to let me leave again. Today I'm in Stuttgart. I received your dear letter and thank you very much. I'm staying here with Faisst the lawyer, where I'll probably remain until Saturday. I hope to arrive in Vienna on Sunday. Much of the time I'm together with Voss, who practically gobbles me up out of fondness. Unfortunately, his health is so miserable at the moment that there can be no talking about our project with him. But he hopes there will soon be an improvement in his situation. Meanwhile, the marquis affords me the best companionship. He also invited me to come visit him at his estate on Lago Maggiore, which I accepted of course. The weather has been beautiful for several days: "heavenly coolness, soothingly sweet air" [*himmlische Kälte, balsamsüsse Luft*]. This evening, or rather night there is a moonlight excursion planned to Degerloch—an hour out of town. I'm looking forward to it. The stay here is especially enjoyable for me, and the association with my friends here (and I have only too many of them) is extremely pleasant and stimulating. Herr and Frau Klinckerfuss, in particular, outdo each other in their attentiveness to me. What a shame that you cannot witness all the love and admiration being shown me in richest abundance here.

My friend Faisst shows me no end of kindness. He anticipates my every wish. There is never any arguing or quarreling, for we are one in body and soul. This marvelous person really lives only in my sounds [music] and he can't do enough to prove his unlimited attachment to me over and over again. Ah, not until I was away from home did I really come to know what friendship is. When I think of my so-called Viennese friends, I literally shudder. From this you will understand why I am very happy in this pure atmosphere. I sense, too, that I'm gradually becoming a better person and I'm starting again to acquire belief and trust in people. May this uplifting feeling soon express itself in artistic realization.

Faisst has just come to fetch me for a walk. And so the very sincerest and very kindest greetings from your always respectful
Hugo Wolf.

114

To Vienna
Graz, April 13, 1894

Dear gracious lady!

Having been on the point of writing several times, I was prevented from doing so each time by important visits or other bothers. I've just returned from a dinner at Schey's, two hours before my concert, and found your note. Originally, I had intended to rest and sleep a little. However, I find it more pleasant to chat with you by writing. You probably already know that Jäger canceled. We'll just have to manage without him.

Regarding Frl. Zerny, I can give you complete reassurance about my behavior toward her. You are absolutely right. She is an egotist and capable of everything but loving. If you knew how coolly and disinterestedly I behave toward her! I hardly give her a glance. She has actually become repulsive to me. Fortunately, my visible disinclination appears to make no particular impression on her, and so I hope to get rid of her gracefully soon.

The concert tonight is taking place without Jäger and without the songs he was to have sung.

Tomorrow evening Hofmann is giving a big party in my honor. Therefore, I can't yet come on Saturday. I'm also busy on Sunday. We're driving up to the Schöckel with Baron Schey, where we'll spend the day.

Monday evening, however, I'll be arriving in Vienna *for certain*. How *I* look forward to our reunion. Faisst is already leaving here tomorrow.

My theory of waiting it out has been well tested, to my greatest satisfaction. I always told you: let's wait and see. I've become uncommonly clear-sighted since then. The sincerest greetings for today in haste from your

Hugo Wolf.

115

To Traunkirchen

Vienna, May 31, 1894

Dear gracious lady!

It is already evening. Mama's still in town and so there is just enough time until supper to finish this letter, which is a necessity for me. I've just come from a walk in the Türkenschanze [park]. God knows exactly why it was the Türkenschanze that was the destination of my stroll; be that as it may, my two black steeds [i.e., feet] were absolutely determined to strike out in a *westward* direction, and so I gave in to their liveliness and allowed myself to be dispatched up to the Türkenschanze. Very odd thoughts, indeed, came to me there, and for a moment I was even a strange curiosity to myself. But more about that another time. To give you an idea, however, I can tell you now that I was overcome by a feeling of unspeakable emptiness and desolation. Be it only out of habit, or be it something else which I would conceal,—I was just terribly bored today for the whole long afternoon, and I literally longed for the compulsion that has recently called me so regularly before your throne. Now that I'm free, I long for chains; but feeling myself so bound, I'm driven again to freedom. What's to be done? I'll reflect on it, and when I've come to a rational conclusion, I'll let you know further. For today, however, I'm thinking of you in the sincerest way and wish you every possible good and pleasant thing for the first part of your stay there.—I was in the garden salon for a moment where I greeted Mama today for the first time. She thanked me coldly and hardly gave me her hand. Thereupon, I excused myself from this evening's supper on the pretext of having spent a sleepless night. She bade me good night very coolly, again hardly stretching out her hand to me. I thought to myself: Goose!

From tomorrow on, I'm no longer eating at Mama's, as I would rather leave this confounded Döbling than anything else. More details shortly! I'm enclosing a letter of Wiesner's from Stuttgart, to whom I gave my photograph at the time.

Sincere greetings to Heinrich and the children. Always your

Hugo Wolf.

116

To Traunkirchen

Vienna, June 1, 1894

Dear gracious lady!

In order to put your mind at ease, I must tell you right away that my remarks about Mama in the last letter were due to a misunderstanding. I thought she was displeased with me because I had stayed away from a tarok game, but learned today from Dlauhy that only fatigue was the cause of her very cool behavior. This morning Mama greeted me in a very friendly way, from which I may gather that Dlauhy was right. I've already silently apologized to Mama and taken it upon myself to be more considerate in the future.

Today the weather is dreadful, rainy, cold. How it must appear at Buchschach (spelled correctly?)! Frau Faisst wrote me a very pleasant note yesterday, inviting me to be their guest in Heilbronn whenever I would like. For the present I can bore myself just as well in Döbling. It probably wouldn't be much different in Heilbronn. Besides, my library affords me such good company that I could hardly find sufficient substitutes for it in Frau Faisst and even the excellent Prof. Mayser.

Boller put me off again for tomorrow evening, for a change, as Oberhauser is prevented from appearing. We're going to try our luck on Tuesday. Surely something will go wrong again. You are probably very busy during the first days with trunks and suitcases and similar matters, which always cause a certain amount of diversion, albeit not the most pleasant kind. I'm valiantly orchestrating away here, in order to finally finish the thing [*Dem Vaterland*, second version]. The new score will sound glorious, because I'm going about it with great care. Earlier I wrote much too much at random, which I notice on almost every page. This time I'm completely sure of the aural effect I have in mind. The piece will have an immense impact in its present form. Perhaps the local men's choral society will perform it sometime. Given the lack of good new things, the people could only congratulate themselves on this one.—

Time to eat. I'm being summoned. So, must close! The very kindest and sincerest greetings from your always devoted
Hugo Wolf.

117

To Traunkirchen
Vienna, June 13, 1894

Dear gracious lady!

The afternoon sun is once again shining so cheerfully through my window that I don't want to resist the temptation of a diverting chat with you long-distance, even if it means the work slows down for a little while. In writing these lines I'm also allowing myself a rest period, for the last stroke of the pen in the orchestration of the hymn [*Dem Vaterland*] has just been made. Now I can turn my full attention to the corrections of Feuerreiter, which will give me enough to do in the next few days, since every single page is just crawling with mistakes. But today, when the sky is so blue and the sun looks out so cheerfully again, I'll have myself a good day, and I think there's no better way to fulfill this intention than chatting with you in the dear, familiar way. As this "familiar way" doesn't preclude revilement and grumbling, I'll begin right off by damning "dear" Smatosch to the very devil and flinging the worst curses on his old graying sinner's head. What on earth is the fellow thinking of, playing around with his customers in *such* a manner! It almost seems to me as if the old fox Pfeiffer is behind this, who set off his invisible mines at the restaurant table at "zur Sonne" and put some sort of bug in good Smatosch's ear. The situation strikes me as highly suspicious. The devil take these old-biddy-Cassandras [pessimists], if they absolutely don't want to make fools of themselves, because unfortunately Pfeiffer is right this time. So I'll have to console myself with August, by which time the evil spell which is now cast over Buchschach will be broken. By then the joy of a reunion will be that much greater. Did I ever tell you that Oberhauser paid me a visit in the meantime? And that this visit pleased and satisfied me in every respect? We hit it off first over Berlioz, whose Cellini [opera] had remained unknown to him except for Fieramoska's aria. So I played him a large portion of it, over which he went into complete ecstasy. Then I introduced him to Fussreise, which made such an impression on him that he immediately sight-read through it again most excellently. He also sang the Wächterlied, Biterolf, and König bei der Krönung most admirably. We're going to undertake Prometheus next, which he's particularly eager to do. Invited to supper at Mama's, he also revealed social qualities that left reason to presume there is a solid core. In a word: I like the man and am indeed happy to have made his acquaintance. I hope that his difficult artistic as well as financial situation will soon be improved by an upward swing, because I hear things are going really badly for the poor fellow.

Am enclosing a letter from Schey and Hansi. Sincere greetings to Heinrich and my three loyal ones. All good and best wishes from your

Hugo Wolf.

118

To Traunkirchen
Vienna, June 18, 1894

Dear gracious lady!

For several days now I've been in possession of a photograph by Dr. Heid, which I must count among the most successful ever issued by this photographer's studio. When I come to Buchschach, I'll bring the picture along, which will surely give you much pleasure, quite apart from the personality portrayed in it. As to the personality, I must leave you in the dark, as much as I'd like to reveal it openly and candidly right now. Nevertheless, it's your own fault that you won't learn more about it at this time. According to my youthful friend Ilse's report, Hansi will move to Traunkirchen this summer. I hope she won't neglect inviting me there occasionally, since the chances of your house being inhabitable soon are becoming increasingly slim. But Joseph [Schey] shouldn't take too long to consider the matter, or he'll be out of luck again, like two years ago when the Hambrecht villa was snatched from under his nose. That *amico* Fritz has gotten himself engaged is very heartening. I hope his fiancée won't have any reason to sing, as does my minstrel [*Musikant:* Eichendorff setting]: "when the two of us were together, my singing left me" [*wenn wir zwei zusammen waren, möcht mein Singen mir vergehen*], although such an assumption is not out of the question. But let's assume the best.

Mama, Helene, children, Fraülein, and Tini went to the country this afternoon, i.e., to Weidling am Bach. Unfortunately, they are just now coming home. It's 9:45 in the evening and I'll be called to supper. Must close with this, but not before complimenting Ilse on her skillful writing accomplishment. I was quite amazed by it. Sincerest greetings to the Buchschachers and, let us hope, a reunion at Traunsee. Always your very most devoted

Hugo Wolf.

119

To Traunkirchen
Vienna, June 20, 1894

Dear gracious lady!

Following the old Germans' custom of asking women for advice in difficult situations, I come to you as the decadent offspring of our upstanding forefathers to elicit your opinion about a very touchy matter. The situation involves the dedication of Elfenlied. My publisher has decided to print a new edition and to use the current one as scrap paper. I was informed at the same time that at my request the dedication in the second, which will now be considered the first printing, will be omitted, as this new printing will be considered the first edition.

The peculiar manner in which Frau v. Lipperheide reacted to the dedicatory inscription of Elfenlied leads one to assume that she attaches no particular significance to the dedication, indeed that it came quite unexpectedly and was perhaps even undesired. This could easily be remedied by elimination of the dedication. The question is only whether it would be advisable to inform Frau v. Lipperheide of my intention or whether to simply ignore her curious behavior, retain the dedication, or to remove it. In my opinion, it seems to me most appropriate to write the lady a polite letter begging her pardon for the liberty I took and requesting her permission to withdraw the dedication under the existing circumstances. After that everything will probably clarify itself. Don't you agree?

Please send me your viewpoint on this *immediately*, which I trust implicitly as always being correct in matters of feminine tact, and accept the reassurance that I will act only in accordance with your judgment.

With sincerest greetings (including Heinrich and the happy trio) your very devoted

Hugo Wolf.

120

To Traunkirchen

Vienna, June 23, 1894

Dear gracious lady!

After a heart-pumping walk in the Himmelgegend [park] this morning your letter arrived and by afternoon the promised book as well. I seized upon the latter as a vulture upon its prey. The first thing I turned to involved the newspaper comments on Keller's election to state clerk of Zürich. What godless ranting and raving, what petty nitpicking, what narrowmindedness regarding such a man! No one would think it possible if it weren't there in black and white. I was a little disappointed in the portrait of the poet. It might do for a state clerk. I can't perceive the poet in these broad, coarse features. At any rate, I'll have to grow accustomed to them first. How I envy the dull Robert

Franz, who was recommended to Keller (nota bene by Wagner) as an "important composer." They weren't well matched at all. Unfortunately, Wagner's association with Keller is only fleetingly mentioned in this book. I was hoping for more details about this relationship. Nevertheless, it contains a wealth of interesting information about the poet and his works, and I'll have enough to do in the coming days to get through this vast amount of material. A thousand thanks for sending the books; you couldn't have given me more pleasure.

Today was the first marvelously sunny day in a long time; how pleasantly you must have spent it on the shores of the Traunsee. With the wish that many more such days be granted you, I greet you and your loved ones, as your always devoted
Hugo Wolf.

121

To Traunkirchen
Vienna, June 26, 1894

Dear gracious lady!

I have always received your letters and have always welcomed them most joyfully as well.

This time I'm enclosing the conclusion of my friend Grohe's letter, which of course sheds another light on Frau v. L[ipperheide]'s behavior. Unfortunately, my letter to Frau v. L. had already been posted when Grohe's letter arrived. But it won't hurt if the good lady receives a tiny reprimand, as she could just as easily have written to me as to Grohe. The dedication, accordingly, will remain in place in the second printing. Yesterday I was in the store twice and met Heinrich both times. He told me in detail about Paris, which does not seem to have particularly enchanted him. However he did arrive there just in time to catch a glimpse of the President of the Republic, who in the meantime has been cut down in such a terrible manner. Poor Carnot! Such a good, kind man and to meet his end in such a way! Monsters, these anarchists. May the hangman claim them all.—

What I learned about Buchschach wasn't very comforting unfortunately. According to Heinrich, taking possession has apparently been put off quite a while by the delay, which has also been accompanied by stupidity and confusion. The gods themselves cannot help in this case, and one just has to be patient. It all has to end sometime.

The letters of Gottfr[ied] Keller are my only diversion at the moment. But I couldn't wish for any better. I've already read over half the book, despite the many letters that have to be read carefully. His views and essays on modern drama are extremely interesting, for which his instinct is as correct as his talent is weak. For all his desire and perseverance, he doesn't even produce a complete draft, [which is] clear proof of his totally undramatic nature. I showed Schalk the poet's portrait and he was just as perplexed as I. Perhaps the third volume, for there's one coming out soon, will have a picture from his younger days, although such [a photograph] would have been more appropriate to the first volume. When I've devoured the Keller volume, I'll return again to Simplicissimus by Grimmelshausen, my reading of which was interrupted by the arrival of your package. You must get to know this book. I'll bring it to you.

Yesterday was a dreadfully sultry day, unbearably hot and muggy. By contrast, it's almost cold today, which is not surprising either, as it's raining cats and dogs. How it must be where you are! Sincere greetings to my three loyal ones and Heinrich.

Respectfully as always, most truly your

Hugo Wolf.

122

To Traunkirchen

[Vienna], June 28, 1894

Dear gracious lady!

In my haste and absentmindedness I forgot to enclose Grohe's letter in my last note. Frau v. Lipperheide has also sent word in the meantime. I'll enclose both letters—with the request to return them whenever it's convenient. How glad I am that I followed your advice. Why are you so totally silent? Give me some sign of life please, I implore you. The Keller letters are still making me delirious with *plaisir*. Hope to finish the book today so that I can start all over again from the beginning.

In between I read a little in Der grüne Heinrich [novel by Keller], then in the Züricher Novellen, then in the poems—apropos! Poems! Are you acquainted with the Apotheker von Chamonix? Utterly droll and superb. It's a satire on Heine's imitators, done entirely in the style of Heine, yet wonderfully rich in fantasy and actually quite mystical at the same time. Do you have it at the moment? If not, I'll bring along my copy of the poems when I come.

How are you? And the children? Is Heinrich sailing around diligently? Today the weather is beautiful. For several days now I've been getting up at 5:30 in the morning and taking energetic walks.

A thousand greetings! Always your

Wolferl.

Fraul Sirke has not shown her face at my place since the 4th of the m[onth]. Where does she live?

123

To Traunkirchen
Vienna, July 3, 1894

Dear gracious lady!

I'm very happy to know that you're so terribly busy, despite the curtailment that our correspondence has suffered as a result of your exhausting activity. Continue to work away at your domestic managing and organizing, which I practically envy you. If it is a pleasure in itself to be busy, the more enjoyable it must be when it's coupled with a good purpose, which in this case involves not only you, but especially your family and even me a tiny bit. So dig in and work hard so that the project for which you're in the process of doing the final—corrections, to use a word that has become very familiar to me—will soon be crowned by moving in.

Let me know immediately what day you are moving in; I would like to be present, preferably as a participant, at the celebration. I can't begin to tell you how much I long for the day that will abduct my tormentors to Rinnbach (primarily cook and kitchen maid, because of the confounded sugar grinding). The little toad Gerda becomes more repulsive to me every day and, well, the others aren't exactly a joy either. I hope I'll be liberated in ten days. This afternoon I'll ask Ignaz for Frau Sirke's address.

The good woman appears to have an amnesia potion in her system.

A month has gone by since she picked up the laundry and never brought it back again. In the end, she'll turn out to be sick, or even dead; I suspect the latter, as she never does this kind of thing. Well, I'll know shortly what's going on.

I'm reading nothing but Keller now, and again more Keller. Yesterday before falling asleep I picked up a Wagner volume, but closed the book again quickly, as I found this long-winded, tapeworm style of writing so offensive. In this respect, the gnarled Gottfried is a completely different man, at least in terms of style. I feel even more at home with his prose than with Goethe's, to which it bears a strong resemblance, by the way. But Keller's language is more pliable, more colorful, and in its deftness stronger and more objective than that of his great role model. Sometimes, of course, his word constructions are stilted and produce strange effects, particularly when he's trying to find the shortest, pithiest expressions. But these are exceptions that serve to adorn his crystal-clear style rather than detract from it. I can't thank you enough for such a splendid gift as the complete works of Keller, with which you have given me a lifetime of happiness.

Kauffmann, whom I already owe answers to two letters, wrote me today. He was prepared in my last letter, by the way, for a long interruption. To keep him in a good mood, I intend to send him my sacred choruses, composed in 1881, which I recently copied in my own hand. Perhaps he'll perform these in one of his concerts and thereby provide proof that not everything the Wagner Society disdains is trash.

Today I'm putting my score of Dem Vaterland (copy) in Löwe's hands to be passed on to the conductor of the University Choral Society, Ed[uard] Kremser. God willing, the piece will be performed and be a success in Vienna. 'Twould be high time.—Many, many greetings from your

Hugo Wolf.

124

To Traunkirchen
Vienna, July 13, 1894

Dear gracious lady!

I just received the first proofs of the Feuerreiter piano
score, which I'm sending you so that you can feast your eye on
the beautiful engraving. When you have a chance, be kind
enough to send the music to B. Schotts Söhne in Mainz, but not
before I give you word to this effect. Yesterday I was with Löwe
at Kremser's, not the café, but the choral conductor, although
we went right away from Kremser's to Kremser's. The Herr
Choral Conductor liked the piece immensely. He was enthusiastic about it to such an extent that he promised on his word of
honor to perform the piece in the coming season. May God grant
that he keeps his word of honor. I'm going to offer the work
to Schott for publication and endeavor to hammer out the best
possible terms for myself, in which, let us hope, I'll be able to be
successful. On the occasion of the departure of my housemates
tomorrow, Herr Beckmesser's noble air will not leave my mind:

den Tag seh ich erscheinen,	I see the day appearing,
der mir wohl gefallen thut.	which pleases me full well.
Da fasst mein Herz sich einen	My heart is seized with
guten u. frischen Muth.	fine and renewed courage.

And of this I am truly in need, for I feel myself terribly dragged
down by daily contact with people who go so entirely against my
grain. In the meantime, I await the fervently desired healing
from my consoler and loyal companion, Solitude. I'm thinking
of staying here until around the end of July after all and com-
muning with myself in complete peace and seclusion. I've become such a stranger to myself during this long time and have
led such a superficial existence that I cannot resist the urge to
make a journey of discovery into my other world, a world so
entirely different from that which has held my aspirations imprisoned until now. In short, I'm going to try to climb down

"into the abyss of contemplation." So don't be angry if my visiting is put off for a little while. Regarding the Wächterlied, I had already decided to set this for large orchestra even before your approval arrived. Nevertheless, my concurrence with your point of view provided me with great reassurance, and I'll be able to get to work now with more confidence.

I spent yesterday evening very pleasantly and cheerfully with Heinrich in Kührer's newly opened beer garden. Crabs, draft beer, fresh air, friendly chatter, plenty of food, reasonably priced as well—what more can one wish?

Heinrich shouldn't forget to write to Faisst, and don't you forget either to write a line now and then to him who greets you most sincerely

Hugo Wolf.

Many greetings to Heinrich and the girls.

125

To Traunkirchen

Vienna, July 17, 1894

Dear gracious lady!

First of all, please send the Feuerreiter piano score to *me* immediately, i.e., do *not* mail to Schott, and [send it] at the book rate, for which a three-kreuzer stamp is enough. I received the enclosed card this morning. Moreover, a letter came at noon from Faisst, wherein he announces his anticipated arrival in Traunkirchen beginning of August (8–15th).

Have you moved in already? I wouldn't mind coming to Traunkirchen as early as next week, since in the last few days it's begun to be unbearably hot. Also, my dear Weinhappel is starting to be stubborn, so that I'm forced to take my noonday meal at the restaurant. Dlauhy is leaving tomorrow, thank God, and will be gone for ten days. Sunday morning there was hail and rain and it wasn't until afternoon that the sky cleared a little bit. Went to Werners' in Perchtoldsdorf around 3:00, but ran into a soaking downpour, hence nothing came of the skittles game.

Mitz was in good voice and sang several things from the Mögele operetta Friedrich der Heizbare.

Went back to Döbling with a terrible hangover about 9:00 p.m. Am now reading Zola's Doctor Pascal [1893]. Very boring so far. Am closing with many sincere greetings as your very devoted

Hugo Wolf.

The handwritten paper from R. Wagner to Brandt has been found. All further details in person.

126

To Traunkirchen

Vienna, July 21, 1894

Dear gracious lady!

Perhaps the long-awaited move into your new home is just taking place as I write these lines. May my best wishes for you and all your loved ones be with you. In accordance with the wish you expressed, I will arrive in Traunkirchen on the 28th of the m[onth]; it will be early in the morning, as I intend to travel overnight Friday on the mail train. Thank you very much for thoughtfully mailing me the newspaper clippings. I found the article on Emerson and Nietzsche to be truly deplorable; pure journalistic drivel. Last evening—oh miracle—Sara [i.e., Karl] Bernhard Öhn—visited me; it was (as he confided to me apologetically) by order of his wife, who, through him, bade me come to supper. Of course I accepted the invitation, because of his wife, and stayed with them until about 11:00, discussing all things possible and impossible. I've even been invited to a skittles party next Thursday. You can see, I'm starting to have some success with the Oehns.

My good Weinhappel has finally calmed down and is now fervently currying my favor. In spite of my serious intention never to speak a kind word to her again, I feel the ice of my severity gradually melting in the face of her humble and wistful attempts to bring me round. She's an odd person, who has definitely missed her calling. Since the air here has cleared again, there is a truly uncanny stillness surrounding me. Ah, how good it feels. Nothing around me but the sky, green leaves, and marvelous sunshine, and over everything the wondrous silence, with its otherworldly magic, its bottomless depths, its familiar,

shaded pathways, its labyrinths of dreams. Can one wish for anything more beautiful? And yet . . . and yet I wish for something
still far, far more beautiful, but I fear this more beautiful thing
will remain only a devout wish for a long time still. Faisst wrote
me today that he hasn't heard a single solitary word from any of
the Köchert family since he left Vienna. He's not planning to
stay in Puchschach either, but in an inn. Why don't you invite
him, please, as Heinrich will not do it.

So, Saturday around 8:30 a.m. at the train station in
Traunkirchen. Sincere greetings to all the Buchschachers from
your faithful

Hugo Wolf.

127

To Traunkirchen

Vienna, July 23, 1894

Dear gracious lady!

The days are so beautiful now and so hot at the same time
that I wouldn't mind coming to Tr[aunkirchen] already early
Thursday morning, assuming that various matters can be taken
care of before then. Shoemaker and tailor play the greatest roles
in this. If no cancellation is forthcoming from me by Wednesday,
please expect me Thursday at 8:30 in the morning at the train
station (I believe this is the time the mail train arrives in T.). In
case of a cancellation I'll arrive on Saturday at the same time.

Yesterday (Sunday) I was in Perchtoldsdorf at the Werners'. There was a bit of music-making (Mizi sang the Wagner
poems) and a lot of skittle-playing. Today a Herr Georg Scherer
sent me his poems from Munich and referred in an enclosed
letter to his close friendship with Ed[uard] Mörike. Enclosed is
the letter in question.

The poems, an all too stately volume, are very beautifully
presented, but that's also the only beautiful thing about them.
In general, a boring whine of heart and hurt, loving and shoving,
moaning and groaning, yearning and burning and whatever other
trash can be drawn from the lyric junk room—nothing but cheap
wares. The publication is even adorned with a picture of the

"poet." To judge from the face, the Herr Poet is in all probability a very good husband and excellent family man. His intellectual children, however, were definitely sired on the school bench.—

During these last few days I read a highly interesting novel by Jacobsen entitled Neils Lyhne, which excels in masterful psychological descriptions, but exhibits great weaknesses in the composition. Nevertheless, it is a book very worth reading.

For a week now I've been afflicted with a terrible head cold, which is in the process of going away, thank God. Hence, no one need be afraid of catching it, even if I were to arrive as early as Thursday. So, until soon. Meanwhile, sincerest greetings from your most devoted

Hugo Wolf.

128

To Traunkirchen
Matzen Castle, Sept. 3, 1894

Dear and gracious lady!

Finally, I can avail myself of a free hour, and I'll use this short span of time for a written message. Grohe didn't get my card sent to Bregenz, which is also why I wasn't met at the train station. So I betook myself to the Hotel zur Post, where I was accommodated quite well. In the morning Grohe hunted me up and we traveled by carriage to Matzen [Castle]. Unfortunately, the baroness is still absent and won't arrive here until tomorrow evening. The number of guests, to be sure, is less by far than we anticipated. Frau Begas, the painter, a young author from Berlin with an unwritable name, which incidentally escapes me, a young man from Munich, a chemistry professor from Prague, and friend Grohe are the only guests. Our daily routine, based on the running of the house, takes the following form: breakfast between 8 and 9:00 in Frau Begas' salon with Grohe and the young author, who by the way is an affected baboon, whom I completely ignore. Then each goes his own way. Usually Grohe is with me. Between 12 and 1:00 *déjeuner*, after which one either remains at the table for a while over black coffee and cigars, or takes leave, just as one wishes. At 4:00 a carriage ride. Usually with three coaches. The baron has twelve horses and three coachmen. Yesterday we drove via Brixlegg and Rattenberg into a mountain village, the name of which I've forgotten. Today we're driving along the Zillerthal [Ziller River valley]. After this there will be an excursion to the Achensee [lake], of course everything by coach. I like the people here quite well, except for the author, who has something in common with Voss in language and manners. Baron L[ipperheide] is a very charming, pleasant, jolly man, always concerned with entertaining his guests. By the way, I'm fairly quiet, except during the coffee hour after the meal, when we three, Grohe, the old professor and I, have a grand time and carry on lively conversations. The talkativeness of the writer from Berlin always makes me quiet. I hope the fellow doesn't stay here much longer. But I'll be tying up my bundle soon as well because frankly, I don't feel all that comfortable here, as much as I like the idea and even the people. The impressive park with ponds and little brooks provides a pleasant change. I, Grohe, Frau Begas, and the writer live in the old miners' house, which offers every comfort. The furnitrue is very beautiful, but better suited to look at than to use. The chairs, for example, are simply awful. They're stylish, but one can't sit on them. So much for today. How are you and your family? How are my three tormentors feeling about the absent one? Greetings to Frl. Elsa and Miss Park. Unfortunately, there's no swimming here. How very much I miss the Traunsee. Please write to me here soon and accept, along with Heinrich and the children, the sincerest greetings of your faithfully devoted

Hugo Wolf.

129

To Traunkirchen

Matzen Castle, Sept. 6, 1894

Most honored lady and friend!

I'm using this morning to check in again with a few lines; who knows when I'll be able to do so this easily again. It's raining torrents and looks as if it will continue to do so for a long time. Grohe left yesterday morning, and there are now four of us remaining. Today at noon Herr v. Szczepański, the Berlin writer, is also leaving us; he became more personable during the last few days, so that we were able to associate with each other pleasantly. The baroness is still staying on in Innsbruck. We await her arrival daily. I'll depart here at the latest on Monday, the day that Frau Begas and Prof. Huppert also want to leave Matzen.

Frankly, I long to be gone from here. I yearn for solitude, for a quiet corner where I can live undisturbed in my own way. Originally, I intended to ramble through the Ötztal for several days and make the trip into Vienna via Franzensfeste. With this bad weather, however, I'll have to forgo this.

My plan now is to make the return trip Monday to Traunkirchen, spend one or two days with you, and then go to Döbling. Is this all right with you?

– – – – – – – – – –

I've just received your second letter and at the same time a registered letter from Frl. Z[erny] with her photograph, with which the unhappy thing believes she can work miracles. She's also written a ten- or twelve-page letter to me here in which she complained most bitterly about Faisst. I have now written her briefly and curtly that she should leave me in peace and that's that. I've saved Z.'s letters to show to you. I think the person is deranged. I really slid into a lovely mess here. God grant that all ends well.

Yesterday, as no one goes to bed before 1 a.m. here—the baroness still isn't here—I played Schubert sonatas to those present at the late night hour, for which all in attendance voted me their thanks. But the dear people understand absolutely nothing about music, so it's embarrassing to accept a word of praise from their lips. The baron even mistook the Feuerzauber [Fire-Magic: Wolf is referring to his setting of Mörike's "Feuerreiter"] for my Elfenlied, and after the ending of Feuerzauber, praised the Elfenlied.

That's really going too far! Grohe sat as if on pins and needles, since he witnessed this bizarre misunderstanding.

I have to break off now. Many, many greetings to you and all from your most devoted

Hugo Wolf.

130

To Traunkirchen
Matzen, Sept. 8, 1894

Most honored lady and friend!

I've also received your third letter here and thank you most sincerely for the detailed reports. Today the sky cleared up again and it's possible that I'll stay here until Tuesday. Whatever the case, I'll wire what day I'm arriving. Tomorrow we're finally going on the excursion to the Achensee. Yesterday the baroness came, who looks very good and is full of charm and grace with me. In the evening I had to play her a group of my songs, in which she shows a lively interest. I'm looking forward to the few days in Puchschach. Give my best greetings to Elsa. I hope she will sing something for me sometime. I've just been called to the noonday meal. It's dreadful. One is almost constantly disturbed and has hardly any time to oneself. The letter addressed to Döbling was from Gericke. In it he writes that he likes what I sent him very much and that he will perform one or the other of the two pieces—why not both of them, then?—in the society's concert.

Many, many and best greetings from your extremely hurried

Hugo Wolf.

I'll write again soon.

131

To Traunkirchen [postcard]
Matzen Castle, Sept. 9, 1894

Honored gracious lady!

If the weather is halfway decent, I'm going to Achensee tomorrow and am arriving *Tuesday*, 5:00 in the afternoon at the Traunkirchen train station. Sincere greetings from

Hugo Wolf.

132

Matzen Castle, Sept. 17, 1894

Dear and greatly honored friend!

Midnight draws near. Flies buzz around me, lazy and feeble. I write these lines in the room where I lived during my first stay here. Ah, if only I had never come here! My only thought

is: away from here. The Lipperheides are really very curious
people. Just listen: I arrive in Jenbach after a pleasant journey.
The coach that was supposed to bring me to the castle is already
waiting for me. We arrive in Matzen (by "we" I mean the coachman and I), and I order the coachman to drive me to the old
Matzen house so that I can clean off the coal dust first. The door
is locked. I ring once, twice, no one opens. Finally, the coachman finds the doorkey. The stairway is lighted, but the door to
my room locked, as well as the door to the room that Frau Begas
inhabited earlier. I betake myself up one floor, thinking that the
Schimpanski room was meant for me. I also found this room lit,
but a glance at the rumpled bedding convinced me at once that
this must be occupied by a guest. Now I considered what to do,
because after all, I had to spend the night somewhere. Since there
wasn't a soul to be found, I collected myself, unwashed as I was,
and went into the new, still brightly lit castle. There I learned
from the servants that the baroness had designated my old room
for me; at the same time, the maids were also astonished that I
had found it locked. Immediately a servant girl led the way and we
betook ourselves to the Matzen house another time, where a key
was found that unlocked my door. But nothing at all had been put
in order here except for the freshly changed bed. There wasn't
even water for washing. So I arranged for some to be provided for
me and at the same time had a snack brought to my room, as I felt
too tired and was also too out of sorts to greet the people of the
house. A warm supper was served me, *without* napkin, a corked
bottle of beer shoved under my nose that I could only stare at, and
a water glass along with it to complete the entire ceremony. Isn't
that scandalous? Under such conditions even Döbling seems like a
paradise and I already regret having come here instead of Döbling.
Will I like it better tomorrow? We'll hope so at least. For today a
most pleasant good night.
Sept. 18

I am sad, awakened like the forsaken servant girl, but not out
of bed. I lay abed until 8:30 sunk in dismal thought, and consid-

ered the things that will happen. My future seems to me to be as hopeless as this morning. Everything shrouded in dreary, gray mist. I'm shivering. There still hasn't been a friendly face to welcome me; the housekeeper who served me breakfast is a grumbling old witch who only grudgingly performs her sloppy service. I want to see now whether my host will be able to put me in a more pleasant frame of mind and am off to the new castle for this purpose.—To be continued.

Sept. 19 morning.

I'm finally getting around to continuing my report. Allow me to proceed chronologically. The baron and baroness received me most kindly and apologized for not meeting me at the train station. Among the guests, I met, in turn, a young married couple and a Herr Rütte, lieutenant in the Prussian army, a very nice young man who thoroughly vented his anger to me over the shabby household service. Additionally, a Count Sarenstein came for a brief visit, an older, upstanding, completely good-natured gentleman who falls into one ecstasy after another over my tinkling at the piano. They all departed Matzen early this morning, so I remain as the only guest. Yesterday afternoon we went on a pleasant outing to the Reinthal lakes, of which the Steinberglsee is especially worth mentioning. We drove for about an hour via Rattenberg and then went upward along an immense wall of rock at a very steep angle for about $1\frac{1}{2}$ hours to a very small lake, or rather swamp, where we rested and treated ourselves to red wine and sweet pastry. The weather was splendid. Since the good weather looks like it's going to stay, I won't delay any longer and will probably make my planned walking tour tomorrow.

I'll discuss the plans in detail with the baron at noon today. First my yellow shoes have to be resoled, unless I want to come home barefoot. Knapsack and other things I can get from the baron. I hope everything can be arranged easily.

Since my predecessor, Lieutenant von Rütte, abandoned the Schimpanski room, I'm going to move in there. I'm very happy about this change, primarily because I won't be molested anymore by the swarms of flies, which make the writing of these lines almost impossible. I can't write a single sentence without having to push away these pesky creatures with my left hand. It's enough to drive one mad. The cause of all this annoyance lies in the horse stable to be found under my room. Enough about Matzen's dark side. I hope from now on to have only good and pleasant things to report about my stay here. If only the postal connections weren't so tedious! This distressing delay is a result of the express train not stopping at Brixlegg, as the letters do not come via Jenbach, but via Brixlegg.

This morning the baron remarked that short hair suits me particularly well on account of my head's fine shape. Didn't you make a similar comment also? I believe so. The baroness spoke admiringly of my walking stick at the same time. It's undoubtedly a token of affection or—she quickly corrected herself—a token of respect. Whereupon I replied that she might by all means consider it a token of affection, as far as I'm concerned. It's touching how both of them admire my fooling around on the piano, which is really nothing special. But there's no convincing them that it's not very good. I can play as I like, I am always admired, while the composer is simply put in the shade by the pianist without making any kind of strong impression. Of course, I try to point up the composer as much as possible, whenever the wish is expressed. It's just caviar for the masses, however. One has to take the people as they are and be satisfied with their good intentions.—The flies are becoming intolerable and make it impossible for me to write, otherwise I'd have gone on chattering much longer.

Write to me, please, very soon and very much. You know how closely I'm affected by all that concerns you. Many greetings to Heinrich, the children, and Miss Park.

As soon as I have another spare moment and the plague of flies has come to an end, you'll get a detailed epistle from him who greets you most sincerely, your

Matzen Castle, Sept. 19, 1894   Hugo Wolf.

133

To Traunkirchen

Matzen, Sept. 19, 1894

Most honored friend!

Having just returned home from a visit to Grützner the painter in Jenbach (it's already 11:00 p.m.), I find the anticipated package from Traunkirchen. Unfortunately, there was no note attached, which pained me somewhat. Perhaps the next day will bring me the gift of a little letter, for which I'm so longing. Tonight is the first night I'll spend in the Schimpanski room. I'm exceedingly happy here now. First of all, no flies, or at least very few; then, no neighbors, for the room is completely isolated; also no constant horse-stomping. The room is very spacious, with a low ceiling, and has nut-brown wood paneling. The furnishing is exceptionally tasteful and at the same time extremely comfortable. A huge bearskin stretches out at the feet of a sturdy sofa. There's a large, priceless canopy bed decorating one wall, an old tile stove, and an elegantly appointed washstand. From my writing desk I enjoy a splendid view to the west in the direction of the Rolandsbogen, which I can see very well from the window. In addition, a very beautiful old carved dressing table decorates my room, on which stands a baroque mirror with a beautifully carved gilded frame. A massive clothing and linen wardrobe next to a second table and seven comfortable chairs of varying quality complete the picturesqueness of the room's furnishings. It couldn't be more comfortable. Besides this, the whole second floor is unoccupied, so that I can live here completely informally. In my last letter I spoke of being the only guest at Matzen. Well, it's not true now. This afternoon a Prof. Brandl arrived with his wife—young people. The Herr Prof., a Tyrolean by birth but who lost his Tyrolean accent in Berlin and is now a prof. in Strassburg, revealed himself right away as a chatterbox of the worst kind. The fellow speaks as if he were standing at the lectrum; he reminds me vividly of the pedantic manner of our upright, stalwart Binder, when he gives lectures on geography and history in sermonizing tone to his skeptical pupil Irmina. Since I had the misforturne to sit next to him at Grützner's, I had to let the flood of his affected talking pour over me for a full five hours, whether I wanted to or not. They were the most tormenting hours of my life. Schimpanski was at least down to earth and almost always witty, but this trained camel always speaks like a book, a book without content to be sure. I hope he goes away from here soon, or I'll flee.— How entirely different Grützner is, the genuine and true artist! There's no trace of falseness or pretense. Quiet and composed in his talking, as in his entire demeanor, no one would suspect the humorist in him, for which he is world-renowned in his fabulous genre paintings. Always pleasant and kind, he contributes just enough to the conversation as propriety demands in order to keep it flowing cheerfully. And he manages this in a most surprising way. I hope to become better acquainted with him, as he'll be visiting the Lipperheides with his wife and daughter tomorrow. He is, for once, my kind of person: one who is capable, but doesn't make an issue of it. Truly a marvelous person! Enough for today. It's almost midnight. For the present I'm only *thinking* about traveling. But when it will happen, I can't yet say. Perhaps in the next few days. So good night and many, many, many greetings from your

Hugo Wolf.

134

To Traunkirchen

Matzen Castle, Sept. 23, 1894

Most honored lady and friend!

Today is a dreary, unpleasant Sunday. The Brandls are gone, thank God, and as the only one remaining, I'm providing for myself in my solitude as well as I can. Now and again Rickelt the painter turns up and asks me to play him something. So far, he's liked my humorous songs the best, particularly the last ones of Mörike. He was quite amazed that texts such as these could be set to music. Basically he's more open to things of a lighter nature, such as Fussreise, Gärtner, and the like, rather than to the more profound ones, for which one cannot reproach him after all. Otherwise we get along very well and enjoy a very pleasant relationship with one another.

Yesterday the grand duke of Weimar came for a visit to Matzen Castle. I used this occasion to take a trip to Innsbruch [*sic*], without informing my host beforehand, something I came very much to regret, however. For aside from the fact that Innsbruck utterly bored me (the museum and even the famous court church do not offer sufficient reward for a special journey there), I was sorely missed in Matzen, because the grand duke, I learned later, would have liked very much to become acquainted with me. Also, the weather wasn't favorable for a visit to Innsbruck. On the way home from Lanserköpfl (a famous scenic lookout), I was surprised by a heavy thunderstorm, with thunder and lighting and a drenching rain shower, so that upon arriving in Innsbruck I looked exactly like a poodle that had fallen into the water. Since the morning had been very lovely at first, I'd decided to take my walking stick instead of the umbrella, and so there I was. On top of this, I still had to survive a two-hour train ride in this condition, during which time my predicament certainly didn't get any better. Luckily, it didn't do me any harm, and I feel completely refreshed and healthy today.

I'll probably have to postpone my planned walking tour with such changeable weather. I was urgently dissuaded from going up to the Stilfserjoch [ridge], as the paths at the top of the pass might well be covered with snow at this time, and a snowstorm could come at any moment. They're trying hard, on the other hand, to talk me into taking the Brenner road from Innsbruck to Bozen, possibly with a side trip to Jodok. So I'll probably decide on a hike over the Brenner, as I certainly have no suicidal intentions and am not willing to immortalize myself by means of a memorial plaque on the Stilfserjoch.

I congratulated Mama on her birthday by telegram. Have you heard any more from the ghost-seer? The story does intrigue me somewhat. Have you read the card of the person in question? I answered in the same telegraph-style by postcard. At the same time, my brother sent me the news, which I received with dubious pleasure, that he's returned from America and has settled in Wilhelmsburg near St. Pöltzen at a friend's, in partnership with whom he's pursuing an unheard of invention, and for which project I'm supposed to help him to the tune of 50 Fl. That's all I needed.

Unfortunately, I have to stop, as the baroness desires to take a walk with me.

Ever so hurriedly, with the request that you write to me very soon, sincerest greetings from your devoted

Hugo Wolf.

The writing pens at Matzen Castle are beneath all contempt. Thank God I'm finished. I've got to get myself other pens.

135

To Traunkirchen

Matzen, Brixlegg, Tyrol, Sept. the 25th, 1894

Most honored lady and friend!

Once again a clear bright sky, after a string of dreary, rainy days. A fragrant, fresh wind blows over from the Zillerthal, which must bring you a thousand greetings from me. How I would have enjoyed spending this morning on my own talking with you; only the "mistress" wishes me to serve as page on her walks, and so I must be brief. Your last letter left me in an altogether melancholy mood. If it's any comfort to you, be assured that I sympathize completely with your feelings.

Starting today I'm going to try to arrange my life here more systematically. Above all I must make an effort to get to bed as early as possible, in order to take full advantage of the morning hours, which are mine to spend as I see fit—today's walk is an exception. Up until now, the evening's entertainment has always gone on until 12:00 at night. That mustn't happen anymore. From now on it's to bed at 10:00 and up at 6:00. I have to think about work again. My hosts will certainly understand this and won't hinder me. I'll discuss the matter with the baroness on our walk today. About the middle of October I'm going to travel to Merano in the company of the two of them. Then there are several excursions I want to make, starting out from Merano. I often play four-hand [piano] with the baroness now. Pleasure from this is quite limited, to be sure, as she plays very badly, but since I can show my gratitude in this way, I'm happy to do it. *Manus manum lavat* [One hand washes the other]. There's nothing else to be done.

Yesterday late at night she asked me to play the Appassionata of Beethoven for her, and when I finished she was quite beside herself with delight over my performance. Nothing beats undemanding people! More next time. For today very sincerest greetings from your faithfully devoted

Hugo Wolf.

Many greetings to H., children, and Miss Park.

Afternoon. I'm opening up the letter again to enclose a note from Bruckner that just arrived for me. The enclosed letter from the aging man brought tears to my eyes. How good it was that I put in my congratulations, even though belatedly. Please return the treasured document to me. I'm planning to compose an extended epistle to the revered man soon.

Along with the Bruckner note, a package also came from Kauffmann, a book entitled: Ed. Mörike als Gelegenheitsdichter [Eduard Mörike as Poet of Occasional Verse], with countless first printings of Mörike poems and drawings from his own hand. I only glanced through it quickly and discovered delightful things. As soon as I've gone through it completely, I'll send it to you. It will amuse you more than a little. I told the baroness about my schedule and she agreed to it. So, again a thousand greetings and all good things.

136

To Traunkirchen
[Brixlegg], Oct. 6, 1894

Dear gracious lady!
Your letter of the 4th of the m[onth], received today, made me deeply happy. How glad I am that I've added something to your enjoyment with Stauffer's letters. Certainly not everyone will agree with such confessions, but we are not counted among those moral cowards who shrink timidly from every natural emotion and anxiously try to paste fig leaves over all nakedness. Devout souls may lament all they wish about how Stauffer blasphemes all customs and morals; he still remains one of the most admirable figures of the fin de siècle, by virtue of his heroic nature and the tragic fate to which he, a man so energetic and strong-willed, was forced to succumb. Even so, one also has to have experienced certain things in order to penetrate with deeper understanding the mysteries of these kinds of psychological occurrences. Such a nature will never be revealed to him who remains glued to the surface. I knew well that the book would make a strong impression on your spirit; that's why I sent it to you and I am doubly happy that my assumption was such an accurate one. One cannot easily read Mörike's occasional poems along with it, which is also why you didn't once mention that book. How well we understand each other, don't we?

Today the sun is shining again after a long wait, and the chill has abated as well.

Countess Sarntheim, along with her father and mother, who were here yesterday for a visit and who are truly lovely and charming people, left us yesterday. Today young Defregger went too. In the meantime, I'm alone again; that is, until evening, for a countess is coming, a Hungarian, who is very pretentious, I hear.

Unfortunately, the baron and the baroness do not get along at all well with each other. There are violent arguments between them, which usually end in a flood of tears on the part of the baroness. It makes a stay here somewhat uncomfortable. Therefore I'd like to get away from here as soon as the opportunity presents itself, temporarily to Eckstein in Vienna V, Siebenbrunnengasse 15. Write me as to when your departure will take place so that I can plan accordingly. I'll give you the key to my armoire in person. I can't begin to tell you how much I look forward to seeing you again. Also find out in Vienna whether D[lauhy] lives in Döbling or in town so that a possible collision with him will be avoided. Schott has sent me a copy of the score and the piano edition of Feuerreiter, as well as the proofs for the choral parts of the hymn [*Dem Vaterland*]. I have to hurry today, as I'm taking this letter personally to the post office in Brixlegg. So just quickly the very sincerest greetings from your

Hugo Wolf.

Best greetings to Heinrich and the children. Also Miss Park.

137

To Traunkirchen

Matzen, Oct. 8, 1894

Dear gracious lady!

This is a heavenly morning. The mists are visibly dissipating and the bluest autumn sky promises a marvelous day. Since the baron is going to Innsbruck today, and the countess is just about to start off on her trip to Vienna, the baroness has decided to travel with me to Maierhofen at the end of the Zillerthal. Zell will be the overnight stop and the next day we'll set off for Maierhofen. One is surrounded by the Zillerthal ice fields in

Maierhofen and you can imagine how I'm looking forward to this outing. If only you were coming along! How much nicer it would be! I probably won't get away from here for at least a week. Since you're not going to Vienna before the middle of October, however, I can just as well wait out the time here. Your last letter cheered me up again very much. The anecdote about Brahms—*si non e vero* etc. [whether or not it's true]—actually isn't bad. I will take the loose-leaf pages of the 7th to heart. It's very kind of you to be so concerned about my good mood. If only I knew how to keep you in a good mood, too. The key to my armoire will be sent to you Wednesday or Thursday. The letters are on the *lowest* shelf in a letter box marked Theyer & Hartmuth. More in my next letter. I have to hurry today, as we're setting out early in order to enjoy the lovely weather and beautiful scenery to the fullest. Accept sincerest greetings from your very devoted

Hugo Wolf.

138

To Traunkirchen
Matzen, Oct. 8, 1894

Dear gracious lady!

I was just in Brixlegg mailing a letter to you when, upon my return, a piece of mail arrived for me just before the excursion we're making into the Zillerthal. You understood me completely regarding D[lauhy]. We must discuss this in person beforehand. A thousand, thousand thanks for your dear words that you wrote me on Sunday. A letter from Zumpe, quite unusual in its way, also arrived at the same time as your letter. They are the first lines Zumpe has ever addressed to me. Do read them and tell me if there still aren't fabulous human beings in the world! I'm completely dumbstruck by it. At the same time, there is a request for an autographed piece of music from a Herr Lumberger in Baumgarten near Vienna, in which he presents himself as an admirer of my "charming songs." This in the greatest haste.

My very special greetings to my dear friend Hilde, also to Ilse and Irmina. From the bottom of my heart your

Hugo Wolf.

Please return Zumpe's letter to me.

139

To Traunkirchen [picture postcard]

Zell, Oct. 8, 1894

I'm taking advantage of the baroness' nap to send you a very cordial greeting from the Zillerthal glaciers. As I write these lines on the veranda of the Gasthof zur Post, they are shimmering before me in the brightest sunshine. In an hour we go on (by coach) to Maierhofen, where we'll spend the night. I hope the beautiful weather continues. Many greetings to H. and my three loyal ones and see you soon!

Your always faithful
Hugo Wolf.

140

To Traunkirchen

Matzen, Oct. 10, 1894

Most honored gracious lady!

You will undoubtedly have received my three letters. We arrived back in Matzen in good shape last evening. The outing was successful in every respect. The route from Maierhofen to Karlsteg was particularly unique in its way, a wild mountain gorge through which the foaming Ziller rushes. One feels totally insignificant alongside such superhuman wilderness and grandeur as is displayed by nature in the Alpine world. Grinzling was the last stop. From there I went on alone for an hour into the Floitenthal [Floiten valley] to see the Floitenspitze [summit] (3200 m). There is an immense glacier surrounding it; the fog settled in soon after, unfortunately, so that the view was only a brief one. Nevertheless, I took away a complete impression of the Zillerthal. The most beautiful spot in it, however, remains Zell am Ziller. Maierhofen lies too far into the mountains. It's an utterly dismal place.

Löwe wrote me today that Elfenlied and Feuerreiter will be performed on Dec. 2nd. It would be too foolish for me to go to Berlin now, since two pieces of mine and possibly a third will be performed in Vienna. Eckstein has most kindly turned over his room to me. In any case, I'll arrive in Vienna before the 20th, as I'd like not to miss the Bruckner concert. The key herewith.

Maybe Larisch will give me his summer place in Perchtoldsdorf. That would be splendid! I'll sound him out about this.

Tomorrow will probably bring me a note from you. For today hurriedly the very very sincerest greetings from your

Hugo Wolf.

141

To Traunkirchen
Matzen Castle, Oct. 12, 1894

Dear gracious lady!

I already received your letter from yesterday this morning, and so that you will have these lines by tomorrow, I'll answer it immediately. I think it wouldn't do you or me any harm to allow a short pause in our correspondence now and then. I'm saying this so that you won't immediately assume the worst, should a few days go by without a letter from me, because frankly I don't have much worth telling you at the moment. On the other hand, it can't be easy for you either, I mean the letter writing now when all the preparations need to be made for your departure. If I haven't yet arrived in Vienna before you do, about which you'll be apprised in time in any case, I'd like you nevertheless to continue to send me my—writings.

Today is a sunny, warm day again for a change. I'm going to take a walk with the baroness this afternoon. Life here is becoming very difficult because of the disgusting quarrels of the baronial couple. Carl Rickelt, the painter and also the baron's nephew, got up from the table at noon today without saying a word when the baroness called him a toady and a flatterer because he behaved indifferently to something she was animatedly defending. After that, she turned on the baron with such vehemence that I grew almost numb. The baroness subsequently left the room, so I was alone with him. Then the baroness was criticized, albeit in more moderate tones than hers. Try to imagine my situation. Each wants to be right. The baroness accuses him of megalomania and vanity. He claims she is a fool and a pathetic creature. And so it goes almost every day.

Luckily, guests are coming to visit for a few days now, and we'll be able to consume our noon and evening meals in peace.

The theatrics usually go on during the noonday meal, because in bad weather we don't get together during the other hours of the day. I spend my happiest hours at the splendid Bechstein grand piano, which has few equals, to be sure. Sternfeld wrote me that songs of mine are to be sung at the Berlin Wagner Society at the end of the month and asks me to undertake the accompaniment. But I have no desire to do this at all. If the arrangement with Larisch works out, I'll stay in the country and make every effort to provide for myself honestly. Regarding the Bruckner concert, I don't know now whether it's on the 25th or the 28th. You wrote the number so indistinctly that I have to ask you to clear this up for me. Did I write you that Elfenlied and Feuerreiter will be performed on Dec. 2nd in Vienna? All the rest, God willing, in Vienna. Many, many greetings to you and all from your always devoted

Hugo Wolf.

142

To Vienna

Perchtoldsdorf, Nov. 8, 1894

Dear gracious lady!

Yesterday's lovely day and the even lovelier one today have restored my old confidence. I revel so in this stimulating fall air, this life-giving sunshine. It was such a marvelous picture to see the pleasant village [Perchtoldsdorf] from the Kreuzberg, shimmering through the thick mist. It was like seeing a fata morgana, the place looked so fanciful, transparent, and fairylike. All at once the fog tore apart and a flood of light and warmth streamed down from the heavens. I wanted to cry out for joy. May this victorious penetration of Lady Sun also be of symbolic significance to me, the mule in the mist.

I'm completely finished with the arranging of the furnishings. The library is also organized and the handsome bindings reflect the morning sun in the early hours. In this splendid weather it would really be a sin to drive into the city. Wouldn't you and H. like to come Sunday with the children, as early as possible, as it's the most beautiful here in the morning. If you don't come, I'll come at 2:00.

Also, a small misfortune has befallen me here. The yard dog has absconded with my good Emmenthaler [cheese] and good butter, so that I'm anticipating a very meager diet. Unfortunately, the food at Koller's is no longer what it used to be; palatable, nevertheless.

All things considered, I thank God fervently that he gave me the idea of leaving Döbling, for compared to Döbling, Perchtoldsdorf is pure paradise.

"Noon—the hour is here" [*Mittag—die Stund ist da*].

Sincerest greetings from your always faithful

Hugo Wolf.

143

To Vienna

Perchtoldsdorf, Nov. 9, 1894

Dear gracious lady!

Don't be angry that I've stayed away so long. It was too beautiful to come into the city on Thursday. Today it's overcast and rainy. In spite of this, I won't come until Sunday, early in the morning, as I'm working now to complete the orchestration of the Wächterlied. I'd like best to spend Sunday night on the divan in the dining room, if I may, as I have a lot of matters to take care of Monday morning, and at Echstein's there's no moving ahead with things. So see you day after tomorrow. Last evening was beautiful moonlight. A shame that bad weather has set in, something not expected with a waxing moon. Sincerest greetings from your

Hugo Wolf.

144

To Vienna

Perchtoldsdorf, Nov. 16, 1894

Dear gracious lady!

Today the morning is of such incredible beauty that I'd most urgently like to request you to come to P[erchtoldsdorf] early Sunday morning with Heinrich and the children, should the weather hold for a few days.

I spend most of my time outdoors, as the temperature outside is warmer than in my room. It is very pleasant to sit in the wind-protected little [garden] house—also a lovely lookout spot and easy to reach.

My head cold has not worsened, fortunately, and the sore throat has diminished appreciably. By Sunday I'll be fit as a fiddle again.

If the weather is lovely and sunny on Sunday, I won't come into the city, even if you don't come to P. But I'm counting for certain on a visit. Notabene: if you come by *coach*, please bring the piano scores of Siegfried and Götterdämmerung with you. However, I definitely advise you to take the train, i.e., with *round-trip ticket*, which would be a much less expensive trip.

Letters were waiting here from Kauffmann and Faisst. I'm enclosing a letter to Kauffmann from Music Director Labitsky, as I find the first half of it very odd. So, see you Sunday in P.

Sincere greetings to all from your faithfully devoted
Hugo Wolf.

145

To Vienna

Perchtoldsdorf, Nov. 19, 1894

Dear gracious lady!

I half expected a letter from you and rightly so, as one came. In your lines you took the words right out of my mouth, so to speak, as I was just about to write you something similar. Since you've anticipated me so well, then let's leave it at that and proceed to everyday matters. I have to mention at the outset that I'm suffering from a very bad cough at the moment, which has made it necessary to heat the room from noon on today. Despite this continuous heating since 1:00, I can't get the temperature above 12 [degrees C]. What will happen when it's really cold! I don't even want to think about it.

Yesterday evening I wrote the baroness and encouraged her to read the writings about the Shakespeare question. A parcel came from Berlin (from Lipperheide). I open [it]: Sang an Aegir für eine Singstimme u. Klavierbegleitung [Song to Aegir for Voice and Piano Accompaniment]. The devil take it. I'm curious about the piece "Es war einmal" [Once Upon a Time]. I hope it comes tomorrow. Edwin Bormann, with his cursed arguments contra Shakespeare, has now become intolerable to me. The man may indeed be right, but what he proposes is actually nothing but empty drivel. I wish I were already finished with this dull reading.

This morning, since the sun absolutely wouldn't shine and it felt very uncomfortable in my room, I took my refuge in Bach's Das wohl-temperirte [*sic*] Klavier and played so long that my neck became stiff and my fingers burned. Ate a good noonday meal afterward at Koller's. If there's no sunshine on Thursday, I'll come into the city in the morning right away. From what I hear, my young friend Heinrich Werner is unfortunately critically ill. I'll stop by the Werners' on Thursday in any case to inquire about the patient's condition. Until then I must wait and see. So, until a happy reunion on Thursday. With sincerest greetings always, your faithful

Hugo Wolf.

146

To Vienna

[Vienna, November 26, 1894]

Dear gracious lady!

The splendid weather this morning seduced me into going to P[erchtoldsdorf]. Don't be angry about it.

Am coming to Vienna Wednesday afternoon for chorus rehearsal.

Yesterday at Griensteidl actually met Golsdchmidt once again. Said nothing to him. Didn't get to bed until 3:30 a.m. Am in a hurry today.

Sincerest greetings and a lovely good morning!

[no signature]

1895–1897

147

Honored gracious lady!
Frl. M[ark] did *not* receive permission from the director. With that the concert *is dropped*. Please inform Jäger of this. Nothing more stands in the way of Frl. v. Spurny's departure now, if she really came here only on account of the concert. More in person.
Best greetings from your faithful
Hugo Wolf.

148

Dear gracious lady!
I'm writing these lines this evening so that you'll be sure to get them tomorrow. My arrival at the flat went very quietly. Nothing to be seen or heard of the gardeners. When I walked into the room the first thing to catch my eye was the cake for my name day, which had been placed ceremoniously on the large round table. A further critical glance convinced me of the housekeeper's care. The beautiful parquet floor had been freshly waxed to the point of reflecting the room's furnishings.—Everything looked clean and polished. You can imagine how this immaculate atmosphere lifted my spirits after the reign of dirt and dust at Siebenbrunnengasse 15. I could have shouted for joy. Shortly after I arrived, my feminine *"spiritus familiaris"* breezed in. There was a touching reunion.—Of course, the temperature in the room wasn't very cozy, but in three hours I did manage to bring it up from 7 to 10 [degrees C], despite the antiquated heating, thanks to the huge supply of coal. Tomorrow I'm shooting for a temperature of 14 to 15.
I found the piano hardly out of tune and Marie's compote still edible. Kitchen and entryway were scrubbed clean and ev-

erything was in its proper place. All this had a most calming effect on me. But how little that means compared to the profound peacefulness that surrounds me here, leading me into the arms of the sorely missed joy of solitude again, giving me back to myself. This indescribable feeling of complete seclusion actually affects me like a narcotic; I almost begin to be afraid of myself, for it seems as if I've turned into someone else in the short time I've been here. A better person, let's hope. Tomorrow morning I start to work early. I don't trust myself to tempt the gods today. I'm still too dazed by the intoxicating first impressions of this sudden change. Tomorrow I'll be more collected and, God willing, will write something beautiful and good. To that end, wish him luck who greets you warmly and always remains your faithfully devoted

Hugo Wolf.

149

To Vienna
Perchtoldsdorf, April 8, 1895

Dear gracious lady!

It's 8:00 in the evening and I took advantage of the falling dusk for a walk on the nearby Hochberg. I've just returned by moonlight from this walk, which, at least in thought, I took with another. Goodness, what a night it is! Cool and brisk, hardly a wisp of cloud on the horizon, and so bright that I could just as easily have written these lines by moonlight. You're probably surprised that I'm writing letters at all, but I haven't written to anyone from here except my sister until now. It just isn't possible, because I'm working without interruption from 7 a.m. (I get up at 6:00) till dusk falls and often far into the night. Yesterday and today I was particularly lucky with inventing things. I've already arrived at the final verses of the 2nd act after having conceived the festive march music at the end of the 1st act yesterday. Don Pedro's "wine-blessed" song, "Wenn dich Einer küssen will" [If someone wants to kiss you], will amuse you greatly. I think the scene with Manuela turned out particularly well. There's something special about it. Tomorrow comes the conclusion of the 2nd act, God willing. I can't begin to tell you how good I feel about myself again; I suspect that I've grown a new skin, however, because once again my music is different now from before. Ha, you'll be wide-eyed over it.—Today somewhat comforting news came from home. The infection is clearing up, although there is still fear of a heart attack, to which none of us is predisposed. Malaga has paid his debts and made Mother very happy. Perhaps, or rather, probably, I'll come to town Friday in order to get myself another sponge, since the one I have is absolutely worthless. The Americ[an] creature is completely unusable. Other than this, I've nothing to send on, except my respect and very sincerest greetings from your always faithfully devoted

Hugo Wolf.

Greetings to the three imps.

150

To Vienna

Perchtoldsdorf, April 10, 1895

Dear gracious lady!

I was just completing an intermezzo that is to be played by the orchestra during the scene change in the 2nd act, when your kind note and your truly formidable gift arrived. Of *this* sponge one can honestly say that one has washed oneself. I can no longer wait for the morning when its magic will be verified. Will that be a treat! Many, many, many thanks!

I'm coming on Friday after all. I *must* play my new things for you, otherwise I'll have no peace. The conclusion of the 2nd act was finished yesterday morning. It is impossible to imagine a better melody for the satirical heroism of the two drinking comrades, Tonuelo and Pedro, let alone compose one. But what am I saying? On Friday you can judge for yourself. Sincerest greetings from your most faithful

Hugo Wolf.

Our next-to-last letters crossed each other. We had the same wish and the same need at the same time. Isn't that lovely?

151

To Vienna

Perchtoldsdorf, April 13, 1895

Dear gracious lady!

Am working at the moment on the 1st scene of the first act, which I'd despaired of earlier and had already decided to cut from the libretto. But an extremely helpful [idea] has occurred to me now, and I think the piece will become quite magnificent.

I'll probably spend the holidays here, as the cold weather will hardly entice a visitor out. The riddle of the missing [shirt] cuff has also now been solved. It turned up in the drawer of my linen wardrobe. In my haste I forgot to put on the second one. On the other hand, I forgot my doorkey in my winter jacket; please bring it with you on the occasion of the visit you are planning to make. I received your cheerful letter this morning and thank you most kindly. Wishing you a speedy recovery and sending you sincerest greetings, your most faithful

Hugo Wolf.

You're coming with your small retinue, aren't you?

152

To Vienna

Perchtoldsdorf, April 16, 1895

Dear gracious lady!

The most sublime things are occurring to me today. I hardly know anymore how to become master of them. For God's sake, come out here soon to your sincerely greeting, blessed beyond all human measure

Hugo Wolf.

153

To Vienna

Perchtoldsdorf, April 18, 1895

Wonderful motive for friend Repela just occurred to me at 1:30 in the afternoon.

Here it is:

The scene between Lukas and Frasquita in the 1st act was completed this morning. "Good luck to your master-singing" [*Glück auf zum Meistersingen*].

Most faithfully your

Hugo Wolf.

154

To Vienna

Perchtoldsdorf, April 19, 1895

A thousand thanks for your speedy procurement of the gold band on the tip of my cigarette holder; that alone makes the tip complete. I also found the missing little gold ring yesterday. I'll bring it along one of these days. I'm writing right before the noonday meal, have to hurry on that account or I'll get the scraps. Heaps of good ideas. Composed 30 measures of interlude early this morning and last night as well, which exceed everything passionate and sweet that has flowed from my pen until now.

Today is a wonderful day for me, though certainly in other respects it is not, as it is cold and unpleasant. But inside me it's burning and glowing as in a crater. Until soon. Most sincerely, your hurried

Hugo Wolf.

155

To Vienna

Perchtoldsdorf, April 22, 1895

Dear gracious lady!
I've been getting up as early as 5:00 a.m. the last few days, because I feel absolutely no need for sleep. I'm already at work by 6:00. It's going splendidly. Repela is already "done and taken care of" [*besorgt u. aufgehoben*]. The scene is exquisite. And I also got to the conclusion of the ardent duo between Lukas and Frasquita, thanks to the marvelous verses of my partner [Rosa Mayreder], which were sent to me several days ago, and today the following scene with Tonuelo was completed for the most part. All that still remains is the admittedly long scene with the Corregidor and the 1st act is finished. For the present, though, I'm planning to undertake the 2nd act, specifically the scene in the alcalde's house. I hope Frau M[ayreder] doesn't let me wait too long for the desired verses.

So much for my activities. Today was a splendid, indescribably beautiful day. Unfortunately, I got very little from it, as I was busy with the opera almost the whole day. The letter sent to me is from Baron Lipperheide. The blasted fellow writes me that he's already been hanging around Vienna for two weeks, but still hasn't come to his senses. I believe it, because otherwise he would have given me his address. Now where am I supposed to look for this jackass? He asks me for a rendezvous, but the devil grant him one when I don't know how, when, or where! So I must ask you most kindly to send our scout Ignaz to reconnoiter.

In the vicinity of the Schillerplatz there is a branch of the

Lipperheide business; one is most likely to find out there where the distracted gentleman is staying, since he certainly won't be in the shelter for the homeless. Incidentally, the devil also take him for coming here just now, at a most inopportune time.

With sincerest greetings, requesting the soonest possible news, your

Hugo Wolf.

156

To Vienna

[Perchtoldsdorf, April 24, 1895]

Dear gracious lady!

Thank you for letter and news. Please don't come here in the next few days, however, as I am expecting Lipperheide and Rickelt the painter. I'll probably come into town Friday or Saturday in order to set my new pages.

A thousand greetings!

Faisst wrote today. He's as delighted with the picture as with the libretto. Kauffmann has it already. Zumpe is supposedly annoyed because of my letter. The donkey! The grapevine is at work.

[no signature]

157

To Vienna

Perchtoldsdorf, April 26, 1895

Dear gracious lady!

I'm writing these lines right after my arrival in P[erchtoldsdorf]. A minute's later arrival at the train station and I would have had the pleasure in this bad weather of making my way from Liesing to P. *per pedes apostulorum* [on foot] and at midnight, too. Fortunately, I made the train and thus arrived safely in P. at 8:30.—Lipperheide received me most cordially. He was very surprised to see me before Sunday, because he and Rickelt the painter had agreed to Sunday. He let me tell him a great deal and is immensely interested in my opera. He's not acquainted with the novella, but from my description, he found the subject charming. The matter of Matzen is settled. The hunter's cottage is available to me anytime, but he insists that I take the noon and evening meals at *his* table. Otherwise he grants me complete freedom. After a while Rickelt came, with whom the baron joyfully shared the news that perhaps I would become a "Matzner" in a very short time. So that's all taken care of. He really is a very nice fellow! The inevitable "red" [wine] was served and our health toasted. He looks quite marvelous and was in the most jovial of moods, as is normally his manner.

The first thing I did upon arriving in P. was to take the eggs out of the sawdust and store them away in a cool place. Only two were slightly damaged; I consumed these raw for supper. They tasted delicious. You really look after me like a mother hen her baby chicks. The eggs are responsible for this comparison. I'll take this letter to the post office tomorrow morning at 6:00 so that you'll get it by noon. Sincerest greetings for today and a very good night.

Unswervingly, your

Hugo Wolf.

Wonderful morning! Good morning! April 27.

158

To Vienna

Perchtoldsdorf, April 30, 1895

Dear gracious lady!

I've just (5:00 in the afternoon) finished the scene in the alcalde's house, which is followed by the song about the Spanish wine. Now only the scenes with the Corregidor and Repela remain, and both acts are finished. I've worked very diligently in the last days, even on Sunday. Contrary to expectation, *all* of those invited came, despite the bad weather, except for Schalk who canceled the day before. Lipperheide with Rickelt the painter was the first. He rode out in a fiacre. The others didn't come until around 5:00 p.m. Hirschlein [Hirsch] was the last. Now you can imagine what kind of impact the story had. Even Lipperheide was beside himself and assured me that he had understood all of it because he believes music such as that in my opera to be accessible to everyone. Frau Mayreder was swimming in bliss, Ma-

Hugo Wolf (1889)

The music room in the Köchert house

Letter from Hugo Wolf to Melanie Köchert (dated November 9, 1894—No. 143)

Melanie Köchert

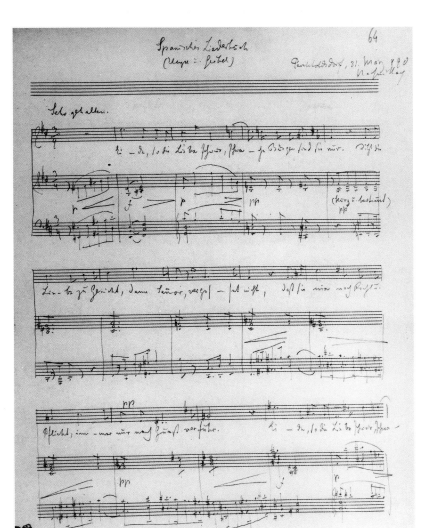

"Eide, so die Liebe schwur"

Hugo Wolf (1892)

Heinrich Köchert

Hugo Faisst

Letter from Hugo Wolf to Melanie Köchert (dated May 23, 1893—No. 83)

Traunkirchen 28. Mai 893

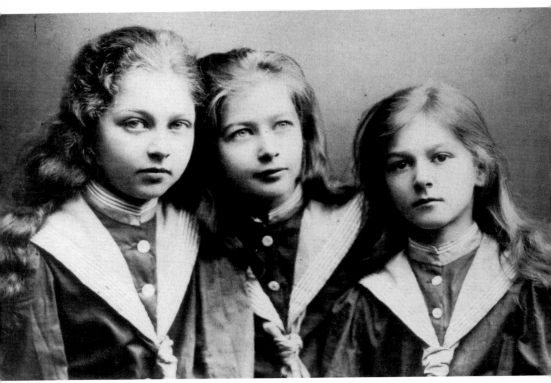

Ilse, Hilde, and Irmina Köchert

Hugo Wolf working on *Corregidor*

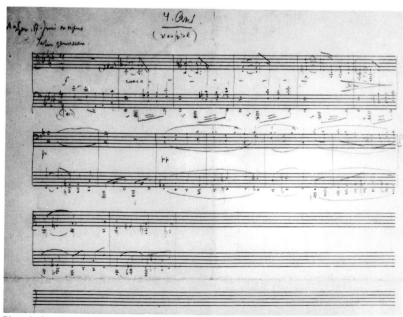

Sketch for *Corregidor*

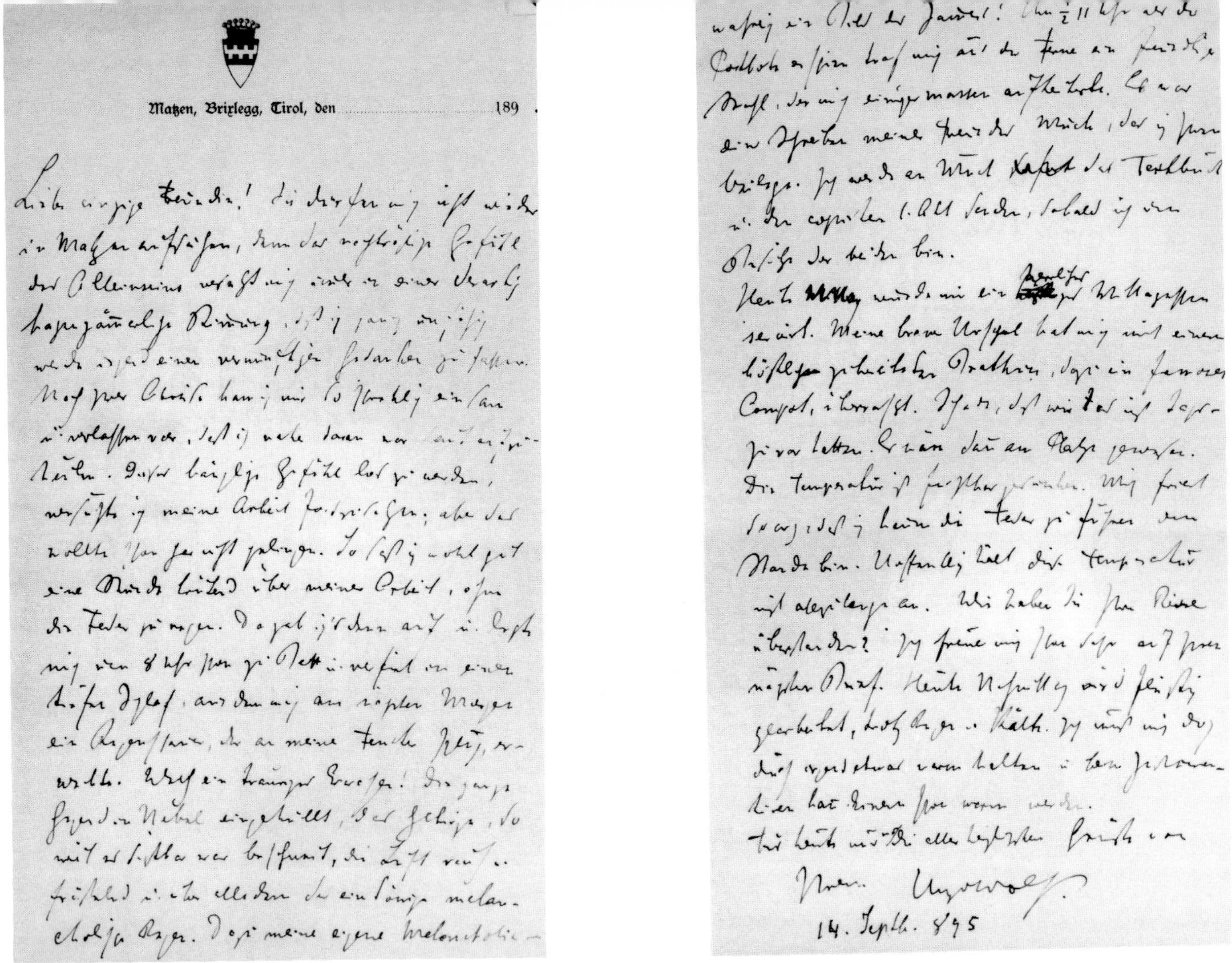

Matzen, Brixlegg, Tirol, den _____ 189

14. Septbr. 895

"Wie soll ich fröhlich sein"

The parsonage courtyard in Traunkirchen

Hugo Wolf's study

Hugo Wolf (1899)

rie [Werner] was of course sobbing, and Hirschlein looked quite dumbfounded. Too bad that Schalk wasn't here. It all broke up at 7:00, except that Lipperheide with Rickelt remained for a few more hours with me, that is, at Koller's, where the unavoidable "red" had to play a part. The weather is dreadful, the chilliness quite abnormal. Today, it's actually somewhat more pleasant, but who knows for how long.—Schott wrote to me. He's very curious about the opera, but urgently advised me not to begin until an expert has expressed an opinion about the libretto's stageworthi-ness. "Poor fool! That's ridiculous," I say with Lukas. The lead pencil gives me great pleasure, because it comes from you, but it's not usable. I'm coming into the city on Saturday. Sunday we all made a date to see and hear the Lachtaube [*Die Lachtaube*] on Sat-urday at the Carltheater. The work is supposed to be based on the same theme as my opera, only in a Polish setting. I'm going to stay overnight at Marie's Saturday, but will visit you in the afternoon. By that time I'll already have written a whole lot of new things. Of course, I'll bring you the manuscripts.

For today then, sincerest greetings from your most faithful
Hugo Wolf.

159

To Vienna
Perchtoldsdorf, May 1, 1895

Dear gracious lady!

I'm answering your perceptive second letter immediately, which more or less nullified the earlier one. You're not quite right with regard to the species of animal, but self-awareness is nevertheless a pathway toward improvement. I just wanted to tell you right away that Frasquita's fandango and the first scene up to the "Schatten meiner Locken" have already been com-posed, i.e., this morning. Unfortunately, I also had some bad news today. Frau Werner has told me in person that I will have to move out on Monday already, as they are planning their move for Tuesday or Wednesday.

Under these circumstances it would be doubly pleasant for me if you came to P[erchtoldsdorf] tomorrow. Come with Schalk, or if you absolutely don't want to, send Schalk word that

I have to be at Lipperheide's in town tomorrow, that he therefore wouldn't encounter me. I'll write to Schalk at the same time that he is expected on Sunday. I'm thinking of traveling with Lipperheide to Matzen as early as Tuesday, which would be the wisest thing, because in Matzen I'd have decidedly more peace than in Unterach. Moreover, the Eckstein family has become insufferable to me, and I'd like to have as little contact with these people as possible.

So hope to see you tomorrow in P. A thousand greetings from your

Hugo Wolf.

160

To Vienna

Perchtoldsdorf, May 3, 1895

Dear gracious lady!

I was thinking exactly the same thing that you wrote in your dear note, the only difference being that *I* considered myself to be the guilty party. Accordingly, you could have saved yourself the letter. Nonetheless, I am still happy to have received a sign of life from you. Today the weather is horrible, rainy and cold. I thank heaven for it.

I hope the Werners don't come out as long as the weather continues this way—and if it only holds!! I'm *not* coming to Vienna Saturday, as I have too much to do. I'll write you when I'm coming. I'm working hard. For today then, in all haste, sincerest greetings from your

Hugo Wolf.

In conclusion, as a special consolation to you, the assurance that I wrote some very beautiful music for Frasquita last evening.

161

To Vienna

Perchtoldsdorf, May 6, 1895

Dear gracious lady!

For today only a few words, because I have to work now as much as is humanly possible. At my urgent request I've been granted a postponement until Tuesday, when I absolutely must vacate the room right away early in the morning. I'll take up quarters at Mayreders' for a few days. They've insisted that I be their guest. I'll see you again Thursday afternoon. A thousand greetings from your

Hugo Wolf.

I'm still hoping to finish the first act here.

162

To Vienna [postcard]

Perchtoldsdorf, May 8, 1895

Dear gracious lady!

I've just learned that the W[erner] family is not moving to P[erchtoldsdorf] until Saturday. Hence, I can keep the room until Friday. Accordingly, I'll pay my visit to you on Friday. Until then, kind regards to you from your very devoted

Hugo Wolf.

163

To Vienna

Matzen Castle, *recte* [more accurately] hunter's cottage,

May 17, 1895

Dear gracious lady!

Many, many thanks for your heartfelt lines, which gave me decidedly more pleasure than the magnificent bouquets of flowers set up on all the tables to receive me in my pretty rooms. A letter also arrived from Schalk at the same time as your lines, but of course I broke open your letter first, so that you were still the first to welcome me in my new home.

Seldom has a train ride passed so pleasantly as this most recent one. I had the clever idea of requesting a 2nd class compartment and learned only upon boarding the train that no more tickets for 3rd class were available anyway, so great was the demand to Salzburg. There were five of us traveling from Vienna to Salzburg. From Salzburg on I had a half-compartment all to myself as far as Jenbach, but the compartments on either side, first and second class, were almost completely empty, so that

there was no disturbance of any kind. The sky cleared, oddly
enough, in the Salzkammergut region and for a good part of the
way Lady Sun accompanied us. The closer the train got to its
destination, however, the darker the horizon became. In Saalfel-
den it actually began to snow. The cold air made itself felt, despite the closed windows. I spent part of the time during the
trip reading Mörike's letters, the first half of which can be said
to be weak and fairly uninteresting. But the other half met with
my approval, although I had imagined the letters to be wittier
and more original. A certain antiquated tone is all too prominent
in them. We "moderns" have a different sensibility. I suspect
we (Mörike and I) would not have gotten along well after all. I
finally took up the poetry of the Corregidor in the absence of
any other intellectual enjoyment, whereupon I felt myself wonderfully refreshed and stimulated. I also have to record several
hours of sleep, notabene just at the time when we were passing
through the most beautiful regions. At 9:15 p.m. I arrived in
Jenbach and was met by the devoted servant Gustav (a valet par
excellence) and delivered to my destination with equipage, i.e.,
directly by coach to the hunter's cottage. Everything was already
prepared. Unfortunately, they forgot to heat the rooms, which
didn't happen until this morning. My bedroom is on the second
floor. It's magnificently furnished. Nothing but *old (antique)* furniture. A Gothic washstand of huge dimensions. Gothic bed,
very comfortable. To be sure no horsehair pillow, but a firm
feather pillow. Of course *plumeaus* [feather quilts] with silk cov-
erlets and very lightweight. Slept fabulously, but didn't get to
bed until 12:00. A cold supper with wine and bottled beer was
already set out when I arrived. I ate it with pleasure. My serving
girl, a good-natured Tyrolean, excused herself and I was alone
in the midst of the splendor. No one around for miles. I wanted
to shout for joy. I got up at 7:00 a.m. It was snowing in large
regular flakes as it only does in December or January. What a
nice surprise! But what to do? My bedroom can't be heated,
because it has no stove. But, on the other hand, it was comfortable in my workroom, a rustic room with a huge green tile stove
surrounded by a wooden bench on which fox skins lie, which
also cover every chair. My workroom on the ground floor is most
charming. Four small windows to the south, two and two toward

the east. A large square table that stands as firm as a stone wall replaces the secretary for me. A natural wood ceiling with a crossbeam, whitewashed walls. (The bedroom, on the other hand, is completely wood-paneled, which makes it very cozy.) There are benches all around the walls. My writing desk is placed so that it's flanked on two sides by benches. At the moment, I'm looking at the Rolandsbogen as the mist is obscuring the view of the Stubaier Alps. As for the rest, meadows and woods in splendidly cared-for condition. I spent the morning today arranging, unpacking, and settling in. The pianino was moved around, so that I now have better light. It was pushed in front of a wall bench, so that I can use the bench instead of a stool. A small, carved wooden cupboard of marvelous workmanship conceals your picture in its velvet frame. It's my holy of holies. Steins of pewter and ceramic, old pictures, and delicate figurines decorate the ledges. In short, it is more livable, homey, and cozy than my most vivid imagination could have dared to envision.—It is almost noontime. I'm dining in the hunter's cottage until the baron comes. The new housekeeper, an agreeable little Tyrolean woman too, set the table for me herself. I'm dining in the workroom, since it is the only one that can be heated. A delicious repast, everything most magnificently prepared. It's being served at this very minute.—I'm breaking off here.—Just gulped down the *first* course. Odd menu. Turnips with cold Braunschweiger.—I'll wait and see. In the meantime, as no one is coming, I can report that I have a fully equipped kitchen at my disposal, with all the kitchen utensils. There are great numbers of baking pans and wooden mixing bowls and whatever all these things are called. And everything shiny, new, and clean. Also new brooms, whisks, dustpans, feather dusters of ostrich plumes, and the like in abundance. The vestibules to both my rooms are splendidly appointed and in good taste. A well-filled credenza in the vestibule provides me with everything my heart could ever desire. In short, a real paradise. *Second* course: veal filet with potatoes and red beets. Very tasty. To finish, radishes, butter, cheese. All in plentiful quantity. Have really eaten well. As I just learned, the food is being prepared in my kitchen. I'm surprised that the people have managed to fix such an opulent meal in such a short time. It's just occurred to me that one of the small pocket handkerchiefs could be in the blue trousers intended for Frau Moser. Please look and see. Three of the small pocket handkerchiefs are missing. I'd like to have all of my new suit here, the one I left behind, because the cold is horrendous. I need heavy socks for the knickerbockers in any case. Please get me two pairs in a pattern that pleases you and add it to my account. I'll send you the money from here for the Engl[ish] material and for the socks. Today it's miserable. Everything covered by thick clouds and mist, and dreadfully cold. I'm taking this letter to Brixlegg so that it will still go out today. After my return I'll get down to business. I hope it'll work. If you hear nothing from me in the next few days, you can assume I'm buried in my work and that I feel my best then. How's my little friend Irmi doing? Give her my best greetings. Schalk didn't come on the evening he promised, because he was held up by Bruckner. He apologized for this in his letter. By the way, the evening at Mayreders passed very pleasantly even without Schalk. Both of Frau Mayreder's brothers-in-law are charming people and fairly musical, especially the one called Prix, who is also a friend and admirer of Bruckner.

And now I'll close! Lipperheide is coming to Matzen Sunday or Monday. Rickelt has been off hunting since yesterday afternoon. I don't envy him the pleasure and prefer a warm room to any tallyho. Please put one or two pairs of thick socks in the package. I brought along only three pairs of the heavy kind. And now thousands, but thousands of sincerest greetings from your always devoted

Hugo Wolf.

164

To Vienna

Matzen, Brixlegg, May 22 (Wagner's birthday), 1895

Dear gracious lady!

I've been frantically industrious these last few days. However, yesterday I had a bad day on account of the workers who had to see to the fence repair along the park paths and whose sawing and hammering drove me out of the workroom. Today it's somewhat better; have gotten a good bit further along with my work. At the moment I'm up to the place "Ach die Nässe, ach der Schrecken, Gott ich sterbe," etc. [Oh the wetness, oh the fright, God, I'm dying, etc.]. The 2nd act must be finished this week. The weather has also gotten better today and it's warm at least, if not especially beautiful. Letter and package have arrived. I haven't had enough time yet to try on the new knee socks. I'm especially pleased with the pattern.

How is Irmi? Have Ilse and Hilde caught it? That would be very unfortunate.

The finches are occasionally bothering me again. I borrowed a rifle from Rickelt the painter to fire warning shots. As yet, I haven't gotten around to shooting, however, as I'm so very absorbed in my work.

When are you moving to the country? Grohe wrote me a very humble and sad letter about his "untimely observations" in regard to the opera *libretto*. He's overjoyed that I've come so far in such a short time. I'm enclosing the letter. Send it back to me sometime, as it hasn't been answered yet. In order to gain time I only eat once a day—at noon—with the baron. In the evening I have a cold supper and a bottle of excellent Kundl beer brought to my room. The baron is in complete agreement with this arrangement. Sometime soon we want to take a hike up the hohe Salve [Hohe Salve] (quite a tame mountain, but with marvelous view), i.e., the three of us: the baron, Rickelt, and I. If only the heavens were more dependable! I'm sending a review of Elfenlied and Feuerreiter by Kauffmann along with this letter. I think it's excellent. Show this to Schalk and then send it back to me. It's 11:30 and I have to hurry to *déjeuner*.

A thousand sincerest greetings from your most resolvedly devoted

Hugo Wolf.

165

To Vienna [letter-card]

Matzen Castle, May 24, 1895

In the greatest haste!
I'm filled with bliss. Have just finished the second act.
Don't come!
Sincerest greetings, your

Hugo Wolf.

166

To Vienna

Matzen, May 25, 1895 in the evening

Dear gracious lady!

Many, many thanks for your last dear and amusing letter, even if the humor is of a somewhat diabolical nature. A bit of the devil should lie hidden in everyone, something like a few drops of cognac in milk, a drink the French particularly like. Too much milk of the pious way of thinking can sour one easily and that's definitely undesirable.

Today I gave myself a day off. Tomorrow it's on to the third act. The newly composed music for the 2nd act satisfies me beyond all measure. I consider it to be the best I've ever written. Everything follows in quick succession in the most economical way, and *every* note has reason and meaning. If you could only hear some of it! How amazed you'd be, how happy! I can't play this music often enough for myself and quite honestly, I'm absolutely reveling in it. God, I'm a lucky person that it lies within me to create such pleasure for myself. If another had written this music, it would certainly not please me less, but since no one else does me such a favor, I just have to do it myself, and God knows, I do it only for my own *plaisir;* for even in my dreams it wouldn't occur to me to write for the public. It pleases *me*—and that's that.—Now, a request: I'd like to enclose with my manuscript the proofs of both Spanish songs that were incorporated into the libretto. Take a look and see whether the things I want aren't to be found among my music, and if that is the case, roll them up and send them to me at Matzen by book post. When you do, please also enclose the Kauffmann review from the Musik[alisches] Wochenblatt, as it's important to me that the baroness see it, although she won't be coming here before July or August, admittedly. I'm very happy to hear that my little Irmi is better. I send her a little kiss.

Now you'll be breathing country air soon also. I can't tell you how much good my being here does me. But the surroundings are really heavenly. And then my little house! But when I *ef*fuse about my little place, I become quite *con*fused, so it's better if I keep silent. Today I shot and killed a finch that was annoying me terribly. When I saw the poor fellow lying there dead, I was overcome with great anguish and wished most vehemently that he were still alive. I stole into the nearby woods with the small dead body and buried it in the earth in a completely out-of-the-way spot. How must a murderer feel who has the murder of a human being on his conscience! I had a fleeting brush with that today. To the devil with killing. But doesn't one *have* to when it gets to be too much?

The weather changes from moment to moment. Sunshine and rain come and go whenever they take the notion. But, fortunately, we've had some very hot days. Tomorrow, on Sunday, I'll be completely alone. The baron left for Innsbruck today and won't be back until Monday. Rickelt is going hunting and also won't be back until Monday. How I am enjoying my solitude. Of course, occasionally one would like to hear a word from dear lips. But one can't have everything, and even if one has a great deal, sometimes the best thing is still missing. And with that, farewell and accept very sincerest greetings from your very most devoted

Hugo Wolf.

What's going on with the English suit? Why weren't a certain four letters received? An answer!

167

To Vienna

Matzen, May 30, 1895 in the evening

Dear gracious lady!

If it were up to me, I'd write you a hundred times a day, because I certainly think about you a hundred times. For the past few days, however, I've been so under the muse's spell that with all good intentions, I haven't gotten around to letter writing. Even now I'm virtually stealing the time. I'm writing by lamplight in my cozy little workroom. For the last few days we've had splendid weather here. The sun shines warm and bright and not a trace of cloud darkens the bluest sky. What joy it is to greet the morning at 5 a.m., breathe in the exquisite, fresh air and take in the splendid panorama that presents itself in majestic beauty to the intoxicated glance—, it's indescribable.

You should really take a little trip over here with friend Faisst; it's truly worth it. There is surely no more beautiful view in all the world than that from the Rolandsbogen, 20 steps away from my cottage. One *must* see this sort of thing. If paradise is only a myth, here it becomes a reality. And if this weren't enough, I enjoy such splendor entirely undisturbed, as if it were here just for me alone. God knows I've already enjoyed much happiness in this world, but I've never felt happier or more blissful than in this wonderful solitude here. And how convenient everything is, how clean and neat everything is kept. My serving girl, a married woman as I learned later, is absolute perfection. Above all, she makes herself as scarce as possible, so that I'm not disturbed in this respect either. Everything is straightened up while I'm having the noonday meal with the baron, which takes place in the castle. Supper is served to me here at the hunter's cottage. I take my breakfast and supper on the balcony that surrounds my bedroom on two sides. Then right after breakfast I get to work. Today I got to the end of the 2nd scene in the 3rd act, but had to break off because the last verses of Frasquita and Repela require a greater expansion. Therefore, I wrote to Frau Mayreder today that she should compose three additional strophes for me. It will be a priceless duet in the most frantic tempo. It's possible that I'll undertake Tio Lukas' big scene already tomorrow, in order not to lose too much time. The two scenes of the 3rd act turned out extremely well. The address to the moon is composed to Frasquita's love motif. The "es ist—, so sprich, es ist—" [it is—so speak, it is—], etc., to Repela's motif. Oh, that I have to explain it all to you in such a cut-and-dried manner. How annoying! Faisst might possibly pay me a visit as early as Pentecost. He's really bombarding me with postcards. He's going to visit you too in the summer, i.e., in August, and then come to me in Matzen again. Grohe, who's now taking a most active interest in my work, wrote an epistle to Lipperheide recently, which I'm enclosing because it is so curious. Lipperheide nearly fell off his chair, as he in no way ever so much as uttered a single word to anyone, or so he assured me, about my being a "difficult" guest. How Prof. Erich Schmidt heard of this will undoubtedly be clarified. Send Grohe's letter back to me and *Kauffmann's review as well*, which I requested recently.

Regarding the song "In dem Schatten," I realized right away that it can't be found. I think Frau Jäger has the proofs. Please arrange to reclaim them from Frau Jäger, as I am urgently in need of them. Enclosed please find an object that constitutes an indispensable component of my atomizer. It isn't functioning properly because the opening is too large. Please have the damage repaired at Reithofer, where the atomizer was purchased, or replace the old top with a new one and send it back to me again soon.

The news of Ilse's illness filled me with the greatest sadness, not so much because of her getting sick as because of the consequences to you; having to stay in Vienna until June 20th, now during this splendid weather, is really no pleasure. Poor you, you have my sympathy. Consequently my stay here gives me decidedly less pleasure when I think about your being exposed to the heat and foul air in Vienna. God grant that you may put this ordeal behind you soon. And now good night and a thousand sincerest greetings from your very most faithful

Hugo Wolf.

168

To Vienna

[Brixlegg, June 4, 1895]

Just quickly a sincere greeting!

Am enclosing letters from Frau M[ayreder], which I'd like you to send back to me again. Did you find the top to the atomizer in my letter?

Tio Lukas is whipping along like mad. Hurrah!

Happy moving!

[no signature]

169

To Traunkirchen

Matzen, June 12, 1895 in the evening

Dear gracious lady!

I've been stumped in the composition's progress recently by Tio Lukas' big scene in the 3rd act. The passage: "Wenn es

Gott gefallen hätte, mich durch schlimmen Schein zu prüfen"
[If it had pleased God to test me by evil delusion] simply
wouldn't let itself be set to music. I brooded over it for three
days before the fortunate moment arrived that helped me over
it. Now the monologue has been finished for three days and
today I've just completed the 5th scene. Now comes the last
scene. I don't think it will give me any trouble, because the 5th
scene also made me sweat much blood. There are some really
devilish things in it. Practically nothing sounds right anymore.—
Something for friend Öhn, who will take pleasure in that. How
well providence treated me, however, by not allowing me to
compose Lukas' scene until *now* instead of at the beginning of
my work. What a superficial piece it would have been without
the previously stated motives. Frankly, it was *never* my intention
to compose it as a first piece. *The fact* that I didn't compose it
then just goes to point up the correct instinct that so steadfastly
guided me from the very beginning, because the drinking scene
in the 2nd act was really the only one (and perhaps the night-
watchman's piece) that could be composed entirely out of context. Meanwhile, Larisch has sent me the score of Meistersinger
so that I can prepare myself thoroughly for the orchestration. I
wrote to Faisst a few days ago and suggested that he hire a copyist in Stuttgart—at my expense, of course, who would copy my
manuscript in his office, since I won't entrust my original to any
copyist. I hope he follows my suggestion. My life here slips by
so peacefully and quietly that I often don't know the day of the
week. No guest is here, except Rickelt the painter. I'll even be
here all by myself in July, as the baron wants to set out on a trip
on the Rhine with his wife, who is still staying on in Berlin. Frau
Mayreder recently wrote me an exceedingly cordial letter ten
pages long, in which she called my attention, among other
things, to the Bernsteinhexe [Witch of Bernstein] as the next
opera that ought to follow Corregidor. She sent me the book
along with it, which I read right away. It's a horrible theme, but
filled with gripping scenes and inspired by an utterly demonic
passion. You should read the book. It's available (Gmunden
[town] has it) in the Universalbibliothek [Universal Library].
The author of the book is Wilhelm Meinhold. I'm sincerely
happy that you are already breathing country air. There's noth-

ing better than life in the country. Today I got my new climbing boots. They turned out very well for a Brixlegg "master," and the best part is: they cost only 5 Fl.

I received the two neckties. And one of them was a *Novum* [new one]. Heartfelt thanks for the surprise. The top to the atomizer arrived in the most deplorable condition, in a thousand pieces. Fortunately, an atomizer of the baroness' is helping me out, so that I can manage without mine. Do give my best greetings to the girls, especially my little Irmi, whom I'm holding particularly close to my heart at the moment. I'm still leading my hermit's life and see the baron only once a day. We always chat very pleasantly then, as we really understand each other exceptionally well. To be his guest is a true pleasure. He is also extremely attentive to his guests and always anxious that something might be disturbing me. In the meantime, I've been faced with the unhappy necessity of doing away with a few more feathered troublemakers. Oh well, one becomes accustomed to everything. Enclosed is the letter from Frau M[ayreder]. And now the very sincerest greetings from your faithful

Hugo Wolf.

170

To Traunkirchen [postcard]

Matzen, June 16, 1895

Have just finished the 3rd act. The sky has cleared up again as well. Now comes the headlong rush into the 4th act. Maybe I'll finish the work this month yet. Everything's going splendidly. Most joyous greetings from your

Hugo Wolf.

171

To Traunkirchen [postcard]

Matzen, June 18, 1895

Many, many thanks for both pieces of mail (poetic and prosaic) and sincerest greetings from your very most devoted
Hugo Wolf.

172

To Traunkirchen

Matzen, June 24, 1895

Dear gracious lady!

Hurriedly, otherwise the letter won't leave here. Have just received the English suit sent me. As an unnecessary extra, friend Bayer has also provided me with a vest. The suit fits *perfectly* and makes me devilishly happy. The material is exquisite and feels as soft as velvet. I'm delighted with it and thank you a thousand, thousand times. I've just delivered Faisst, who came to see me Friday afternoon, to the train at Jenbach. We spent heavenly days here. Played him the 3rd act twice and what is finished from the 4th. Have just now stopped at the place: "Mein Gatte der Corregidor" [My husband the Corregidor], which Mercedes sings. Going to be magnificent. I'll write in more detail very soon.

Why have you been silent for so long? It's not a bit nice of you. I'm very upset about it. For today only the very, very sincerest greetings from your

Hugo Wolf.

173

To Traunkirchen

Matzen, June 26, 1895

Dear gracious lady!

Unfortunately, I can't answer your recent delightfully long letter in the same way, as I'm in a good frame of mind today and dare not lose too much time with letter writing. Only I'm very very sorry that you've taken such a stubborn stand against the Bernsteinhexe. To answer indirectly, I'm sending you a letter of Frau M[ayreder]'s. Maybe it will put your mind somewhat at ease.

Did I send you the letter that has to do with my matadorsponge—also from Frau M.? If not, you should get it later. *Please report about it.*

I've arrived at the place: "Lukas, ich verachte dich" [Lukas, I despise you], and will probably compose one more page of libretto in the course of the afternoon.

Now I have to rush to the noonday meal so as not to be late.

For now then, many sincere thanks for your dear, detailed letter and the very best greetings from your most faithful
                                                                            Hugo Wolf.

174

To Traunkirchen [postcard]

Matzen, July 9, 1895

Dear gracious lady!
Contrary to all expectation I am already in the extremely happy position of being able to tell you that the work was completed today in the afternoon. *Finis coronat opus* [The finale crowns the work]. With the very sincerest greetings, your very devoted
                                                                            Hugo Wolf.

175

To Traunkirchen

Matzen, July 28, 1895

Dear gracious lady!
Today I'm writing these lines on an indescribably beautiful Sunday morning after a short walk in the immediate vicinity. I'm completely in a holiday mood and my thoughts linger over nothing but lovely things; and so it's only natural that I am also thinking of you. I haven't slept a wink since 4 a.m., when the morning bells rang in the day. What a contrast to the real reason for my waking. After coming home late from a visit to Grützner the painter, I was aroused at 3 a.m. by the scratching and nibbling of a mouse. Since I hadn't turned out the light until 1 a.m., I had slept only two hours. Furious, I got up and tried to find the intruder. But nothing could divert him from his sinister business, and he chewed and pawed and scratched away in spite of my vigorous countermeasures. What should I do? The fiend simply couldn't be reached. I couldn't sleep any more, of course, so I got up and wandered around like a dreamer in the half-light of the breaking dawn. When I came back to the room after a

while, the rascal was still working like a maniac, and was as unconcerned as if he were the only one on earth. Furious all over again, I took a hammer and banged on the spot from which the noise came. That did help for a moment, but almost immediately the racket started up again. Then the morning bells began to ring and—as if by stroke of magic, the anger and the rage over the beast were gone. I felt almost grateful to the creature for being the involuntary cause of such an uplifting, exhilarating pleasure for me. The philosopher draws the moral from it, that one evil doesn't have to lead to more evil, but can, on occasion, actually be the source of good. The visit at Grützner's went very pleasantly. The drive over under the burning sun with Rickelt the painter in the baron's carriage was a rather depressing prelude, but the further course of events, and especially the conclusion, compensated for the hardship endured. Grützner, who on the occasion of a visit to Matzen had already invited me to his place for a "shearing," actually kept his word. He sheared my head smooth and bald, and it is just a joy. As a paraphrase to Bruckner's saying (when Wagner presented him with a beer stein) "but *such* a waiter!" I can now appropriately say: "but *such* a barber," or rather "hair whacker," as I've jokingly dubbed him.—

Friend Faisst has now sent me sample music paper from Breitkopf & Härtelschen [Härtel] for the score. The paper is excellent and preferable to the best Viennese music paper by far. The orchestration has already progressed to the first Spanish song, that is, approximately halfway through Act 1. I'm also in possession of the life of Friedrich Nietzsche, written by his sister. Faisst had it sent to me along with the music paper. As soon as I've finished the book, I'll send it along to you. Since so far only the first volume has appeared, one mostly learns only about Nietzche's [sic] childhood and youth. Dear God, how the man did change later on. One can scarcely believe one's eyes when one reads the sentimental outbursts stemming from his student days in Bonn and thinks of the hard and relentless superman he later became. What a gulf there is between! The book is very well written, by the way, and with a truly touching reverence for the brother. You will surely enjoy it.

I will use the stamps enclosed in your last letter only for

letters addressed to you. Do you agree with that? If I shouldn't write for a few days, you'll trust that I'm hard at work; I must diligently write music again, otherwise the performance will come to nothing this season. That would truly be a shame. Many and sincerest greetings from your

Hugo Wolf

176

To Traunkirchen

Matzen, August 1, 1895

Dear gracious lady!

The Mayreders arrived last evening at 6:00. They're quite delighted with the magnificent lodgings of the old Matzen house and above all with the splendid park. This morning we toured the baron's new castle, which elicited admiration from all sides. Nowhere else has he [Mayreder] seen so much good taste with regard to the furnishings and to the designing of the grounds as well. Our housekeeper dreams up everything possible to provide our table with the greatest abundance. Unfortunately, the weather has turned bad. It's raining buckets, so that we've had to give up our planned excursion to the Reinthaler lakes.

While I'm writing these lines, Lino [Mayreder], who proposed the [familiar form of] "Du" [you] to me at the evening meal yesterday, is sitting in a corner of my workroom and making a pencil sketch of it; he is doing it so that I'll be in it too, writing. Meanwhile, his wife is sitting on a bench in front of the house reading Nietzsche's biography. We're both in agreement that the book is written more for cousins and family relatives than for admirers of his philosophical views. There are passages in the book like: Nietzsche's first word was "Omama," i.e., grandmother. I was reminded of a certain Gerda. It's really a torture to wend one's way through this book. Now I also understand why Faisst was able to be so enthusiastic about the book. It's truly reading material for very unsophisticated people, of whom Faisst is one. Faisst would certainly not comprehend or even like the later Nietzsche. I really don't know whether I should send you the book. Incidentally, I've only read half of it up to now.

Faisst wrote me yesterday that my manuscript is just now being copied. I'm furious about such a delay. Faisst is a numbskull, for all his otherwise fine qualities. I still haven't received the music paper for the score either; it's enough to drive one mad.

My kittens, especially the light-haired kitty, are great fun for me. They're around me almost all the time now, watching me as I orchestrate, walking around very leisurely on the table where I'm working. The blond kitty follows me everywhere like a puppy, so that I can hardly make a move without it. I'm not bothered by mice anymore. Our housekeeper is going to put flowers in the hallway tomorrow at my request, i.e., trailing carnations, which will give the hunter's cottage a very festive appearance.

Enclosed photographs probably won't meet entirely with your approval. Besides a certain docility, I was also photographed from my unflattering side. The nose is decidedly not wolfish.

The Mayreders will stay here until Monday, as we definitely want to climb the Sonnwendjoch [ridge]. We have to wait for good weather for that, however. From tomorrow on, I'm spending the mornings on my own and on my work. Afternoons will be devoted to them. Only under these conditions are they willing to stay until Monday. With regard to the Bernstein-hexe, Frau M. would rather await the effect of Corregidor, in order to approach the dramatic technicalities with complete assurance. Her plan seems to be quite excellent to me. It provides for grand stage effects. The trial scenes aren't even included. However, there is a big prison scene, in which the tortured soul will be eloquently expressed. I'm fully convinced that she'll make a splendid piece out of it. Twilight is just falling and Mayreder is stopping his work, to continue tomorrow. And so I'll close too. With very sincerest greetings from your most faithful

Hugo Wolf.

August 2, very early in the morning.

Last night I had a very lovely dream about you and dear little Irmina and woke up feeling quite blissful over it. I thought back on it for a long time and imagined it in further detail. The dream was so beautiful. It prompted me to reopen the letter, which could no longer be taken to the post office yesterday, and add these lines. The sky is clearing and it will be a lovely, sunny day. I only wish you were here now and could take part in our pleasant and exuberant conversations. You would certainly like it. The Mayreders are truly such charming people, but Polyhymnia did not stand over their cradle. You won't find two more unmusical folks in the world. When I put Frau M. to the test, she confused the motif of the Corregidor with that of Repela. Such a thing would never happen with you. Forgive my drawing you into a comparison with Frau M.; however, since I have great admiration for that woman's unusual talent in other respects, the comparison is pardonable to some degree. She is as lacking in her understanding of me in my art as *you* are gifted. That simply cannot be changed, as painful as this admission is for me. The fact that I can't play the opera's last acts for the two of them because Faisst has the manuscript doesn't actually upset me at all, for it would be a useless labor of love. How fortunate I am that your talents are so entirely different from those of Frau M.; whereas she has to call upon her intellect as the only correct perception leading to true understanding, as if solving a mathematical problem, everything to you becomes at once a clear picture. In this regard, you are so much above that woman, who otherwise has no rival among her peers. That which I demand above all in a friendly association with another person, that my unique nature be understood and comprehended, Frau M. cannot offer me; and it is precisely this which makes our friendly relationship so valuable and enduring, this complete fulfillment in each other. (. . .) [one line obliterated]

I've been interrupted by my two kittens, who have started up a dreadful yowling on the second floor. Both animals, especially the one, are already tyrannizing me. When they're not around me, they wail continuously. I feel completely enslaved by the two beasts.—As this mail should go out before noon, I'll be brief and very quickly add yet a thousand greetings to the page. I hope to hear from you again very soon.

Totally yours
Hugo Wolf.

177

To Traunkirchen

Matzen, August 3, 1895

Dear gracious lady!

    Mayreder and I have just returned drenched to the skin in pouring rain from a mountain tour on the Sonnwendjoch (2400 m). We set out last evening at 6:00 under completely clear skies, which augured the best for the next day. Frau M. accompanied us in the coach to the foot of the mountain, from which Mayreder, I, and the caretaker of the castle, who doubled as guide and porter, began our climb to the ridge. After a brisk $2\frac{1}{2}$-hour walk on a fairly difficult path, part of which led through beautiful wooded areas and part through very romantic rocky stretches, we spent the night on hay in a miserable shepherd's hut so that we could climb to the summit of the ridge at 3:00 the next morning. A glorious moonlit night promised us the finest morning for the next day. But, unfortunately, it turned out otherwise. After we had walked about two more hours, in the middle of a wild, craggy cliff area a thick mist descended, which gradually turned into a heavy, stinging rainfall with very strong wind gusts. We had only a quarter of an hour's walk left to the summit, but from that point on, our previously well-trodden path disappeared into narrow windings along an immense wall of rock on the right, and a terrifying abyss opened on the left. Our guide didn't want to risk climbing further in the thick mist, as from that point on, the utmost care was called for, and the thick mist would make such caution difficult at best. So there was nothing else to do but begin our retreat in full view of the peak, which we completed successfully, also in pouring rain. Despite this and even though the wind was whistling around my ears and my fingers holding the climbing stick were completely stiff with cold, I was not deterred from picking a few bunches of Alpine roses, which cover the ground there by the thousands, so I could send you a greeting of flowers from the mountaintop. The Hohe Salve [mountain] greeted me at the same moment from the distant horizon as I spied the first Alpine rose. May these same flowers remind you of lovely and happy hours.

Your dear letter has just arrived. The fact that Spur and Schur have finally found common ground doesn't surprise me. Enemies one minute, friends the next. An old story. Today it's raining continuously. I'm quite melancholy over it. The Mayreders picked a bad time for their visit. But what is there to say about rainy weather in Matzen, where there is every comfort and convenience to help one through it, compared to rainy weather at Achensee? The two will be leaving Monday, rain or shine. Actually I look forward to being alone again.—My kittens have also deserted me in the meantime. When I got back from the mountain tour, I found the spot empty where they had liked to pass the time. Cat temperament!—They flatter and behave lovingly and affectionately—but they're not faithful.—H[einrich] sent me cigarettes from Vienna; I wired him my thanks for them. With very sincerest greetings, always your most faithful

Hugo Wolf.

On my way to the noonday meal just now, I found my friend Larisch with the Mayreders in the Matzen house. Immediately invited him to the noonday meal and will keep him here tonight in the room adjacent to mine in the hunter's cottage. He leaves again tomorrow.

178

To Traunkirchen

Matzen, August 8, 1895

Dear gracious lady!

Of course you are right regarding my most recent picture; as long as you like it, it has my approval also. You'll receive the drawing of my workroom very soon, which is quite wonderfully done. Mayreder really did excellently with it. I've just gotten a letter from Frau M[ayreder]. It's too amusing for me to withhold it from you. Send it back to me at your convenience. "Frl. Obexer" is our housekeeper and cook at the same time; she's also a foster mother to me particularly. The latest news I can pass on is that the light-haired kitten has returned. At the moment, she's sitting on my back and is watching over my head as I write. She's whirring and purring away, so that it makes me feel very cozy. Miez is an absolutely adorable animal and follows me around like a puppy. If I'm gone for even a moment she starts to whimper right away. The place she decidedly likes best is on my back. She stays there very quietly, except for her cozy purring, and since she doesn't disturb me with it, I let her be.

You'd be delighted with the kitten, if you could see its cunning ways. I think it would be something for my little Irmi. Wouldn't she like to have a little kitten? I could get her one.— Faisst wrote me today that the copyist is already at work. The orchestration is proceeding slowly, since I'm doing the final draft now and must be very careful with the notation, because erasing causes great difficulties. Sunday I'm going to the Achensee, as the Mayreders are leaving there Sunday afternoon. I'm also going to meet Kapellmeister Röhr from the Mannheim Hoftheater there, who's a very good friend of Grohe.

Grohe wrote me that he's not coming until the beginning of September. Fine with me if he doesn't come until later. Must close now. The meal is waiting for me. Very sincerest greetings from your most faithful

Hugo Wolf.

179   To Traunkirchen

                                  [Brixlegg], Sept. 14, 1895

Dear only friend!

You must never come to see me in Matzen again, because the subsequent feeling of loneliness always puts me in such a disconsolate mood that I'm completely incapable of forming a single rational thought. After your departure I felt so horribly alone and forsaken that I came close to sobbing aloud. To rid myself of this anxious feeling I tried to continue with my work; but that didn't succeed at all. So I sat for a good hour brooding over my work without ever touching the pen. Then I gave up and went to bed at 8:00 and fell into a deep sleep, from which a rain shower beating against my window awakened me the next morning. What a sad awakening! The whole region enshrouded in fog, the mountains, to the extent they were visible, covered with snow, the air raw and chilly, and the monotonous, melancholy rain on top of it all. Along with it, my own melancholy— truly the picture of misery! When the postman appeared at 10:30

a pleasant gleam greeted me from afar that cheered me somewhat. It was a letter from my friend Muck, which I'm enclosing for you. I'll send Muck the libretto and the copied 1st act as soon as I'm in possession of the two. Today I was served a splendid noonday meal. My good Urschel surprised me with an exquisitely prepared roast chicken, along with a fabulous compote. What a shame that we didn't have that the day before. It would have been the perfect time. The temperature has dropped drastically. I'm so cold that I can hardly guide the pen. Let's hope this temperature doesn't last too long. How did you withstand the journey? I'm looking forward very much to your next letter. This afternoon there will be much hard work, despite the rain and cold. I'll have to keep myself warm by some means, and orchestrating can certainly heat one up. For today, then, very sincerest greetings from your

Hugo Wolf.

180

To Vienna

Matzen, April [mistakenly written

instead of October] 14, 1895

Dear gracious lady!

Your friendly lines arrived earlier than usual today. The sun, which arrived somewhat later than normal today on account of the dense fog, came into my room at the same moment your letter arrived. I now have morning sun, you know, which I missed desperately in the spring and summer. My room seems twice as cheerful in the sunshine as it does otherwise. Fortunately, the weather has changed again for the better; yesterday was a warm, marvelous autumn day. How beautiful it is here now in the fall; it's beyond all description. I'm basking in this melancholy, which robs nature of its charms, but bestows a new one simultaneously. It is the time of ripening, and this milieu is so attuned to my own feelings. How sorry I am for you, that you must spend the most beautiful season in the city, and how happy I count myself to be in the opposite situation.

The baron still hasn't shown up. But it's possible that he'll come today.

I did write to Faisst, but a jovial, high-spirited letter. I too suspected that love had played a nasty trick on him, to which I gave veiled expression with Repela's words: "Ist's ein Herz-schlag, der ihn traf?" [Has he met with a blow to the heart?].

I wired Muck yesterday; am wondering if he'll respond to it. A second letter arrived from Brockhaus at the same time as your dear lines. I'm enclosing it and ask that you return it to me immediately. Since I've not signed the contract with Heckel yet, I wouldn't be opposed to handing over the whole affair to Brock-haus, who has a very well known name, i.e., on commission for the present, because what he'd offer me today would be child's play compared to what I'll be able to demand after the perfor-mance. Nothing will come of it. Later yes, when he has to shell out properly, he'll have to shell out through the nose. *'Yes, that's what you're going to pay me!'* This is going to be my motto hence-forth with regard to publishers. There is no need to return the enclosed card, which I received yesterday. What do you suppose Schalk will have to say about it?

I'm also sending you the current installment from Pot-peschnigg so that you can see what a nice fellow he is.

Thank God I'm finished with the opening scene, which caused me *terrible* difficulties. I've already written down the pas-sage: "Schenk ein du Blume von Castilien" [Pour, you flower of Castile]. Now it will go smoothly again.

You'll have a lot to do in town during the first days. A few lines will be enough for me; you needn't make the effort for a proper letter. These lines are intended to welcome you at the threshold of your house; I hope I'm the first of your friends to greet you there. A happy return. Greeting you from the bottom of his heart, your always faithful

Hugo Wolf.

Today is a gloriously beautiful day. Bluest sky and the most golden sunshine.

181

To Vienna

Matzen, Oct. 18, 1895

Dear gracious lady!

Just the quick news today that the baron and his wife arrived by coach on the evening of the 15th from Tegernsee. I didn't greet them until the next day. Both were very happy to see me again. The baroness is tremendously kind to me. Last evening she came up to me and brought me flowers and fruit. I played for her from the 1st and 2nd acts and she was absolutely delighted with it.

This morning she sent me a tea service with flowers. The tea service is a present from her. More than ever, I am her confidant. She pours out her whole heart to me. I sympathize as much as I can, and "I helped as much as I could" [*ich half, so gut ich konnt*], as Mime says.

This morning was a strange awakening. The entire landscape was covered by an inch of snow. It was the loveliest sight. The trees looked like Christmas trees, a picture-perfect winter landscape. I had my rooms heated very well, however.

Frau Werner reported to me that the neighboring flat in Perchtoldsdorf, where Mitzie used to live, is available. I've always had my eye on that flat, but it was already taken, unfortunately. Since it's now available, I've asked Frau Werner to look it over and report the findings of her inspection to me. The flat costs 120 Fl. I'd be happy if I could get the flat out there. What do you say to this?

In my orchestrating I've already gone beyond the song of the Spanish wine.

I'm planning to arrive in Vienna end of Oct., beginning of Nov.

Muck has not yet responded to my telegram. It's been almost a week since I wired. Sternfeld wrote me that Director Pierson in Berlin is very interested in my work and that he's going to propose it for performance in any case.

The snow has already melted, but the air is raw and cold. Must close. Adieu.

Many, many greetings, your
Hugo Wolf.

A letter from Potpeschnigg enclosed.

182

To Vienna
Matzen, Oct. 21, 1895

Dear, esteemed friend!

Today I received four letters all at once, yours, then one from Frau Werner, one from Baroness Bach, and the last, but not least, from my dear friend [Frau] Mayreder,—so, from four ladies. Isn't that charming? I'm enclosing Frau M.'s letter because it is a one-of-a-kind, as all her letters are. Frau Werner's letter depressed me a great deal, as it contained extremely regrettable news. The flat in Perchtoldsdorf, she writes me now, was, unfortunately, already promised a long time ago. I was dumbfounded. Therefore, I won't be coming to Vienna so soon and will have to stay here for a still longer period of time in any event. I had looked forward so very much to our seeing each other soon, and now here we are. Yesterday I drove with the baroness in horribly cold weather to Schwaz, a small town of which I'm particularly fond. In the evening I played the 1st act of Corregidor for both of them. My willingness was very much appreciated. Unfortunately, the two of them understand next to nothing about my music, but they pretended that they liked it exceedingly. Baroness Bach has already written me a second [letter] (the first was addressed to the Siebenbrunnengasse), wherein she pesters me to accompany her in her benefit concerts. The goose! For just three songs (notabene the shortest of all my things) she expects me to make a fool of myself for her. How presumptuous people are! On top of that, with genuinely touching consistency, she persists in writing my name with two f's. Such negligence infuriates me. She considers herself to be one of my admirers and can't even write my name correctly. "Best not to pay her any attention" [*Am besten, wenn ich sie gar nicht beacht*]. On Nov. 16th in the small Musikvereinsaal, for the benefit of the Child Protection Society, she wants [to sing] "Blumengruss," "Du willst in die Ferne reisen" (instead of: "Mir ward gesagt, du reisest in die Ferne"), and "Frühling" (instead of: "Er ist's"). The goose doesn't even know the titles, and a person like that wants to latch onto me! "I've gotten myself into a fine mess!" [*Da hab ich mir was Schönes erblasen!*].

I've heard absolutely nothing from Muck. It's been 10 days now since he received my telegram. And neither an answer nor a package. I really no longer know what to do to regain possession of my things. I'd probably best turn the matter over to a lawyer. It is unbelievable that an educated person can behave in such a way. Speaking of lawyers, I'm reminded of my kind, dear friend Faisst. The poor fellow is lying in the Stuttgart hospital, so Grohe has told me, laid very low with typhoid fever. I wrote immediately to Frau Trost to send me more information. Frau Trost is his housekeeper.—

In the meantime, I've been to the noonday meal in the castle. The baron will send an authorized person from his business to Muck, who will demand the manuscript from him. Let's hope this measure helps.—The weather is grayish and terribly cold. I've already gotten up to Manuela with the orchestration. From now on, it will go quickly to the end. I'll stay with the Mayreders when I come to Vienna. I've also written to Schott, but not yet received an answer. Sincerest greetings from your most faithfully devoted
Hugo Wolf.

183

To Vienna
Matzen, Oct. 25, 1895

Dear and esteemed friend!

I'm writing these lines in all haste. Am in the process of finishing [the orchestration of] the 2nd act, which will be completed this afternoon. Am stopping on the final page. Just received a card from Frau Trost, from which one learns that Faisst is better. *Do write him a few lines*. I'm also enclosing the forgotten letter from Frau M[ayreder]. Guests came yesterday. I haven't seen them yet. A general who treasures my songs, I understand, and also sings, along with three women, daughters of the poet Karl Stieler and related by marriage to the general. Today at noon I'll probably have to meet the people. Through the good offices of the baron, Muck was formally questioned by an authorized person about my manuscript and asked to deliver up my things. Muck replied that he had *already sent me* the manuscript. Were this really the case, I should already have it in my possession. The devil knows what this creature has done with the manuscript. Maybe he lost it during the move. I'll wait until morning and then go back to sending wires again. This is one of the most unbelievable stories.

It promises to be a beautiful afternoon today.—The letter from Frau M. must compensate for my short little note. Sincerest greetings from

Your
Hugo Wolf.

Schott has answered. He is ready to hand over everything to Heckel, and he's giving me back the Italian [songs] upon restitution of the honorarium, the same with Feuerreiter.

184

To Vienna

Matzen, Oct. 28, 1895

Dear friend!

The long-awaited package from Muck has just arrived,—as could be foreseen, without an accompanying letter. What caused Muck to proceed in such a loutish manner and never offer me a word of apology, or any word at all, is something I cannot comprehend. A madman could not have behaved more strangely. The main thing is that I'm now again in possession of the manuscript. Moreover, Muck can go fly a kite. It is snowing constantly here. The walks are all impassable. It looks really wintry here. The company at the baron's is so disagreeable, dull, and boring that I want to take off soon. I intend to leave within the week and am only waiting for news from Frau M[ayreder] whether she's still staying in Plankenberg or is already in her town apartment.

Herr Hutschek (or whatever the good man's name is) should send me 50 Fl. I only have 25 Fl left from the 86 M, as I sent 25 Fl to my sister Modesta, who was in need of money. Too bad that the autumn was of such short duration, as we're in the middle of winter here now in Matzen.

Certainly I'd like to have the piano score brought out before the performance. Or are you opposed to this?

I won't be needing my winter coat. The train compartments at this time of year are already heated and I have a fairly warm suit. I'm longing for Vienna tremendously and can hardly wait for the day of my departure. The people here have all become repulsive to me, and since there are guests here, it's not to be tolerated at all. I've canceled my appearance at meals today and tomorrow. I want peace and quiet. I'd rather eat only bread and butter if I can just consume it with an appetite. But in the presence of such a menagerie as is gathered in the castle, one's

appetite disappears. And so, until soon. Sincerest greetings from
your

Hugo Wolf.

185

To Vienna
Matzen, Nov. 1, 1895

Dear friend!

My departure from here won't come about as quickly as I'd
planned. Frau M[ayreder] is still occupied in Plankenberg, in
addition to which she's putting up a guest at her house until the
15th of the m[onth]; I just have to be patient until then. Moreover, since there are no longer guests staying on here, my sojourn here has become bearable again. Today we even have a
wonderfully beautiful winter day, admittedly very cold. The sun
is shining brightly into my well-heated room. My work [orches-
tration of *Der Corregidor*] is going ahead quickly now. I'm taking
giant strides toward Tio Lukas' big scene, which I'll finish up
here in any event. I've now decided definitely not to write an
overture to Corregidor. The material is really too grand and too
serious for a comedy overture. Also, I still don't know whether
I should call the piece a "comic" opera, since it's as much tragic
as comic. A short but substantial prelude will have to suffice.—

So much for today, as I must rush to the post office to get
the letter out. Am enclosing a letter from Frau Mayreder. Sincerest greetings from your

Hugo Wolf.

186

To Vienna
Matzen, Nov. 4, 1895

Dearest friend!

The day today is so phenomenally beautiful that I cannot
refrain from recording this fact quite explicitly here. We have
suddenly been transported back to high summer, so warm is the
sun shining and so mild the air. There's not a cloud in the sky.

Even the flies are making their presence felt again, unfortunately. In short, Indian summer is very beautiful this time. Unhappily, I have to sit in my room and work. Am already at the beginning of Tio Lukas' scene. If the good weather—your prayer seems to help—hangs on a while longer, I'll definitely remain here for all of Nov. and complete the 3rd act. But I have a feeling it's only going to be of short duration. Received the money. But I find it not at all nice of you to withhold the photograph from me for so long. I expect it *immediately*.

Today Frau M[ayreder] sent me half of the printed libretto. Unfortunately, it's printed in Roman type; I would have preferred Gothic. It looks very grand. I still haven't sent my copy to Heckel, as I can't find time to enter the necessary corrections and write in the correct performance directions. The piano score probably won't be out by Christmas.

The very sincerest greetings then, from your
In great haste.

Hugo Wolf.

187

To Vienna

Matzen, Nov. 9, 1895

Dear friend!

For today, just the short message that Elfenlied and Feuerreiter are causing a huge sensation in Mannheim. Concertmaster Schuster wrote me an enthusiastic letter about the reception of the work[s] and thanked me for the pleasure my things have given him. What gives me the biggest kick over this is that Strauss and Humperdinck are really flattered as a result. The two pieces were repeated everywhere—naturally, in the city where one lives and has his "good friends," such a thing doesn't happen. The success in Mannheim makes me very happy because of Heckel, who is now my publisher, as you know.

But your picture gives me the most pleasure of all; the successes cannot compete with it. All else fades away in comparison.

I have an awful lot to do now. Lukas is holding me up terribly and this damned letter writing—I won't write for a long time now—robs me of my best hours. I have to enter changes in the piano score now as well, because it would be a shame to leave out the counterpoint that I'm using in several passages of the Lukas scene. The place "lachen werden sie, ja lachen" [they'll laugh, yes, laugh] will make everybody shudder. I've come up with completely new ideas there. But now, must close.

We have lovely, warm weather again. Today was particularly beautiful.

A thousand greetings, your

Hugo Wolf.

188

To Vienna

Matzen, Nov. 16, 1895

Dear, beloved friend!

With your most recent package you have more than abundantly requited mine.

Against my will I've interrupted my work—I am already in the liveliest musical debate with the entire worthy crowd—and have devoured greedily the highly interesting correspondence [the epistolary novel *Amitié amoureuse*], which flashes with a real crossfire of will-o'-the-wisps. What a fantastic story! The demonic element of human nature celebrates actual orgies in it. I was left completely breathless by it. What a devil must have resided within this female [Hermine Lecomte du Nouÿ]. Poor Maupassant! How astonished he must have been. By the way, he acquitted himself rather well, even though she is stronger than he. If I could only read the diary of this gifted creature. Unfortunately, it has still not been translated into German. Once again, a thousand thanks for this splendid surprise. Too bad that the correspondence wasn't drawn out longer. One doesn't tire of reading it. I'll read the letters to the baroness. She's always grateful to me when I bring her something new.—

Today we're having a truly God-given day. Only in the country can one appreciate the magic of a beautiful autumn day. I'm sorry that I must sit in my room and work, but there's no alternative. The 3rd act has to be completed in a week at the latest; for this reason I must finish this scribbling too.

A thousand sincerest greetings from your
                                        Hugo Wolf.
Your picture is my unending joy. I look at it all day.

189

To Vienna [postcard]
Matzen, Nov. 23, 1895

It never has nor ever will be the case. "Submit!" and in Hamburg?! No, Herr Pollini will have to knock at my door if he wants to perform the work, but not I at his. Who in the world startled this wild duck?—Today is a dreary, cold winter day. Everything's covered over with frost. Quite unpleasant. Perhaps I'll come earlier than I'd planned. Sincerest greetings.
                                        Hugo Wolf.

190

To Vienna
Matzen, Dec. 8, 1895

Dear, esteemed friend!
I'm answering your dear words right away. Outside the snowflakes are joyfully swirling about and have already covered the ground ankle-deep. The snowscape is delightfully pretty. I've never experienced such a splendid, comfortable winter. In winter now I find the surroundings to be full of charm and feel sorry for all city people, who have absolutely no idea of a winter idyll. Yesterday, in spite of a snowstorm that drifted over all the pathways, the baroness came to fetch me for a walk. We walked valiantly around the park for an hour and were both delighted with the wonderland that winter has clothed in its clean white robe. Nothing is quite as fantastic as a wooded winter landscape. One has to see it; it can't be described.
My friend [the baroness] has just sent me a half-dozen potted plants. Primroses and cyclamen. Today after dinner black coffee will be partaken of in the forest hut up on the mountain. She's having the dishes brought up so that she can prepare the coffee herself there. A terrific idea, really chic! The baroness

and I are alone today, as the baron is traveling to Innsbruck, as he usually does on Sunday. I am very much in favor with her; but we also understand each other exceptionally well. Soon the sleigh rides will begin; the ground is already suitable for it. I'm looking forward to it very much. My work is moving happily ahead. At the moment, I've stopped at the place "An der Wand des Schlafgemaches stand der Herr Corregidor" [at the bedroom wall stood the Corregidor]. Work doesn't cause me many difficulties at all anymore and I'm just savoring the orchestrating.— J. J. David's broken leg has something tragicomic about it. I feel sorry for the poor devil, however, because I know from experience what a miserable affair a broken leg is.

I'm sending you a few clippings today from the Munich Neuesten Nachrichten [newspaper], some of which will really amuse you. That Hans Pfitzner has outdone me as composer for "Fest auf Solhaug" is really entertaining. He may well be good enough for the folks in Mainz. Schott will prefer him to me in any case.

And now *vale* [farewell]. I still have to advance a good bit further today; I've already arrived at the 300th page. A thousand sincerest greetings from your

Hugo Wolf.

191

To Vienna

Matzen, Dec. 16, 1895

Dear, beloved friend!

By the time you read these lines, I will have finished my composition. I've already written out the voice parts of the final chorus movement; hence, I don't have to do any more with text. To be sure, it will still be quite a bit of work to add the large orchestra. But I still hope to be finished with it tomorrow. You can well imagine my excitement. Now I'll start becoming a human being again, since the work load these last days was really rather inhuman.

Today I received the finished copy of the 1st act from Graz. Unfortunately, Maresch made a pretty bad mess of my score; he stained it with coffee and did other sloppy things. I've complained severely to Potpeschnigg about it and given orders that such improprieties are not to occur in the future.

It's snowing murderously here; one has to wade knee-deep through the snow to get anywhere. I'll depart on Friday or Saturday after the holidays. We'll soon celebrate a happy reunion. Sincerest thanks for sending the Balzac. The book, which put me off at first because of its dissolute tone, is captivating me powerfully, now that I've somewhat accustomed myself to Balzac's style. I'm in the middle of the novel at the moment. I can only read before I go to bed; it's usually 1:00 a.m. by then. At 7:00 a.m. I'm already back on my feet again, as I don't have much need of sleep.

And now a further request. I'd like to have dress fabric (winter dress fabric) for Frl. Obexer (our housekeeper) and make her a present of it for Christmas. Would you do me the great favor of procuring this for me, as I have no experience in such matters. Maybe you could write me what the thing costs ahead of time. Frl. Obexer is as small as a dwarf, i.e., even smaller than I. So we don't need much material. Carl Rickelt is painting me in pastels. I think the picture's going to be good.

I must hurry and take the letter to Brixlegg myself today in order to get it mailed in time. So quickly then, very sincerest greetings from your

Hugo Wolf.

On May 17 I began the continuation of the composition of the 2nd act here in Matzen. And on Dec. 17 the score will be completed.

192

To Vienna

Matzen, Dec. 20, 1895

Dear, beloved friend!

The prelude to my opera is now providing me with the greatest pleasure. Yesterday morning I was still brooding in utter desperation over the piece, which was supposed to be executed according to a plan conceived a good while ago. But this plan no longer pleased me. I no longer knew what to do with it. Then suddenly toward evening I had a glorious inspiration. A completely new melody of unspeakable depth and passion occurred to me,—and so the curse was broken. Now the conclusion has become entirely different from what I originally intended. The piece concludes now in radiant splendor, prepared by a powerful crescendo. The effect is overwhelming. I'm ecstatic. And I've been extraordinarily successful with the symphonic character as well. It's a small masterpiece. I'm basking in happiness. The orchestration will be taken up yet today. I feel superhuman powers within myself and am convinced that my next dramatic work will leave Corregidor far behind. I feel ready to take on the whole world, so victorious is my mood. Life has taken on meaning for me again, and everything combustible that has been accumulating inside me will lead to a terrific explosion in my next composition. Ha, how I'm looking forward to it! Now to something else.—

I like the fabric so much that I have to ask you to send me a second package for my servant girl. She's a very respectable person and was once in very good circumstances. I can't very well offer her money and would like to show my appreciation with a Christmas present for the fine service she has provided. Therefore, please send off the fabric immediately so that it still arrives in time. Today Rickelt took six new photographs of me with the camera. Unfortunately, he's traveling back to Munich today. He'll send the picture to me in Vienna. Twilight is suddenly setting in. I have to hurry to the post office in Brixlegg. The sincerest greetings in all haste and wishing you happy holidays, your

Hugo Wolf.

I think the fabric is very inexpensive. We'll take care of "business" in Vienna.

193

To Vienna
Matzen, Dec. 22, 1895

Dear beloved friend!

I did not deny myself the pleasure of giving you a modest, little Christmas gift too. The book I sent you has often made me laugh, but has also often moved me. I recommend above all that you read the small novella "Bei Sedan." It's an immensely heartening episode from military life. However, I've found all the stories to be very skillfully told and keenly observed.

Today Grohe surprised me with a charming Christmas gift. Complete Beethoven quartets (score) in book form. Of course the notes are very small, but still very distinct, so that it can be read quite easily. This will now become my favorite reading. The leather binding is unusually tasteful, which was definitely unexpected, as the Germans in general have little taste. Grohe has made me extremely happy with it. Also thanked him immediately and offered him the orchestral score and piano reduction of Corregidor.

I won't be at all tempted to open your parcel earlier than Christmas Eve because the postman routinely stays away on Mondays; formerly it was on Sundays. That's Brixlegg postal service for you. So with all that it won't come until Tuesday. But I'm curious nevertheless. Today was a wonderfully sunny day. In the evenings we have very pretty moonlight. I'm still going to go to Brixlegg this evening to dispatch these lines, and so I will have the advantage of moonbeams shining on me the entire way. I'll stay here just long enough for the full moon. I'm leaving here on the express train early the 27th (Friday). During the course of the morning on Saturday, I'll make my visit to you with the score. On Saturday I'd also like to present myself to Director Jahn to discuss with him what comes next. The baroness is still in bed. It's been almost two weeks now since we've been able to see her. Let's hope I'll still see her before my departure. Is my winter coat being held in readiness? I've gotten along quite well to date without it. There will certainly be no need for it on the trip, as the [train] coaches are really overheated these days. I'm orchestrating the prelude very leisurely now. It will be finished tomorrow.

And now Merry Christmas in your family circle. Forever your
Hugo Wolf.

194

To Vienna

Matzen, Dec. 24, 1895

Dearest friend!

Your dear letter on the 23rd moved me to tears, even though I wasn't at all in a weeping mood. I received letter and package at the same time and so I laughed and cried all at once. My, what splendid things this exquisite little treasure chest holds! But too much, just too much! I sink beneath such a burden. I inaugurated the marvelous cigarette holder immediately, unfortunately only with some vile Herzegovina and with just a mangy butt of that. The new holder is even far more beautiful than the former one. And then the handsome, practical toiletry kit, the extravagant gold cufflinks, undoubtedly a present from your husband, for which I sincerely thank him. I almost forgot about the fabulous Malaga grapes, Frasquita's grapes. Goodness, how could one forget something like that!

Unfortunately, I can't give myself the greatest joy for Christmas, as the prelude is still awaiting its conclusion. While I was orchestrating, I came up with another new idea and have enriched the piece by an addition, with which it has gained a great deal. But I hope to be finished with it tomorrow, on Christmas Day. Nevertheless, I'll have to postpone my departure for one more day, as I won't get the crate until Friday. Thus, I'll leave here early Saturday and won't be able to visit you until Sunday. We're having splendid weather again, sunshine by day and moonshine by night. One couldn't wish for anything more beautiful.

Christmas Eve [festivities] at the barons' are at 6:00 this evening. I suspect a box of cigars or cigarettes will turn up [under the tree] for me.

The fabric arrived. My servant girl was very pleased with it. And now a thousand sincerest greetings from your

Hugo Wolf.

195

To Vienna

[Vienna, February 16, 1896]

Honored gracious lady!

If these lines should still arrive today, please send me *all* the bank notes by means of Ignaz. Although I need only 50 Fl at the moment, I want to be rid of all these boring embarrassments once and for all. I'm supposed to have the money as early as this morning, but how is that to be arranged?

So send it immediately. Please.

With respectful greetings

Hugo Wolf.

196

To Vienna

Vienna, March 23, 1896

Dear friend!

In spite of the most intense searching, I cannot find my Italienisches Liederbuch. Please send me your copy. I'm going to Perchtoldsdorf tomorrow afternoon.

Sincerest greetings from your

Hugo Wolf.

197

To Vienna

[Perchtoldsdorf, March 28, 1896]

Dear, beloved friend!

With the first ray of beautiful sunshine the ideas began to come again. Today I composed the handsome, hungry Toni— how? It's impossible to describe. I know only one thing: that humor in music had never set foot in the world until this song. Even I am speechless over it and ask myself: was it you, really you who invented this music? Heaven only knows who inspired me with these sounds. Today (a splendid day) I'm so in the mood that I'll probably compose yet a second song. On Monday at 3:30 p.m. I arrive at the Südbahnhof.

Meanwhile, very best greetings from your

Hugo Wolf.

The second song was done today (as I predicted) without a hitch.

198

To Vienna

[Perchtoldsdorf, March 31, 1896]

Dearest friend!

Right now (it's 3:30 p.m.) it's snowing down the roofs as in December. God knows when the sun will break through again. Yesterday toward evening I hastily sketched out a new song and filled it in today; since the accompaniment requires extremely careful treatment, I used today's morning hours to finish up the little piece completely. Here's the text:

Lass sie nur gehn, die so die Stolze spielt,	Let her go then, she who plays the haughty one,
Das Wunderkräutlein aus dem Blumenfeld.	The wondrous little herb from the flower field.
Man sieht, wohin ihr blankes Auge zielt,	One can see whither her shining eye travels,
Da Tag um Tag ein andrer ihr gefällt.	As from day to day another one suits her fancy.
Sie treibt es grade wie Toscana's [*sic* Tuscanas] Fluss,	She carries on just like Tuscany's river,
Dem jedes Berggewässer folgen muss.	Which every mountain stream must follow.
Sie treibt es wie der Arno, will mir scheinen:	She carries on like the Arno, it seems to me:
Bald hat sie viel Bewerber, bald nicht einen.	Now she has many suitors, soon not a one.

Yesterday I received a 12-page letter from Paul Müller, very interesting in part, which I'll show you eventually. I've sent him a variant for the passage "Dahin, dahin möcht ich mit Dir" [There, there I should like to go with you], etc., which has caused shock almost everywhere; I wrote it out from memory; it will benefit both the composition and the accompanist. Balzac's "Modeste Mignon" is delighting me endlessly. All the scenes until now have taken place in a cozy, intimate environment; there are still no conflicts in sight; rather, everything is in the loveliest harmony, and the heroine herself is the most charming creature Balzac ever created. This fits so well with the small world into which I've spun myself musically.—Many thanks for the two volumes.

[no signature]

199

To Vienna
Perchtoldsdorf, April 3, 1896

Dear Friend!

I didn't get the score until 10:00 this morning. You can imagine how very eager I was to get it. But I'm horribly disappointed; I'm so angry; I'm seething. My whole day is ruined because of this beastly misunderstanding of this capital idiot named Rollinger. This sheep should have *immediately* printed the title *exactly* as I gave it to him. What does this mean:

Der Corregidor.

Hugo Wolf.

Score.

That is simply nonsense.

I'm sending the score to Rollinger today and will put to him the expressed condition that he charge nothing for the change, *not a kreuzer.*

Oh, these dunces!

I was so looking forward to today and now—this disappointment. I had just begun an exquisite song when the postal package was delivered to me. But I'm so angry that I certainly won't work anymore today. The devil take this nincompoop.

I composed a song yesterday too and wanted to write out the text to both for you today. But I'm too distraught and too annoyed. See you soon. Always your

Hugo Wolf.

200

To Vienna

Perchtoldsdorf, April 3, 1896

Dearest friend!

My anger subsided the moment the beautiful score, which had been deformed through the arbitrary addition of pages by the miserable bookbinder, was out of the house. In addition to this, a few chapters of "Modeste Mignon" also helped to restore my lost equilibrium. My mood has become most peaceable and gentle again, and now I must admit to you that the cover delighted me. It was not the least bit soiled either, which consoled me to some extent. I wrote to Rollinger that *he* must bear the cost of the change, as the blame lay solely with him. Now I'm writing out both enclosed poems, the latter of which, however, is still coming into existence.

No. 7 composed yesterday:

Wie viele Zeit verlor ich, dich zu lieben!	How much time I have lost in loving you!

Hätt' ich doch Gott geliebt in all der Zeit.	Had I but loved God all this time.
Ein Platz im Paradies wär' mir verschrieben,	A place would be reserved for me in Paradise,
Ein Heil'ger sässe dann an meiner Seit!	A saint would sit at my side!
Und weil ich dich geliebt, schön frisch Gesicht,	And because I loved you, lovely fresh face,
Verscherzt' ich mir des Paradieses Licht,	I forfeited the light of Paradise,
Und weil ich dich geliebt, schön Veigelein,	And because I loved you, lovely little violet,
Komm' ich nun nicht ins Paradies hinein.	I won't get into Paradise now.

This poem is treated quite simply in the accompaniment and kept in a very naive tone, which is to say, easier to understand for weaker souls. No. 8 begun this morning:

Und steht Ihr früh am Morgen auf vom Bette,	And when you arise from bed early in the morning.
Scheucht Ihr vom Himmel alle Wolken fort,	You banish all the clouds from the sky,
Die Sonne lockt Ihr auf die Berge dort,	You entice the sun from behind the mountains
Und Engelein erscheinen um die Wette	And little angels appear to vie with each other
Und bringen Schuh u. Kleider Euch sofort.	And bring shoes and clothes to you at once.
Dann, wenn Ihr ausgeht in die heil'ge Mette,	Then, when you go out to holy mass,
So zieht Ihr alle Menschen mit Euch fort,	All people are drawn to follow you,
Und wenn Ihr naht der benedeiten Stätte,	And when you approach the holy place,
So zündet Euer Blick die Lampen an.	Your glance kindles the lamps.
Weihwasser nehmt Ihr, macht des Kreuzes Zeichen,	You take the holy water, make the sign of the cross,

Und netzet Eure weisse Stirn
  sodann
Und neiget Euch u. beugt
  die Knie in gleichen—
O wie holdselig steht Euch
  alles an!
Wie hold u. selig hat Euch
  Gott begabt,
Die Ihr der Schönheit Kron'
  empfangen habt!
Wie hold u. selig wandelt Ihr
  im Leben;
Der Schönheit Palme ward
  an Euch gegeben.

And then moisten your white
  brow
And bow and bend your knee
  as well—
Oh, how graciously
  everything suits you!
How nobly and blessedly
  God has endowed you,
You who received the crown
  of beauty!
How nobly and blessedly you
  go through life;
The palm of beauty was
  given to you.

I've arrived at about the halfway point with the music of this splendid poem. Whether it will still be finished today is doubtful. I think it will be better to wait for my mood in the morning, and as compensation, I'll finish reading the Balzac novel, which is quite unique in its way.

The sky has also grown dark and I need sunshine for my poem. Until tomorrow then! And now many, many thanks and sincerest greetings from your

Hugo Wolf.

201

To Vienna
Perchtoldsdorf, April 4, 1896

Dearest friend!

Thanks for your dear lines. Could you send me the notice in the "Freie Presse"? I woke up this morning with a head cold, which took on very serious proportions during the course of the day. Fortunately, I finished the 8th song in the morning, because by afternoon I was unfit for work. I'm gnashing my teeth. Am going to go to bed early and will avoid cold baths for a while. This involuntary pause in my activity comes at a very inopportune time for me and, what's more, when I don't have anything to read;

nor are there any more proofs [for correction]. I'm very surly today because I can barely swallow, a painful feeling that always makes me completely kaput. Pepi is taking this note to the post office. I'll close, as she's already grumbling. Happy Easter.

Always your

Hugo Wolf.

Parcel received this morning. Thanks very much.

202

To Vienna

Perchtoldsdorf, April 9, 1896

Bulletin.

Head cold completely gone. Pharyngitis abating. Already smoked cigars today. Also working on a song. "Corregidor" arrived. Magnificent. Am delighted.

Sincerest greetings. Always yours.

Hugo Wolf.

203

To Vienna

Perchtoldsdorf, April 12, 1896

Dearest friend!

Read—and then be amazed—

No. 10

Wie soll ich fröhlich sein u. lachen gar,	How can I be happy, let alone laugh,
Da du mir immer zürnest unverhohlen?	When you are always openly angry with me?
Du kommst nur einmal alle hundert Jahr	You come only once every hundred years
Und dann, als hätte man dir's anbefohlen.	And then, as if you had been ordered to do so.
Was kommst du, wenn's die Deinen ungern sehn?	Why do you come, if your people frown on it?
Gieb frei mein Herz, dann magst du weitergehn.	Give back my heart, then you may go your way.

Daheim mit deinen Leuten
  leb' in Frieden,
Denn was der Himmel will,
  geschieht hi[e]nieden.

Halt Frieden mit den
  Deinigen zu Haus,
Denn was der Himmel will,
  das bleibt nicht aus.

Live in peace with your
  people at home,
For what heaven desires,
  comes to pass here
  below.
Keep peace with your people
  at home,
For what heaven desires
  cannot be averted.

No. 11

O wär' dein Haus
  durchsichtig wie ein
  Glas,
Mein Holder, wenn ich mich
  vorüberstehle!
Dann säh' ich drinnen dich
  ohne Unterlass,
Wie blickt' ich dann nach dir
  mit ganzer Seele!
Wie viele Blicke schickte dir
  mein Herz,
Mehr als da Tropfen hat der
  Fluss im März!
Wie viele Blicke schickt' ich
  dir entgegen,
Mehr als da Tropfen
  niedersprühn im Regen.

Oh, if your house were as
  transparent as glass,

My noble one, when I steal
  past!
Then I would see you inside
  continually,
How I would gaze upon you
  then with all my soul!
How many glances my heart
  would send to you,
More drops than the river has
  in March!
How many glances I would
  send your way,
More drops than rain can
  sprinkle down.

I wrote out these two delightful little things in finished form, the first one this morning and the second one in the afternoon. Since it's only 5:00, it could well be that still a third one will come along. Isn't this a blessed day! And rightly so, a Sunday! Now the sun is shining as well. Of course it's a little bit late, as the evening sun doesn't have much significance as far as my cold room is concerned. Surely it will be an even dozen tomorrow; consequently, the halfway mark will have been passed. I'm taking courage again.

Confound it, I have to come into town on Tuesday. Nevertheless, I will come *in any case*.

See you soon and best greetings from your
                                    Hugo Wolf.

204

                                              To Vienna
                              Perchtoldsdorf, April 16, 1896

Dear friend!
    Kosak was here this morning. He'd like to construct the bed
sooner, since he is going to Buchschach, and hopes his arrangements with me will enable him to stay in Vienna until the 28th of
the m[onth]. What do you say to this? Of course I would like it
very much if he constructed the bed earlier, because it ought to
dry for a period of time and I want to move into the new flat in
any event before my departure for Mannheim. The bed will cost
only 18 Fl, as I did without the wood carving, date of the year,
etc. He requested another advance payment of 20 Fl; I couldn't
give him anything, as I hardly have enough for my own needs.
However, I've given Gilbert instructions to send to Kosak the 25
Fl I have coming on the 20th of the m[onth]. Please let me know,
and Kosak as well, whether he can stay here until the 28th of the
m[onth], or whether he must definitely leave on Saturday.—
    Today there's a terrible storm. It makes me feel really des-
perate. I haven't composed a thing. Am really out of sorts. Have
finished reading "Eugenie Grandet." It's really very nice too.
    Reviews from Graz enclosed. Am very melancholy today
and not disposed toward anything, not even to reading, let alone
writing. Many, many greetings. Always your
                                    Hugo Wolf.
Stowasser has requested me in writing to be patient until
Sunday.

205

                                              To Vienna
                              Perchtoldsdorf, April 17, 1896

Dear friend!
    Since nothing can be changed, I will submit stoically to
my fate. I hope you've already notified Kosak; if not, please

do so immediately. As Kosak will only be away until the 1st of May, the bed can still be constructed. The wire mattress [bedsprings] has been ordered but is not yet manufactured, since Iskra, the wise cabinetmaker, told me that the wire mattress manufacturer hadn't been to his place to take the measurements.

By the way, I'll make inquiries myself at Leopold Walter's [manufacturer]. Unfortunately, I know only that he lives in Margareten, but neither the street nor the number. Please, look it up in Lehmann under iron furniture; the address is listed there. Pass on this information to me by return post. Now I know too why no idea has come to me these days. I was continuously thinking subconsciously about the two songs, which I had considered weak and had put aside unfinished. Today I took up one of them again, and lo and behold! All of a sudden I like it again. Sat right down and finished it off with a single stroke. It's the song "Gesegnet sei das Grün," etc., etc. Now to the other one.

Sunday I'm having visitors. Mayreders, Miz, the unavoidable Hellmer Jr., and Werner Jr. will be coming in the afternoon. What do you have to say to Tilgner's sudden death? As I picked up the Tagblatt [newspaper] at noon today at Koller's, I caught sight of a feature article entitled "Viktor Tilgner," and thought to myself, he's getting pretty good publicity. You can imagine my astonishment when, according to the first lines, the topic was his death. This sad news surprised me so much that *I* practically had a heart attack. The poorest yet fortunate man! One really cannot die more beautifully. The unveiling of his memorial will be the most beautiful and worthiest funeral for him. Today was a horrible one for me otherwise. From early morning until late in the evening the masons have been making noise above my window, which looks out on the garden. A new chimney is being put in place. Tomorrow the row begins all over again. This eternal repair of the Werner lodgings is making me ill by now. Not a year goes by, but what some such bedevilment is perpetrated. Happily the sky has come to its senses again and put on a happy face. I hope it will last. Sincerest greetings from your

Hugo Wolf

206

To Vienna
Perchtoldsdorf, April 18, 1896

A thousand thanks for Balzac and the "Freie Presse." At the same time, I received an invitation from the Mozart Monument Committee to attend the unveiling. As an enthusiastic admirer of Mozart and a friend of Tilgner, I'd best make an appearance. However, I need a set of tails for this. Therefore, please send the suit to Mayreders', with the instructions that it *not* be sent to Perchtoldsdorf, as I'll probably stay overnight with Mayreders on Sunday, since the unveiling is scheduled at an early hour (10:00 a.m.).

The second rejected song is already finished too. Now things can get going again.

Shall I see you at the unveiling perhaps? Then see you soon.

Always yours,

Hugo Wolf.

207

To Vienna
Perchtoldsdorf, April 19, 1896

Dear friend!

I will *not* be coming to Vienna for the unveiling of the Mozart Monument. Not having a top hat as head covering is part of my reason for staying here. Also, I don't wish to find myself in the company of our musical dolts and, finally, I can use my short time here to better advantage. The Mayreders, Werner, Jr., and Hellmer were here. Miz didn't come. I played only from Corregidor. Stowasser, as I anticipated, did not send the money. The man apparently wants to make a fool of me. In spite of this I'll wait a few more days. Today I completely rewrote the 2nd of the two rejected songs, as it was giving me no peace. Now it's finished in its final form. I'm really afraid that my days here are numbered. Maybe I'll have to leave as early as next week. And I still have so much to do! The story of my life!

For today, then, a very sincere greeting from your

Hugo Wolf.

208

To Vienna

Perchtoldsdorf, April 23, 1896

Dearest friend!

In all haste! Today was, or rather *is* a superb day for me. I've written two little pieces which go beyond all those composed so far. Herewith the text:

Nicht länger kann ich singen,
    denn der Wind
Weht stark u. macht dem
    Athem was zu schaffen.
Auch fürcht ich, dass die Zeit
    umsonst verrinnt.
Ja wär ich sicher, ging' ich
    jetzt nicht schlafen.
Ja wüsst' ich was, würd' ich
    nicht heimspazieren,
Und einsam diese schöne
    Zeit verlieren.

I can no longer sing, for the
    wind
Blows strong and makes it
    hard to breathe.
I fear too, that time is
    running out in vain.
Indeed, were I sure of this, I
    wouldn't go to sleep now.
Indeed, if I knew something,
    I wouldn't go home,
And lose this lovely time by
    being all alone.

The same cautious fellow sings the song that follows [in Heyse's book] in the same way, though in serenade form as shown in the accompaniment, for his sweetheart snubs him as follows:

Schweig' einmal still, du
    garstger Schwätzer dort!

Zum Ekel ist mir dein
    verwünschtes Singen.
Und triebst du es bis morgen
    früh so fort,
Doch würde dir kein
    schmuckes Lied
    gelingen.
Schweig' einmal still u. lege
    dich auf's Ohr!
Das Ständchen eines Esels
    zög' ich vor.

Shut up for once, you
    irksome chatterer out
    there!
Your confounded singing is
    making me ill.
And even if you kept it up
    until early morning,
Not one pretty song would
    occur to you.

Shut up for once and put
    yourself to bed!
I'd prefer to hear the
    serenade of a donkey.

These two pieces are separated in the book. But they obviously belong together. Now 18 are assembled. God willing, I'll already have completed 20 by tomorrow. But then it must still become 24. I won't be satisfied until then. Unfortunately, the sky clouded over completely this afternoon.

Let's hope it'll be better tomorrow. Balzac's "Verlassene Frau" [*La Femme abandonnée* (1832)] is splendid and ennobling. I thought a lot about you all the while; you must read it.

See you very soon. Always your

Hugo Wolf.

209

To Vienna
Perchtoldsdorf, April 25, 1896

Dearest friend!

I want you to know by tomorrow that in the course of the late afternoon today I wrote the *21st* song. I know this poem is one you will particularly like, so it pleases me even more that this will not be missing from the collection.

Here the little thing:

Heut' Nacht erhob ich mich
    um Mitternacht,
Da war mein Herz mir
    heimlich
    fortgeschlichen.
Ich frug: Herz, wohin
    stürmst du so mit
    Macht?
Es sprach: Nur Euch zu
    sehn, sei es entwichen.
Nun sieh, wie muss es um
    mein Lieben stehn:
Mein Herz entweicht der
    Brust, um dich zu sehn!

Last night I rose up at
    midnight,
As my heart had secretly
    stolen away from me.

I asked: Heart, where are you
    rushing with such force?

It said: It has escaped just in
    order to see you.
Now behold, just how it is
    with my love:
My heart escapes my breast,
    to see you!

A thousand greetings from your

Hugo Wolf.

210

To Traunkirchen
Stuttgart, May 14, 1896

Dear, beloved friend!

I've just finished a generous breakfast at Faischtling's [dear Faisst's], after which I played the song "Ich hab in Penna einen Liebsten wohnen" for him by heart, whereupon he fell into a completely cannibalistic ecstasy. He wanted to hear it again and again. It affects me the same way and probably will you too.— Faisst just now rushed to the telephone—Kauffmann is on the line from Tübingen. I'm supposed to be in Tübingen Saturday and Sunday. For God's sake.—My trip went very well. Faisst traveled to Ulm on the Swabian border to meet me, like a potentate, and from there we traveled 1st-class to Stuttgart. Our meeting involved something immensely amusing, which I'll tell you about in person when there's a chance, as time is short today. Dined yesterday noon at Lamberts' with Faisst and Nast the bookseller. In the evening in the hills at the Klinckerfuss villa. Played two acts of Corregidor there on a magnificent new Bechstein. Today Faisst and I are traveling to Heilbronn and will stay overnight there. Tomorrow we're back in Stuttgart. Saturday and Sunday in Tübingen. Monday it's off to Mannheim. I'm staying in Hotel Marquardt, but it's very noisy here. Today is a magnificent day. At the moment Stuttgart is truly enchantingly beautiful. All the trees are in bloom. One can hardly imagine anything lovelier. It's probably also marvelously beautiful where you are now. Faisst will also come to you again this time. Do make a special point of inviting him. He sends many greetings, as does most sincerely and hurriedly your

Hugo Wolf.

We have to rush immediately to the train station, thus the haste.

211

To Traunkirchen
Mannheim, May 18, 1896

Dear friend!

I'm using the first free moment today to tell you a scanty bit of news about myself. I had to leave Stuttgart yesterday at noon and get myself over to Mannheim, at an urgent summons from Röhr and Grohe. Had hardly arrived—am being put up quite miserably, unfortunately—at Herr Hildebrandt's—when I immediately had to take over a remedial woodwind rehearsal at the theater. The conducting was somewhat difficult for me at first, although it went tolerably enough as things progressed. Piano rehearsal came later, during which I made the acquaintance of the excellent performers, among whom the performer of the Corregidor and of Tio Lukas won my approval. I was less satisfied with Repela, least of all, however, with Frasquita. The lady in question who is playing this role suffers from a speech defect, a dreadful fault. Otherwise she sings her part quite well. Röhr is taking great pains. He doesn't find the orchestra difficult, only the many errors in the orchestral parts make the learning difficult. Had a rehearsal of the 3rd act today, on Sunday, with him to uncover the mistakes. This afternoon there's another piano rehearsal. Tomorrow orchestra rehearsal of the 3rd act for the first time. I'm dead tired; hardly sleep at all and as a result, walk around all day like a sleepwalker. I wish the whole thing were already over. After the performance, which in all likelihood will take place on the 31st of the m[onth], I'm going to spend two weeks at Nast's in Degerloch near Stuttgart, to recuperate from these grueling ordeals and upsets. I'm so tired today that I'm hardly able to guide the pen.

What's going on with Kosak?

Please write me at the address: Dr. Oskar Grohe, O 7, 18.

Hildebrandt is getting me a lodging in the vicinity of the theater, as I announced to him that I absolutely cannot stay in his noisy house. It will consist of two elegantly furnished rooms and is supposed to be very quiet. I'm going to move in tomorrow. So much for today, as I'm dying of fatigue.

Sincerest greetings from your

Hugo Wolf.

212

To Traunkirchen
Mannheim, May 19, 1896

Dear, beloved friend!

I've just returned from the theater (10:00 in the morning), where a full rehearsal of the singers with piano was to have taken place. The instrument that was placed at our disposal on this occasion was so badly out of tune (notabene an age-old crate from the Biedermeier era) that I declared the rehearsal over, as I contended I did not feel the least bit obliged to undergo an attack on my auditory nerves. "Where there's one prank, the second soon follows," I say with Max and Moritz. I announced to the personnel that I would make no concessions regarding diction and tempo, unreasonable requests for which having been made to me. If the ladies and gentlemen didn't wish to follow my directions precisely, I would simply withdraw and let things take their course. Let them see just how ready they would be without my assistance. Scene: yesterday, for example, rehearsal was called for 4:30 in the afternoon. I appeared punctually, but not a creature was to be seen. Since my lodgings (a charming apartment in the Hypothekenbank consisting of two elegantly furnished rooms) are right across from the theater, I went home, thinking that the rehearsal wasn't scheduled until 5:00. When I reappeared in the auditorium at this time, there was once again no one to be seen. I had waited for a good half hour when finally the Capellmeister entered, apologized that he'd forgotten to inform the singers of the rehearsal, and asked me to wait for the singer of Frasquita. After a long time a theater employee came with the message, Frl. Hohenleitner (the name of Frasquita's interpreter) asks to be excused; she feels too tired to rehearse. Whereupon I announced to Capellmeister Röhr that I would not tolerate such inconsiderate behavior, that I am not an employee of the theater, that I would be glad to be of service to the theater, but that I insist on respectful cooperation. Röhr was very upset about it and promised everything possible to keep me in a good mood.—Today he (Röhr) is holding an orchestra rehearsal, asked me not to attend, however, as they are still working at a rough level. I can hear the orchestra playing the *forte* passages here in my room.

In an hour I'll go out and pay a visit to the theater manager. I've already spoken with him fleetingly in the theater. He seemed to me to be very congenial. A distinguished, as well as jovial, gentleman.

I dine alternately at Hildebrandt's and Grohe's. Haven't spent a penny up until now. A Frau Reiss, to whom I am making a visit today with Grohe and who lives in grand style here, is giving a soirée very soon, at which my Tio Lukas and Corregidor are going to participate and at which a number of my songs will be performed by these two. Please address letters to me to Grohe's flat: O 7 18. We want to make use of the next pleasant and free day for an excursion to Heidelberg.—The Italian [songs] have still not arrived, in the meantime being continuously tossed about in the mail from Vienna to Stuttgart, from there to Tübingen, from Tübingen to Vienna, from Vienna back to Stuttgart, and so forth. I have my dear Potpeschnigg to thank for this, whom the devil should take for sending the songs to Vienna instead of to Stuttgart. I'll tell you the story in more detail here; one could make a second Comedy of Errors out of it. And now, sincerest greetings from your

Hugo Wolf.

213

To Traunkirchen
Mannheim, May 21, 1896

Dearest friend!

After a vain attempt to take a midday nap today—several young scamps were making a terrible racket on the playground under my window—I'll at least try to concentrate my somewhat scattered thoughts on this note, although even this business will be fairly difficult for me in the midst of the devilish noise that surrounds me. Today I received your third letter. Since then, several unpleasant things have occurred. I find the most unpleasant by far to be the latest postponement to the 7th of June, which was decided yesterday. Frl. Hohenleitner, singer of Frasquita, can barely sing half the role from memory and has announced that she would be unable to have it ready by the 31st. Not only that, but the orchestra plays so miserably, the conductor Röhr will let no one tell him anything, and the affair consequently has taken such a disgusting turn that the performance for this season will probably be canceled. In an hour the theater manager is coming to see me in my flat to discuss with me the remuneration with regard to my work. The singers are the most narrow-minded people in the world. The slightest criticism is immediately perceived as a personal insult. Ditto Röhr, who has also revealed himself to be a very run-of-the-mill musical soul. This business disgusts me from the bottom of my heart. I will have nothing more to do with any theater. That is now my sole desire. Maybe I'll leave Mannheim as early as the next few days. Then I still want to spend a few days in Stuttgart and Tübingen *(where I haven't yet been, as there wasn't enough time)*, and then come back to Vienna. You could have the chests from your flat put into mine, since one cannot entrust this idiot Kosak with any responsibilities long-distance. God knows what sort of stupidity this brute will come up with again, if I order chests from him. I only want to keep the two chests you've offered until I have another pair built by Kosak or someone else. But for the time being, please have these two chests transported to my flat.

Tomorrow is the grand soirée at Madame Reiss's. She is a millionairess, lives in terribly high style, and is very enthusiastic about my songs. Was a friend of Liszt's, is now an old spinster, but very alert and bright. There are more than 70 people invited, all of whom will make an appearance for my sake. The singers of the Corregidor and Tio Lukas, Rüdiger and Kromer, will perform an ample number of my songs (each one about a dozen). In addition a couple of women, whom I will not be accompanying, however, are singing things of mine. Among others, Kromer sings *"Sänger"* with splendid voice and excellent delivery. Then "Grenzen der Menschheit," "Erschaffen u. Beleben," "Biterolf," "König bei der Krönung," "Anakreon," etc.; Rüdiger [will sing] almost the entire Eichendorff cycle [i.e., songbook]. It's going to be a big to-do. Naturally, I must appear in formal dress.—The Italian [songs] finally arrived yesterday, after Faisst had sent them from Stuttgart to the Mayreders in Vienna—all from absentmindedness. I've been suffering from a terrible chest cold the last few days, which as I feared, is gradually turning into a husky throat and then a regular head cold. That's all I need right now. And I'm getting this damned nuisance only because of the confounded cold bathing. If I had only left the infernal india-rubber [bath]tub at home. I'll probably make an excursion to Heidelberg with Grohe for the Pentecost holidays.

— — — — — — — — — —

The theater manager has just left after an almost hour-long visit. We tossed the matter back and forth. I told the manager quite frankly that the theater conditions here disgust me, that none of them, from Capellmeister to the last supernumerary, is worth anything, and that I've really had enough of the whole

thing. He asked me in the kindest manner to wait it out nevertheless. He promised that he would attend the rehearsals himself and will grant me everything I want if I'll only be present
at the performance on June 7th (for that has now been agreed
upon!). I threatened him with my earlier departure, however,
should the performance be scheduled for the 7th of June. Perhaps this threat worked, as the performance is still being
planned for the 31st after all. It won't be a good one in any case,
not even on June 7th. Meanwhile, I'll do everything possible to
bring about the performance on the 31st.

I'm writing in a very confused manner. I'm staying home
for the first time today and am going to bed early. Must make a
chest poultice and perspire thoroughly.

More soon. In greatest haste, sincere greetings always from
your

Hugo Wolf.

214

To Traunkirchen
Mannheim, Pentecost [May 24,] 1896

Beloved friend!

I haven't been inside the theater for three days, although
I live directly across from it. Inasmuch as Capellmeister Röhr
used me solely for the musical drudgery for which he had me
summoned from Stuttgart, I have been deemed superfluous and
very disruptive. My wishes in regard to tempi and execution are
simply not heeded. It's exactly the same way here as it was that
time with Gericke. One can't open one's mouth without running
the risk of being smacked. So I'm quiet. In all probability the
performance will not take place until the 7th of June, assuming
that nothing interferes in the meantime. I'm behaving from now
on in a completely docile manner and letting everything proceed
as it will. I've become thoroughly fed up with the stage, its unending shallowness and depravity. How well I understand Nietzsche's aversion to the theater now, where one becomes the
"neighbor." How vividly I can now imagine Beethoven's abhor-
rence of the theater! No, the theater is absolutely not for solitary
people. I'm longing to return to my solitude again. I'm planning
to return to Stuttgart tomorrow via Heidelberg—Grohe will ac-

company me that far—and to spend a week with Nast the book-seller. The peace and quiet at his estate in Degerloch (he occupies a magnificent villa all alone with his wife there) will do me good. I'll arrive back in Vienna during the early days of June.

Yesterday there was a large soirée at Frl. Reiss's in my honor. The evening went very well and was very lively. Rüdiger and Kromer from the theater sang an endless number of songs of mine; unfortunately, the performances of the two dilettantes weren't very captivating. The theater manager, who was present (a totally kind, charming gentleman), gave a stirring speech about me, which contained a very great deal that was flattering to me. He even offered me his flat and is filled with an uncommonly tenacious concern for my work. Unfortunately, he can't conduct, otherwise he would just as soon take the whole matter into his own hands. However, inasmuch as nothing can be done about Röhr, since he stubbornly persists in his interpretation, I'm no longer going to trouble myself about the further course of the event. I'm also not going to attend the performance, as I'm convinced the thing is going to go all wrong. If I had only stayed in Vienna! How many bad experiences I've had here! I think I've had enough to last me my entire life.

The Italian [songs] arrived on Thursday.—Meanwhile, still address me care of Dr. Grohe, who was promoted to *Counselor of the Provincial Court* the day before yesterday. Letters will also be forwarded to me wherever I'm staying. Maybe the attitude of the singers involved and of the Capellmeister will change under the influence of the theater manager.—Maybe! In that case I'll notify you *immediately*. It's possible that the performance will take place on the 31st after all, although the chance of this is slim. Frl. Hohenleitner, so I hear, is now diligently learning her role [Frasquita] with the theater's musical coach. However, I don't hold out any great hope for her performing capability. Above all, it was a serious misjudgment on the part of the theater manager to assign such a difficult role to a novice. I would have much preferred to have Frau Sorger, whom I recently saw perform the title role of Carmen here. Unfortunately, they found themselves compelled to entrust this excellent artist (the prima donna) with the role of Mercedes [in *Corregidor*], which she sings and acts truly splendidly and indeed nobly.

Today at Grohe's I'm also going to meet his brother-in-law,

Hugo Becker, who is coming here from Leipzig for the day. This afternoon we are going for a drive around the area in Frl. Reiss's carriage. Despite her 60 years, Frl. Reiss is an extremely gracious and charming lady, who has a great appreciation for my things (out of pure love of the art she was an opera singer in her day, a friend of Wagner and Liszt). I am very grateful to Grohe for this acquaintance. My chest cold is already better. The dreaded head cold did not come to pass, thank goodness. How are you? What lovely thing are you reading? I don't get around to reading now at all; although there's a volume of Bülow letters lying right here, I haven't had time even to open it. I always feel so tired and drained, probably because my rest at night is so minimal.

As soon as something new develops, I'll write again. Meanwhile, very sincerest greetings to the entire Buchschach [clan]. Always your most faithful

Hugo Wolf.

Dr. Oskar Grohe's address O 7 18

215

To Traunkirchen [postcard]

Mannheim, May 27, 1896

Honored gracious lady!

I can already let you know today that the performance has been definitely scheduled for the 7th of June. The dress rehearsal takes place the morning of Saturday the 6th. More details in a letter. Sincerest greetings!

Hugo Wolf.

216

To Traunkirchen

Mannheim, May 29, 1896

Dearest friend!

Faisst arrived here this morning and is stretched out on the sofa in my study smoking a Virginia [cigar] while I write these lines. Unfortunately, he's traveling back to Stuttgart tonight at midnight. He only came to discuss a Liederabend, which he wants to stage for me in Stuttgart. The Liederabend is to take place three days after the premiere, and it would be very nice if you were able to be there. I heard from Gilbert today that he's already been to Stowasser's twice, but didn't find him. Thereupon, I instructed Gilbert in writing to bring suit against him *immediately*.

Leopold Walter has taken back the already delivered bedsprings, so Gilbert tells me, because he wasn't paid right away. I'll buy an iron bed at Kisch's then and have instructed Gilbert to notify Kosak that he shouldn't construct the bed frame. Gilbert has also been directed to order two chests of softwood from Kosak, made to measure. So you needn't send the two chests over to the apartment. The desk (according to Gilbert's message) is already in the flat, but is supposed to be taken away, as they are worried about their claim (480 Kr). I hope Gilbert straightens out this situation. Kosak is already in Vienna then? I'm planning to arrive in Vienna by around the 24th, on which date my ticket expires. Meanwhile, there is only the piano and the writing desk in the flat; Kosak hasn't delivered any furniture.

The attitude in the theater is better for me now. However, I fear that the performance will not be particularly good. I'm feeling quite wretched, as far as my health is concerned. I have a horrible cough that plagues me night and day. God knows when it will end. Yesterday, by chance, I read in the paper of Paumgartner's death, also of Archduke Carl Ludwig's. No one told me a word about it. . . .

Unfortunately, I have to go out into society again today. Faisst is going along. He sends cordial greetings. Must close for today. Always in sincerest faithfulness, completely yours,

Hugo Wolf.

The letters between Traunkirchen and Mannheim are really flying. Yesterday's letter from you of the 28th arrived this afternoon on the 29th. More soon!

217

To Traunkirchen

Stuttgart, June 10, 1896

Dear, gracious friend!

I arrived in Stuttgart yesterday at 2:00 in the afternoon and was welcomed by my host Nast and Faisst at the train station. I spent the trip to Stuttgart in the company of the Mayreders. The evening at Frau Sorger's was very stimulating. Frau Sorger will not take part in my concert in Stuttgart, by the way. Faisst is appearing in her place and will sing five new Italian [songs] along with "Prometheus," the unavoidable "Grab Anakreons" [*sic*], and "Phänomen." The concert will be on the 15th of the m[onth]. I'm being accommodated very well here; took an invigorating walk in the surrounding vicinity today in magnificent weather, which did me a great deal of good. The reviews in the Mannheim newspapers were so tasteless that I decided it was better not to send you any of them. There is a great drawback here, of course, and that is the endless number of chaffinches that bedevil this place. I even have to use my antiphon [earplugging device] during the day. For this reason, I'll shorten my sojourn here. I'd prefer to be in Vienna by the 20th. Have you read the Frankfurter Zeitung? It still says it best, although the "youngster" exempts himself, oddly enough. Tomorrow I'm going to discuss with Obrist the details concerning a performance of "Corregidor" in Stuttgart. Today I still have to write my mother an account of the performance, hence ever so quickly many, many sincere greetings from your

Hugo Wolf.

218

To Traunkirchen
Vienna, June 29, 1896

Dear, beloved friend!

I'm answering your recent lines by return mail. Many thanks for sending the pocket handkerchief. Enclosed is a review that Faisst sent me today. Apparently they are interested in "Corregidor" in Düsseldorf. Director Staegemann (formerly in Leipzig) has made written inquiries concerning the conditions under which "Corregidor" would be available. Wrote to Staegemann today.—It's going ahead very slowly with the furnishing of the flat. Kosak, the lout, won't be finished with his work until Thursday. In addition, there are many adjustments to be made on the doors, locks, stoves, and such. The whole thing is going to cost me plenty. My bedroom has to be repapered. Was at a wallpaper store with Frau Mayreder day before yesterday. Picked out a pretty pattern and a reasonably priced one (22 kreuzers a roll). So far, there's just the piano, the Beethoven [picture], and the desk in the flat. Picked out chairs at Thonet with Frau M., who is a big help to me. Ordered only three pieces, 3.40 per piece. Look very smart. Tomorrow the papering will be done. The servant girl is supposed to clean the rooms in the afternoon. I hope she'll do it well.

I haven't gotten together with Fuchs yet, as until now he's always sent word to cancel. A strong wind prevails here constantly. Maybe I'll be able to move in as early as Friday. However, on Saturday for sure. I still have to write letters in all directions. Thus, must close now. Many, many sincere greetings, also to the girls. Always your

Hugo Wolf.

219

To Traunkirchen
Vienna, July 1, 1896

Dear friend!

I'm half-dead from doing errands. The wallpapering and lock work is finally finished. Kosak is supposed to bring the furniture tomorrow. But since my servant girl has let me down, I'm going to have to cancel Kosak. O this servant girl! Frau Jäger really recommended a good one to me. Today I learned from my landlady that the servant girl, after she had already carried dustpan and broom into the flat, collected them again and announced that the job was too strenuous for her. I need to look around for a replacement. The goose didn't say anything until *today*, after having looked at the flat four days ago. Dashed over to Neuer Markt [the Köchert family's Vienna address] to discuss the matter with Ignaz. It was Ignaz's day off, so of course he wasn't there. Ran over to his flat and fortunately encountered the entire family. Ignaz's wife is ill and, therefore, can't take on anything. After much talking back and forth, she thought of a person who will come tomorrow to clean the flat. If this person seems adequate to me, I'll hire her. The servant girl recommended by Frau Jäger stole a good pair of scissors that I had left behind in the empty flat. Am glad that I won't have any more to do with this good-for-nothing. Was at Denk im Eisgrübl [a fine china and housewares store] today. The consignment from certain barrels has still not arrived, but is expected any day. So that's being taken care of. As everything is always so delayed, I'll probably not be able to move in this week. Ordered an iron bed with springs today at Kitschl's Söhne; costs 31 Fl. Am rushing over to Kosak's now and will take the opportunity to pay Gilbert a visit, who must give Stowasser a nudge.

How is your cough? Drinking Ems water diligently [mineral water from Bad Ems]? Should I send you Emser pills? I found some in a half-filled cigarette tobacco box. The weather here is really ghastly, but still better than if the sun were shining. One doesn't perspire. There's nothing to be done with Fuchs for the present, as examinations which Fuchs must attend are being held at the conservatory now. Otherwise, nothing new. Many, many greetings to all.

Always your
Hugo Wolf.

220

To Traunkirchen
Vienna, July 3, 1896

Dear friend!

Most of my possessions are packed up. Early tomorrow morning Kosak comes with the furniture and the move will be accomplished. On Saturday I will spend the night in the new flat, Schwindgasse 3, II. Stiege [staircase], 4. Stock. The cleaning woman got the flat in shape today. I'm quite delighted with this comfortable home. The imposing writing desk fits very well in the study and makes me immensely happy at the moment. It looks terribly grand. The bed has also already arrived. I forgot to tell you that the windows throughout have been provided with very modern green venetian blinds, so I don't need to purchase any such thing. Frau M[ayreder] is going to lend me a sofa for the present, until I buy one myself. I can't wait any longer for that moment, which will make me the happy occupant of such a lovely and quiet flat. Lipperheide is coming to Vienna in about ten days. He'll be astonished when he visits me. Am in a big hurry today, as there is still much to do.

Sincerest greetings. Always your

Hugo Wolf.

221

To Traunkirchen

Vienna, July 10, 1896

Many, many thanks, dearest friend, for your recent kind and detailed letter. I'll take up only matters of business today and report on the sequence of events in my new flat.

Yesterday the bedroom was treated with sulfur [fumigated]. I'm not sleeping in the study, as you mistakenly assumed, but rather in the large room, that is to say, in the drawing room. The hallways to the two other rooms were well sealed on account of the sulfur fumes, so that my olfactory nerves were in no way affected by the stink of the sulfur. My bookcase is now in place and my workroom fairly well in order. Today the venetian blindmaker was here and put on completely new bands and cords. Looks quite handsome now. In the workroom the curtains are already parading across the windows too. Unfortunately, the curtains for the other windows don't fit, as they came out too short. I'll probably have to have them pieced. I'm anticipating the embroidered tablecloth with great joy. I've been making do with a handtowel until now. Heinrich was here yesterday noon and was quite delighted with the flat. The bedroom treated with sulfur stays closed until Saturday evening. Today is a dreadfully hot day, a real holiday for the bedbugs. Found an especially well nourished little creature right on my dressing gown, which was not at all encouraging. I'm going to hand over the rug to Ignaz.

Yesterday I went to visit Lipperheide at the Hotel Imperial and found him all by himself in the dining room with pork chops. He was overjoyed to see me, immediately had them bring out a half carafe of wine, and we drank to the Mannheim success. At the same time, he offered me the use of the hunter's cottage again for an unlimited period of time. He wants to invite Paul Müller to be his guest as well. "Die fromme Marta," a comedy by Tirso de Molina (the author of "Don Juan," which da Ponte adapted for Mozart's libretto), has amused me very much indeed. It is unbelievable how much wit and intellect is amassed in this piece. A real fountain of high spirits and humor. Exquisite language, moreover, even in translation. And such things have completely disappeared. Unbelievable! A blanket cover has come to light that most certainly was not intended for me. Why did you pack so much junk? Books and, among other things, music that doesn't even belong to me, not stolen by me either. That was way too much ballast. What should I do with it all? The ballad from "Fest auf Solhaug" has been found in a copy. But I haven't yet unearthed the piano score of the two Gudmund songs [also from *Fest auf Solhaug*] from the mess. More shortly. Sincerest greetings to all.

Always your
Hugo Wolf.

222

To Traunkirchen
[Vienna, July 12, 1896]

Dearest friend!

I'll answer your dear lines right away, as you'll most certainly be interested in learning what's new with my flat. The sulfur-treated bedroom was opened up on Saturday evening. The procedure went very well. The sulfur burned right up to the end and the result appears to have been effective, judging from the dead creatures sprawled about near the baseboards. Now that the bedroom has been aired for two days, it will be moved into again today. Let's hope the scourge has been taken care of once and for all. There are already five pictures adorning my workroom. Beethoven and, on the same wall, a picture by Piranesi (copper engraving), portraying a square in Rome, which the Mayreders gave me framed as a present. In addition, there's a playbill of "Corregidor," the American picture by Katzer in watercolor that Marie had framed and put under glass, and the Mayreder sketch of the room in the hunter's cottage, also framed and under glass. Curtains have been hung on all the windows. Today I purchased a small table made of bamboo for 3 Fl in a Japanese import store on the Kärtnerstrasse extension. It's been a desire of mine to own one of these little tables for a long time (do you remember one like this in my flat in Perchtoldsdorf?). I'm very happy about owning this. I'm also very pleased with the piano stool—it swivels and is made of pressed leather—which I bought at Thonet's for 15 Fl. Yesterday, on Sunday, I had intended to go to Perchtoldsdorf. I found it so comfortable in my apartment, however, that I spent the entire day in it, and only went out on the street for my noonday meal (at the Hirsch [restaurant]). My rooms are pleasantly cool in summer. I leave the windows open overnight and during the day they remain shut with the venetian blinds closed. In this way I've managed to bring about a lovely cool temperature.

Schalk sent me his wedding announcement today; it doesn't say when the wedding will be, however. [The second page of this letter is cut off.]

223

To Traunkirchen

Matzen, August 5, 1896

Honored, dear friend!

I'm sitting here this morning, rain pouring down, at my workroom's small low table in the hunter's cottage, and I write these lines while Paul Müller, who sends you his regards, slurps his morning coffee. Everything here is the same as before, except for a second bed in my bedroom, which will be taken away today however.—My trip passed quite pleasantly. I didn't get quite to the end of the novel by Jacobsen, which I like more and more, though I read avidly during the ride. Müller and Potpeschnigg were at the train station to pick me up, as I imagined they might be. The latter did not partake of supper, and so I was all alone with Müller, as the baron is currently staying on in Innsbruck. We chatted into the night until about 2:00; consequently, didn't get up today until around 9:00.

Potpeschnigg, to whom we are going to pay a visit now, lives where the post office is. I'll make use of this situation to send this note along quickly.

P. Müller was already here yesterday and enthusiastically

made music with Potpeschnigg. Despite the rainy weather, which has now let up a little, by the way, the surroundings here have reasserted their charm over me. I feel happy and satisfied here. As I've just learned, the baron will arrive sometime today.

I have to close. Many, many greetings to Heinrich and the girls. Always your very devoted

Hugo Wolf.

Have just received Faisst's card. Am writing at Potpeschnigg's.

224

To Traunkirchen

Matzen, August 8, 1896

Dear, honored friend!

I had hardly sent off my letter with Faisst's card when Faisst arrived with young Kauffmann from Tübingen. The two of them are putting up at Vogel's Inn in Brixlegg, but taking meals at the baron's. At the same time, a Dr. Rudolf Mayr, friend of Paul Müller's and also an excellent baritone, is staying here, living at the inn as well, but eating at the baron's. Potpeschnigg always attends our mealtime pleasures at noon and evening too. Yesterday Faisst deserted us, without saying a word ahead of time. Today we accompanied friend Mayr to the train. Only Müller, Kauffmann, and Potpeschnigg remain here now. We're going to make a long trip on Monday into the Stubeier Alps with the two of them, which will take three to four days. Potpeschnigg will take care of outfitting me. I'm getting a wool shirt from him and jersey shorts; the climbing boots are his wife's; they fit me perfectly. The baron is in the best mood. We never get to bed before 2:00 in the morning. The weather has been dreadful until now. Rattenberg is completely under water. Today there was a glimpse of sun once again. Now we're hoping for good weather for our planned trip into the countryside. Today we are all going swimming, the Potpeschnigg family as well. The water is supposed to be 18 degrees [C].—What news do you have from Ignaz? Has the cigarette holder been found? I have to hurry, as Müller and Kauffmann are waiting for me. Müller is departing tomorrow. Just between us, he told me that

he's completely enchanted by you and sends you his best regards. Maresch is already copying the score. The printer's proofs
of the Italian [songs] were sent off to Röder today, after Müller
and Potpeschnigg looked through them and still discovered all
kinds of mistakes.

    And now sincerest greetings to Heinrich and the girls. Al-
ways your

Hugo Wolf.

The conclusion of "Marie Grubbe" is indeed mystifying and
very depressing. Do such things really happen in life?

225

To Traunkirchen [picture postcard]

[Cortina d'Ampezzo], August 16, 1896

    Cordial greetings! I have finally gotten acquainted with the
splendid Dolomites, and in gorgeous weather. The trip was
completely improvised. In Toblach it suddenly occurred to
Potpeschnigg that we could have a look at the nearby Dolomites.
No sooner said than done. Before we knew it, we were in Cortina, from where we'll begin our return by way of the lake tomorrow. Once again sincerest greetings. More about the trip in a
letter.

Hugo Wolf.

226

To Traunkirchen [picture postcard]

Misurina, August 18, 1896

    Set foot on Italian soil for the first time today. In my card
from Cortina I forgot later to add the name of the lake. Herewith
a dim likeness of it. The trail up to this point was enchanting.
There is nothing comparable to it. I'm going totally out of my
mind. We'll spend tonight in Klagenfurt. I arrive in Graz with
Potpeschnigg at 12:00. At this moment guitars and mandolins
are sounding. Sincerest greetings.

Hugo Wolf.

I'm sending a special word to Hilde that "Finiculi, finicula" is
being sung this very moment, but in Italian. Fabulous!

227

To Traunkirchen [postcard]

[Vienna], Sept. 14, 1896

Have just received a telegram that arrived belatedly (addressed to Plösslgasse 4) with the sad news that Baroness Lipperheide died of a heart attack on the 12th of the m[onth]. Am very grieved. Greetings.

Hugo Wolf.

228

To Traunkirchen

Vienna, May 26, 1897

Most honored friend!

A letter from Mayr enclosed, which I ask you to return as soon as possible. Grohe wrote me too, but hasn't yet expressed himself regarding the libretto. I'm putting in his note as well.

Yesterday I met Frau M[ayreder] at the Langs [Edmund and Marie]. We were just discussing the libretto quite enthusiastically, when Frau M. appeared unexpectedly. Naturally, nothing further was said about it, so as not to upset Frau M. unnecessarily. Frau M. has not yet been apprised of our plot; she still thinks that the matter will be resolved by making a few insignificant changes. She will awaken from a horrible misconception. I am most profoundly sorry for the poor woman. In the meantime, Dr. Hoernes, an excellent poet, has been busy with the novel. He has offered to sketch a scenario first of all. We're going to meet on Friday, Haberlandt, Hoernes, and I, in the Natural History Museum, where Hoernes is a curator, as is Haberlandt. Hoernes will use this opportunity to develop his views. That with which Dr. Mayr found fault regarding Frau M.'s language is decidedly not to be feared with Dr. Hoernes, as he is a master of expression, a poet by God's grace, so to speak. My opera librettos are really quite a story. Nothing seems to happen without intrigues. Before, Schaumann was the victim, this time it would seem to be Frau M. I hope this recent affair will end more peaceably, although I think of the resolution only with trepidation.

Meanwhile, I've received the package of eggs. At first, while clearing away the mounds of sawdust, I thought that Nazl had played a bad joke and sent me *only* sawdust, such mountains of this stuff had already piled up on the floor. But finally, one by one, the two dozen eggs made their appearance. With greedy hand the gingerbread was scooped out. Unfortunately, a part of it had become completely soft, so that all that remained from some of the pieces was a sticky mass that clung to the paper. Most of it was in good, if also quite soft, condition however. Immediately devoured a respectable portion, which did me a great deal of good. A thousand thanks. Bohatsch has just sent me the colored shirts, which look really elegant. Will inaugurate them on the holiday to-morrow and present myself to the astonished Perchtoldsdorfers. Since I still want to have Haberlandt look at Mayr's letter, my let-ter will be sent off from Perchtoldsdorf. Today I'm going to see Edmund [Lang] to show him Mayr's letter. It will interest you to learn that Edmund has opened an office in partnership with Etelsberger the lawyer. He's drawing the salary of a licensed clerk, but along with this, can take care of his own clientele. I think that such an arrangement for Edmund as a beginner is not so unfavorable, as he is thus spared all the administrative expense. I can share with you the happy news that my tormentors on the 4th floor chugged off to Ischl today.

Mahler has still not put in an appearance to date. As the "Freie Presse" reports, he is ill. Instead of "Walküre," "Caval-leria Rusticana" will be given.—Oh, this damned "Venegas"! If only I were already rid of this devil! Sincerest greetings to you and all the Puchschachers. Always yours,

Hugo Wolf.

Are you acquainted with the book by Laura Marholm: "Wir Frauen u. unsere Dichter" [We Women and Our Poets]? If not, I'll send it to you as very interesting reading.

May 27. Bad weather. Am not going to Perchtoldsdorf. The new shirts fit badly. Bohatsch has to let out the collar and cuffs. Also, the sleeves too long. Good morning!

229

To Traunkirchen

Vienna, June 1, 1897

Most beloved friend!

Yesterday I finally had a conference with Dr. Hoernes, which took place in the Natural History Museum; our meeting last Sunday had come to naught because of a wretched misunderstanding. Dr. Hoernes had sketched out a scenario in the meantime, which he read to Haberlandt and me. There simply is no doubt that his sketch far surpasses the work of Frau M[ayreder]. Remarkably enough, the exposition in his version begins in almost exactly the same way as Frau M.'s libretto (Dr. Hoernes is not familiar with Frau M.'s libretto), only fewer secondary characters are used and everything is conveyed to the listener in a more condensed fashion. Soledad and Manuel already see each other in the first act at the celebration before the lottery ball, i.e., where Manuel, who is taking part in the procession, wants to draw his daggar at Soledad, but is prevented from doing so by Don Trinidad. It can be seen from this that the 1st act is already loaded with dynamite. It would take too long to report on the entire content of the outline here. Unfortunately, Hoernes had written out his sketch in shorthand. I'll ask him today to have a readable copy sent to me so that others may have a look at it too.—I'm in a real quandary as to how I should convey to Frau M. that her work will not do. For the moment, I'm cloaking myself in silence and remaining as invisible as possible. But in the long run this will not work. I dread the moment when it must come to a final explanation. On Saturday the young and pretty, but rather uninteresting, daughter of the Wecker couple in Heilbronn visited me. She came in the company of a machine manufacturer named Haaga, a friend of Wecker. Since they were planning to travel to Mödling on Sunday, I joined them (the whole Haaga family) as far as Perchtoldsdorf. Stayed there then, moving back and forth between Haberlandt and Werner until later at night, unfortunately without having met Hoernes. (. . .) [Three lines are cut out of the letter.]

Schwarzwald [Black Forest]. Otherwise nothing new. The heat here is very dreadful. How I envy you and everyone else, who can breathe pungent country air at the moment.

Today, on the 1st of June, I'm going to inaugurate the newly cleaned English summer suit. Am already looking forward to it. Edmund recently talked me out of 5 Fl. Yesterday the same thing happened again with Marie. If things go on like this, all my savings will soon be gone. Under these circumstances I'm going to curtail my visits to the Langs somewhat. Edmund will at least pay me back, so it doesn't matter. But Marie, with her weak memory when it comes to money matters, is risky.

I'll send you Hoernes' sketch shortly.
A thousand greetings from your

Hugo Wolf.

230

To Traunkirchen
Vienna, June 8, 1897

Most honored friend!
On my return today, Tuesday morning, I find besides your dear lines, also a very interesting letter from Heckel about "M. Venegas" along with a few very kind and friendly lines from Frau M[ayreder]. While fully acknowledging Frau M.'s poetic talents, Heckel expresses his opinion very candidly about the libretto and permits me to show the letter to Frau Mayreder. I'll send Heckel's letter to you when I have a chance. I have seldom read such a sensitive discussion on literary matters as this letter. Perhaps Heckel is indeed the man who has the calling to write the most suitable libretto for me. I'll make the suggestion to him in any case. Nothing ventured, nothing gained either. Anyway, the good thing about him is that he's *very* musical and knows exactly what works for musicians. Hoernes has made some changes in his sketch. I will send these to Heckel as soon as I have them, and ask his opinion about them. Hoernes is damned unmusical, although I can completely rely on his poetical strengths. I'm going to put every wheel in motion to finally achieve an absolutely perfect libretto.
I spent the Pentecost holidays very pleasantly. On Monday in the earliest morning hours I went up to the Franz Joseph Warte [lookout], the "highest mountain in the distance" [*höchster Berg in der Weite*], all by myself. This hike refreshed me very much and was terrifically good for me.
Frau M. is evidently still in Gmunden, where she spent the holdays with her husband. I'll visit her one of these days. Otherwise, nothing new has happened.
Sincerest greetings from your

Hugo Wolf.

The missing nightshirt has been found. It stayed behind in Perchtoldsdorf. Have used it for two nights recently.

231

To Traunkirchen
Vienna, June 10, 1897

Dear, beloved friend!

I received your recent dear letter today. I have all kinds of news to report to you. First, I was finally at Frau Mayreder's just a few hours ago. I met her very calmly. She was exceptionally nice to me. We talked at first about Gmunden and such things until we got around to the actual topic of conversation. I gave her the enclosed letter from Heckel to read, which she accepted with extremely good grace. She invited me to the noonday meal on Sunday. However, since I have a conference with Hoernes about "Venegas" Sunday in Perchtoldsdorf, I politely declined, whereupon she engaged me for Thursday. Frau Mayreder is very interested in Hoernes' sketch. I'll have a copy of it sent to her tomorrow.

Second, a big piece of news: Frau [Joseph] Schalk has given birth to a girl. As chance would have it, I walked into the house just one hour after the event, in order to learn Schalk's address in Döbling. I met none other than his sister, who naturally let me in on the secret at once. And so it came about that I was the first to be told of this happening. Since Schalk's sister was having difficulty finding a messenger who would relay the joyful news gently, I offered myself for this. She happily accepted my offer, and so I made tracks right away for Döbling. As I'd initially intended to acquaint Schalk with Hoernes' new sketch, it could all be taken care of at once. Schalk is quite delighted with the sketch and congratulated me on it, whereupon I replied that my opera children are all of the male sex in contrast to "Fidelio," "Carmen," "Genoveva," etc., "Iphigenie," "Armida," and so forth. What would he have to say to a little Soledad if one were to be born to *him*? That a little bird in the forest had confided this to me, and that I thought there might be some truth to it, and so forth, until I finished it off with the fait accompli, and the poor fellow sank down speechless in his chair for a moment and covered his face with his hands, whereupon he hugged and kissed me.—Everything went in the best of order. The child is said to be immensely strong. So I was able, then, to deliver my stork's message in fine fashion. We stayed together until after 11:00 p.m. chatting intimately (his other sister is with him). A certain Dr. Schneller, a pupil of Schalk's, has turned over his winter flat on the Billrothstr[asse] to him until Sept. It is magnificently furnished, has a lovely garden, and is on the ground floor. So he's very well accommodated. His wife is coming out in two weeks. Boller also turned up for a little while and I read him the sketch too. Was really delighted with it as well. I'll send you the scenario on Monday, which should then be sent at once to Herr Carl Heckel, Musikverlag [music publisher] Mannheim. Very best greetings to all, always your most faithful

Hugo Wolf.

N.B. I would be very obliged to you if you would have the servants gather up the used tea leaves and save them. The small amount of tea I use doesn't help me much. I need the tea for rug cleaning. Send me a little package at your leisure, when you've accumulated an appropriate amount.

Faisst wrote me today. He wants to visit you the end of July, beginning of August, but will stay at the Gasthof zum Stein, as he's traveling with a Stuttgart friend.

232

[To Traunkirchen; visiting card]
Vienna, June 14, 1897

Beloved friend!

The sketch follows today, which I discussed in the greatest detail yesterday with Hoernes, after which a few more things were changed, therefore the crossed-out lines. Frau M[ayreder], to whom I read the sketch day before yesterday, finds it to be excellent and certainly much more effective than her work. Hoernes is already starting to work on its completion. He's going to turn over all his free time to it. Spent a splendid day in Perchtoldsdorf yesterday and a no less magnificent moonlit night. Didn't get back to Vienna until early this morning and was already up at 4:30, thanks to a pesky fly.

Thanks for your dear lines. Please *also* send Heckel the letter from the Strassburg director. Maybe you could enclose your card and write on it: at the request of Hugo Wolf. Frau Werner gave me beautiful roses from her garden to take with me. My writing desk is now adorned with flowers like the picture of the Christ child. Sincerely greeting all the Puchschachers, your

Hugo Wolf.

233 To Traunkirchen

Vienna, June 28, 1897

Most honored friend!

I've just come from Perchtoldsdorf, where I spent Saturday and Sunday. After a refreshing bath, my first [act] is to answer your last letter immediately. Along with it came the announcement of the death of the aged mother of a Mannheim acquaintance, Alb. Müller, who made me a present of the book by Anselm Feuerbach. I received your next-to-last letter, as well as the package of tea, and thank you for both. Concerning the consignment of tea, my Poldi requested that she be permitted to use it first, before she actually devotes it to its special purpose. Naturally, I complied with this modest wish; consequently the cleaning of the rug will be postponed for awhile. I have taken to heart your loving misgivings regarding my bicycling and agree with you completely. I won't take any more lessons with Eckstein and will give up cycling until such time as my circumstances are improved and I have a more substantial reason for cultivating the sport of bicycling. Under existing conditions a bicycle would indeed be only a burden and, over and above this, would also reduce my budget considerably—so, no bicycle. I've already accustomed myself to this idea. The evening at Bokmayers' went very well. Besides Haberlandt and Werner, there were approximately 20 others invited, who listened to Bokmayer's recital with the most rapt attention. Herr and Frau Bokmayer were quite touched at my appearing and outdid themselves in showing me their respect and admiration, so that it became very awkward for me. Bokmayer, by the way, doesn't sing at all badly, and in any case, *con amore* and with a fair amount of understanding. Unfortunately, I forgot to take a printed program with me.

I'll obtain one and send it to you. Löwe accompanied very beautifully, but hurried many of the tempi. I'll tell you more in person about the evening, which concluded with a solemn supper (buffet). No one left until 1:30 in the morning. Haberlandt, Werner, and I rode in the fiacre, which Bokmayer ordered, as far as Perchtoldsdorf, Löwe to Vienna.—The next morning was the procession in Perchtoldsdorf, famed far and wide, which was presided over by a bishop. There was a terrifying horde of people, along with a murderous heat. We watched the spectacle from Larisch's flat. It was a magnificent sight. The whole town was festively decorated with banners, the ground strewn with grass and flowers. I was all the more interested in the whole thing because of the procession in "Manuel Venegas" and hence had the best opportunity to make observations. A half dozen bands were moving with the procession, playing in turns. In between was the monotonous singing of the rural populace, to the extent that one could scarcely see or hear a thing.—Unfortunately, Hoernes wasn't there. He'd gone on a bicycle tour for three days, but I heard from Haberlandt that the 1st act is completed in verse up to the final scene. Day after tomorrow the 1st act will probably be sent to me. Meanwhile, Marie Lang has turned up with a scenario that appealed to me very much when she told me about it, but that looks really ridiculous the way she has put it on paper. One sees again what a difference there is between ecstatically discussing something and, as is the case with an artist, keeping a cool head in order to hold fast to the experience of the previous excitement and give it shape. Naturally, I will refrain from submitting her sketch to Heckel as she requested, because one would make an undying fool of oneself. Her work is nothing more than a paraphrase of the novella in unrestrained passionate accents, often quite awkward in expression and, in its excess, sometimes actually offensive. Ah me, if writing poetry were so easy, I would already have made my own libretto long ago. One must just be born a poet. There is no other way to become one.—For now then, very sincerest greetings from your most faithful

Hugo Wolf.

I'm going to spend tomorrow's holiday in Vienna in quiet seclusion.

234

To Traunkirchen
Vienna, July 1, 1897

Most honored friend!

Letter and package have just arrived from Bokmayer. You will see from Bokmayer's letter that he's a very intelligent and well-educated person; except for the exaggerated tone of respect in which the letter is unfortunately written, he shows himself to be a valiant combatant before the Lord, who is not to be trifled with. I'm enclosing the program [of June 28] along with this. Müller's letter may interest you as well. Potpeschnigg wrote me today on the inevitable postcard that his mother is already moving about outdoors in a wheelchair. It's terribly hot here and barely tolerable anymore. A speedy cooling-off would be highly desirable. I'll be in Perchtoldsdorf again on Sunday and will visit Bokmayer from there. Sincerest greetings to all!

As always yours,
Hugo Wolf.

235

To Traunkirchen
Vienna, July 7, 1897

[Beginning is missing]

. . . among which are true pearls. The procession in the 1st act sings one of my sacred Spanish songs—"Führ mich, Kind, nach Bethlehem"—, which is interrupted after the various verses by Manuel's outbursts, as for example after the 1st verse:

Manuel (to Hauptmann)

Carlos, Carlos! dieses Lied,	Carlos, Carlos! This song,
So vertraut u. ach so fremd	So familiar and yet so strange
Meinem Herzen!	To my heart! Childhood
Kinderjahre,	years,
Ach, wo seid ihr?	Ah, where are you?

(Moved, he glances about and looks over to Soledad on the balcony)

Ha! Was seh ich!	Aha! What do I see!
Sie! Doch nein, das Weib des andern!	She! But no, the other's wife!
Unrein, ungetreues Weib!	Tainted, unfaithful woman!
Schändliche Verrätherin!	Shameful betrayer!
Schwarzer Dämon meines Lebens,	Black devil of my life,
Der die Seele mir vergiftet!	Who has poisoned my soul!

Chorus of the procession

Rüttle mich, dass ich erwache! etc., etc. (eine Strophe)	Shake me, so that I awaken! etc., etc. (one verse)

Then again *Manuel*

Und sie wagt's in eitlem Putze	And she dares, in vain adornment
Hier vor allem Volk zu thronen!	To be enthroned here before all the people!
Brüstet sich im Licht der Sonne	Preens herself in the sun's light
Noch vor dem, was sie gethan.	Even before him, what she has done.
Wie? sie zittert nicht.— Unsel'ge!	What? she trembles not.—Ill-fated one!
Zittre für dein Leben! Ahnst du	Tremble for your life! Don't you know
Nicht, dass dein Verhängnis nah.	That your destiny approaches.
Dass der Rächer, Richter da?	That the avenger, judge is here?

Chorus of the procession

(Barefoot male and female penitents)

"Von der Sünde schwerem	"Deathly ill from sin," etc.

Kranken," etc.   (verse)
(Strophe)

This scene should make an excellent effect on stage. Quite on
his own Hoernes had the idea of incorporating the song in question into the libretto. I had no notion of it beforehand. My associate could not have made a happier choice, as the song in its
piano setting is a pure *a cappella* melody, and the words, as I just
now tried, fit marvelously well under the piano line, i.e., vocal
line, so that not a note of the piece will need to be changed. I'm
having the vocal line done by a *prayer leader* (tenor solo), who of
course must sing very well, over which float the soprano and alto
voices with their eighth-note figures in thirds, the same underneath with the basses and tenors, which will create an indescribably tender and devotional mood. I'm quite delirious over it all.
When I come for a visit, I'll bring along the libretto, naturally.
I hope it is finished by then.—Yesterday I was at the Venice
[restaurant] with the Mayreders at the Praterstern. I was led
around like a youngster celebrating his confirmation. First we
went to the theater, where exquisitely trained dogs were presented that performed the most unbelievable tricks that amused
me endlessly. Less entertaining was Miss Titi Sidney in her
tights, offering living tableaux. After this we got on the giant
Ferris wheel, which was immensely entertaining. One enjoys
the most marvelous bird's-eye view as from a hot air balloon.
Riding up and down extremely pleasant and highly recommended. Afterward was supper, excellent risotto served with
chianti in an Ital[ian] restaurant, and then back to the theater at
10:00. The ballet was first-rate, the program very lavish and varied. The Icarian games (clown tricks) were mystifying and the
snake dance simply overwhelming. We were all in the happiest
mood and didn't leave this showplace of so many delights until
after midnight. In addition to everything else, the weather was
also splendid, not too hot and not too cool. In short, we were in
the highest spirits.

In the same mailing, I'm sending you the evening's program and a widely read and respected Berlin weekly newspaper,
in which Dr. Sternfeld wrote about me once before. This time
Nodnagel has distinguished himself. The article is very good,

with the exception of a few spots. Faisst sent it to me. He is quite delighted about the respectful mention of my name. I only regret that another name was also brought up. The article should be returned to me. And so then, very sincerest greetings and see you soon.

[no signature]

236

To Traunkirchen

Vienna, July 10, 1897

Beloved friend!

Yesterday I was at Schalk's in Döbling the whole afternoon and read the 2nd and 3rd acts to him. He was quite delighted and excited by it. Schalk is going to travel alone to Reichenhall soon and will stay there six weeks. Finally Franz came as well, and much was discussed with him about "Corregidor." He still wants to give the opera at the beginning of the season. Bokmayer paid me a visit today and was very moved by my friendly reception. I played him the Michelangelo songs and presented him with a copy of the hymn "Dem Vaterland." He was so uplifted by this that he felt obliged to reciprocate immediately. Shortly after his visit, then, he sent me an electric lighter that looks uncommonly smart, is very easy to use, and that I had very much admired when I was there one time. So I've written him a very nice letter today also. Bokmayer is also bearing the costs of Schalk's stay in Reichenhall, without Schalk's knowing about it. He really is a nice fellow, a terrific person so to speak.— Hoernes, who is now spending time in Hungary (near the border), wants to change some things in the 1st act, which is why I haven't started to work yet. I'm spending tomorrow afternoon with the Mayreders at the Kobenzl. Why aren't you writing me anything about Nodnagel's article, which, taken as a whole, is quite respectable? So, in 10 days I'll arrive. Am looking forward to it immensely. The heat here is beginning to become bothersome again. Marie [Lang] moved to the country yesterday and threw in the towel as far as "Manuel Venegas" is concerned. It's just as well too. I've been using the Du-form [familiar *you*] with Hoernes and Haberlandt since the day the libretto was finished.

I sang Hoernes a lot of my Spanish songs at Haberlandt's on the same day, and it seemed to dawn on him gradually concerning the music. The song about the auction impressed him particularly. He wants to do a modern Don Quixote for me as an opera libretto. That could be superb. If only I had already conquered Manuel. What a lot of work it will be!

For today then, a thousand greetings.

[no signature]

237

To Traunkirchen

Vienna, July 31, 1897

Beloved friend!

Haberlandt was just here, prevented from traveling further by the bad weather. In honor of his arrival, I dare not miss being in Perchtoldsdorf tomorrow, and so I'll give myself a real Sunday, despite the fact that I'm already well into things. Yesterday Edmund visited me, and I read him the libretto, which really delighted him tremendously. I've already sent the original text to Dr. Mayr. A card from him enclosed. I have given up completely my idea of smuggling the chorus from "Fest auf Solhaug" into the libretto, because with God's and friend Hoernes' help, I'd like to make *an opera* out of the Ibsen piece. When I recently set to work on the Solhaug music score, I felt terribly sad that these refreshing sounds would never be heard. And it evokes such a genuinely dramatic atmosphere. Haberlandt, to whom I gave sections of it today, was quite surprised by the popular idiom and liveliness of the expression and supported me in my intent to make an opera out of it.—Fortunately, I don't have to rely on borrowing from my older compositions, and so the day before yesterday quite a fine inspiration came to me for the 1st chorus, which I've already laid out fairly well too. It will be a splendid piece. Of course it's no longer a girls' chorus, as the composition stipulated tenor voices alternating with soprano and alto, which hardly troubled me at all. So you can see then, dearest friend, that I've already steered into the correct channel. Now things should start happening.

As I gather from the newspapers, it must look pretty dreary

in the Salzkammergut. But up on your "sunny hill" you're well protected. The rain seems to have gone to the head of the shabby Vienna [river], because it has become terribly unruly and gives the appearance of being at least a Volga or an Amazon river. At the Stubenthorbrücke [bridge] it's kicking up such a commotion that a Rhine whirlpool is pure meekness by comparison.

For a change, my electric cigarette lighter is kaput once again. I think I was royally taken in with this one, even though it's the second, *improved* edition.

12:00. Mealtime. Forgive me, most honored friend, if I am common enough to allow myself to be hurried to a conclusion by a good beef roast. Don't fault me.

Sincerest greetings from your very most faithful
Hugo Wolf.

238

To Traunkirchen [picture postcard]
[Perchtoldsdorf], August 8, 1897

Most honored friend! For today just a hurried, but all the more sincere, Sunday greeting. I'm writing these lines on the airy veranda at Haberlandts', for whom I played the first scenes of the new opera today and who were quite delighted with the motifs. They also send best greetings. I'll write in more detail tomorrow. Have already a lot of news to pass on. I'm in a bright mood, as is always the case when things are inspiring me.

Your
Hugo Wolf.

239

To Traunkirchen [visiting card]
Vienna, August 19, 1897

Hurrah! The cursed Morisco-motif is *finally* born. The baptism took place very quietly this afternoon over a small glass of Südtiroler (I always drink this inexpensive and light wine now instead of beer). The motif is truly Malaga-ish, nimble, mischievous, and yet gallant at the same time. Ah, I can breathe again.

Now I can get going again. How I'm looking forward to it! Am going to "Meistersinger" today. Have invited Hellmer and Edmund to it. Must dash to the opera right away, therefore sincerest greetings only quickly from your blissfully happy

Hugo Wolf.

240

To Traunkirchen

Vienna, August 23, 1897

Beloved friend!

I've just returned from Perchtoldsdorf, where I'm in the habit of spending my Sundays, and found your dear lines this morning, which made me extremely happy, as always. Along with your letter, unfortunately, arrived the package of the newly written score of "Corregidor" from Graz, and so now I have the very dubious pleasure of checking out this new score from beginning to end with great care, as the final autographed copy will be done from this score. So I'm forced for the next period of time to perform musical drudgery, despite Potpeschnigg's friendly offer to take over this job for me. However, since I discovered in glancing through it hastily that in some places changes are still necessary in the orchestration, as well as in the performance markings, I've no choice but to go ahead with the task myself. "A bitter assignment and now above all" *[Ein saures Amt u. jetzt zumal]*, when I'd much rather be working further on "Venegas."

Despite now having a motif available for Morisco, I still had the intention of giving Morisco his leave to go. On this account, I had a discussion with Hoernes on Friday, who willingly went along with my suggestion. But what Hoernes, who appears to be taking no more interest in the libretto, has offered me now for verses to replace this are so lifeless and insufficient that I sought counsel from Haberlandt, who was also horrified at Hoernes' modifications. So Haberlandt sat down and made changes along the lines of my thinking, and so excellently that I'm now going to stay with the Haberlandt version without saying a word about it to Hoernes. Once the thing is set to music, he won't be able to say any more against it and I'm convinced that he, too, will like Haberlandt's change. Meanwhile, as I said, I'm not going to get around to working on the libretto for a while, as my time will now be completely taken up by the Corregidor score. If you don't hear anything from me now for a longer period, you'll know the reason for it. Of course I'll attend the Nibelungen cycle [Wagner's *Der Ring des Nibelungen*]. Director Krückl in Strassburg is terribly eager for the Corregidor score. Presumably the performance in Strassburg will still take place this year.

Ah, what a long-suffering creature man is! I often hardly know which end is up. As soon as I catch my breath again I'll write. Until then, please have patience.

With sincerest greetings, entirely your

Hugo Wolf.

241

To Traunkirchen

Vienna, Sept. 10, 1897

Dear friend!

A lucky coincidence came about in that shortly after the arrival of the delivery from Paris, the always welcome messenger Ignatius knocked on my door and transferred spiritual inspiration to me in the form of two bottles of Marsala. So I was therefore in the pleasant situation of being able to return the favor immediately, addressed forthwith the unopened small crate to Traunkirchen, and handed it over to Ignaz for further transporting. So that's now been well taken care of. Nevertheless, I would urgently request you to deal more carefully with future instances concerning deliveries from abroad and, above all, to inquire whether, and from whom, I would like to receive a package. Also, you are sufficiently aware of my dislike for the cursed required mailing charges to induce you not to impose this kind of unpleasantness on me in the future. This time I had such a horrifying customs duty to pay, which surely corresponded in no way to the package's contents, that it would have taken very little for me to refuse to accept the package at all. But the high fee made me so distraught that I paid without hesitating. Only afterward did I discover, to my not very slight anger, that Frl. [Vally] Franck had written the address in her own hand; had I noticed this fact in time, I would certainly have refused the box. Now, however, since such a lovely way to be rid of the package was provided, I'm satisfied. May you, and all those who partake of it, enjoy it.—I spent the last holiday again in Perchtoldsdorf, where evenings at the Wednesday Club were quite lively; Bokmayer was there too. I told him in conversation that I would probably have to forgo the trip to Duino (we've given up on Ragusa because of the expense), as my financial situation would be otherwise too overburdened as a result of the planned installation of electric lighting in my flat. What did my good Bokmayer do upon hearing this? He worked out an understanding with Larisch, who is handling the matter, and offered to cover my portion of the costs out of his own pocket. Larisch, deciding quickly, agreed on my behalf and—the case is closed. Truly a terrific person, my little Bokmayer! right?

The work on "M. Venegas" has been at a standstill for almost a week. This confounded 2nd chorus before Manuel's entrance didn't want to come for a long time, until I finally conquered it today. Now I'm going to have to deal with Manuel personally. Oh how I'm looking forward to that!

My laryngitis was over a long time ago, and I'm now once again letting myself enjoy the good taste of Havana cigars that Bokmayer brought me illegally from the "Reich" [Germany]. In short, everything is going as I wish. Sincerest greetings from your

Hugo Wolf.

242

To Traunkirchen

Vienna, Sept. 14, 1897

Dear friend!

I really must describe to you the eventful 14th of Sept., even as little as you deserve it after the carelessly wrapped gingerbread package. The day began with my having put myself in the necessary frame of mind for Manuel's big monologue, which I was burning to set to music. Things did not go well for me in the morning, however, or rather, things went for me as they went for Beckmesser in the 3rd act, as all the unpleasant memo-

ries of the previous night were hovering about in his brain. I
wanted to compose the monologue but was continuously thinking about all that I wanted to say to my sassy Poldi today. In all
this, I was intent upon heaping the choicest insults on her head
and gave long lectures to her aloud by myself in a fierce tone of
voice, assumed a posture, and threw angry glances at the stove,
which I pretended was the delinquent. I was absolutely determined not to keep Poldi for a single day longer. Tensely, I
watched the 6:00 evening hour approach. Meanwhile, midday
arrived. A good, modest meal at the Hirsch calmed me to some
extent. A fine Bokmayer Havana and a glass of Marsala did their
part to improve my mood. I sat down to my work again and
buried myself in the monologue—and, oh miracle! All of a sudden the musical spring gushed forth out of all my pores and with
such vehemence that I could hardly keep up with writing it
down. One verse after the other took on tangible form and
shape; it was as if I were writing down all the notes out of the
air. By evening I was finished with the entire monologue, a thing
I would never have considered possible, as the monologue contains 16 long iambic verses. That was certainly an accomplishment and I became increasingly aware of a certain respect for
myself. At the same time, however, Poldi still came to mind, to
be sure, in the dim background, but just as quickly disappeared
again from the scene.

But, oh horror, the doorbell rang. I open. Heinrich Werner
sticks his swan's neck in the door, a butter twist in one hand, a
bread twist of exceptional quality in the other. Taking this valuable booty quickly and slamming the door was one motion.
Shortly thereafter someone rang again. Damn! I leap to the door,
see through the peephole a person who looked very distinguished and recognize in him the young Scheu. What do you
want, I ask him. Only wanted to congratulate you on the accept-
ance of "Corregidor" by the opera here. I: Damn it all, what
do I care about "Corregidor." Now the watchword is: "Manuel
Venegas"; since he knew no more about the performance than
I—and that's little enough—I showed the donkey what was
written so far of "Venegas," in which this calf indicated no interest whatsoever; thereupon, I graciously ushered him out. He
was hardly out the door when: ding-a-ling, it rang once again.

Confound it! Has the world gone mad today? I open up again. Foll. Well, that can happen. I immediately played him 20 pages from the new opera at his request, and it was touching to see how this icicle visibly began to glow. Yes, yes, the musicians will take notice.

Finally, Poldi appeared. 4th scene, last entrance.

I (friendly): Well, my good Poldi, have you nothing to say to me?

Poldi: I? Not that I know of . . . (this said rather sullenly, after she had greeted me coldly).

I: So, no apology?

Poldi: Apology? For what?

So, I say, then allow me to pay you some compliments on your behavior yesterday. And now I fell into a terrible rage and trembled with excitement and began thus:

Do you know what you are? You are the most impertinent, vile, impudent, brazen, ill-tempered female! Great astonishment on her part. But all the time she retained complete composure, made no reply to the flood of my reproaches and invective, and did not show herself in any way to be upset. That impressed me, on one hand, but enraged me still more, on the other. In the end, I paid her, demanded the key from her, and left the flat, which Poldi cleaned up in the meantime. I went to Edmund to lighten my heart, and told him the story. When I come home, Poldi is still here, red-eyed and quite upset. Suddenly she knocks on the door of my study, throws herself at my feet, and begs me for forgiveness in a flood of tears. Afterward we both sobbed, and the curtain fell. Touching tableau. Reconciliation.

Now you must admit that I can also be a good little boy, since I recount all the stories of my adventures so nicely. What do I get as a reward? It is surely worth a whole sack of Nuremberg gingerbread. I believe this time I've spoken really plainly, or do you still not understand me? Ah, my dear friend, now and then it is so difficult to communicate with you. Meanwhile, it has become 10:00 p.m. I've been working on this epistle for almost an hour, even though it's just flowing out of my pen. Good night and mend your ways. Little Poldi comes again at the crack of dawn from tomorrow on. After the big scene, I had to rush over to Edmund's again to cancel his servant girl. She wasn't at home of course; only Fritz and Edmund were there. Then I had to endure another adventure at Edmund's front door in front of witnesses (three housemaids). I ring. No response. I ring a dozen times. Not a soul opens. I strike the door with my walking stick and rap harder than Repela had ever knocked in the ff [double *forte* sections]. No one stirs. I begin to work on the door with both my feet and have to admit that I've never given such kicks to any other object. Finally Edmund shuffled to the door, whom I greeted with a whole flood of curses. He apologized and said that the weak doorbell was responsible for my trouble. But my rapping? He only heard my kicks. Now that is the absolute limit.

But that's "enough joking" [genug der Witz]. Sincere greetings from your very high spirited

Hugo Wolf.

243
To Traunkirchen [visiting card]

[Vienna], Sept. 15, 1897

Don't you want to come here for a day and listen to "Manuel Venegas" for yourself? The big monologue is really one of the most heartfelt things ever created in music until now. Come! But alone! By that time I'll be up to the 5th scene, entrance of Don Trinidad. In haste your

Hugo Wolf.

On Sunday I'm going to play the opera for all the faithful in Perchtoldsdorf.

244
To Traunkirchen [visiting card]

[Vienna, Sept. 17, 1897]

Potpeschnigg is leaving a mortally ill sister and coming Sunday to Mödling. If you do not arrive on the same day, I will *never* set foot in your house again.

Hugo Wolf.

Have just come up with the love motif. I'm seething like a volcano.

1899

245

My dear friend!

Do send me my flannel suit along with a couple of white starched shirts with collars and cuffs by means of your town porter or servant; I'd also really like to have a pair of my patent leather shoes, i.e., those in the smaller size. Perhaps you could bring the requested items yourself or possibly have them sent by mail. I would be very obliged to you for sending me a new overcoat of a subdued color, which one should be able to get in a clothing store such as Rothberger's or somewhere. I hope your health is better. I would like very much to prevail upon you for a friendly visit, if it could take place without endangering your personal safety; otherwise, I'd rather forgo the visit, as my presence appears to spread harm, particularly with regard to those persons who were very kind and dear to me at one time and of whom I think constantly with pleasure. My cough is pretty much gone. Whether I'll be permitted to leave the asylum is still very doubtful, however, or actually *not* doubtful, because how am I to get out of here without help from my friends? With the sincerest greetings and, nevertheless, still hoping for a final release, I remain your most devoted

——— [no signature]

EPILOGUE

by Franz Grasberger

Not until the publication of Hugo Wolf's letters to Melanie Köchert does this woman's full and critical significance enter into the life history of the great composer. We will now be able to include a new, characterizing trait to the well-known picture of his personality; above all we now have the right to assume knowledge of an essential, human background in the creative process. This fact alone justifies the scope of the introductory chapter. Moreover, many of the contexts are not evident from this fragmentary correspondence, which has come to us with many gaps; to have mentioned them only as footnotes would not have done justice to their significance. Furthermore, it seems advantageous to accompany an edition of letters with a portrayal of the personality as a whole, one in which the portrait is redrawn more precisely in the context of the letters. In the case of Hugo Wolf, this assessment is now especially necessary, since one could not hitherto assume with certainty much about his nature or his relationship with Melanie Köchert.

Frank Walker was acquainted with the letters and used a few of them with great discretion for his definitive Wolf biography [*Hugo Wolf*]. He seems also to have planned a publication of them, for he had many copies in his possession, which he spontaneously handed over to me when he learned of the intent to publish them in their entirety.

That this was possible at all is primarily thanks to Frau Irmina Köchert, Melanie's daughter, who still lives at "Puchschacher" near Traunkirchen on the Traunsee [Irmina Köchert died on August 16, 1972]. She made the original letters available, patiently provided information, and brought to our conversations the spirit [of Hugo Wolf] that she had sensed and experienced as a child. For all this, and particularly for her confidence in every regard, I extend my humblest and heartfelt thanks.

In this publication, the original format of the letters is maintained as far as possible; particular attention has also been paid to preserving their outward appearance, since consistent adherence to this casts a distinctive light on the personality of the letter writer.

The publisher approached this project with idealism and preserved the dignity of the outer form [of the letters] at all times. For this personal commitment of Herr Hans Schneider I am especially grateful. Frank Walker would have been very pleased with this publication, but unfortunately did not live to see it; thus, my profoundly sincere thanks for his unusually generous contribution will no longer reach him.

Finally, I wish to thank my dear wife and Dr. Grete Müller for their constant, unfailing support and also, in the same spirit, Frau Agnes Ziffer and Fräulein Renate Albinger.

Vienna, December 1964

ANNOTATIONS

The Annotations in the German-language edition have been adapted and supplemented by the translator.

All writings annotated here are letters unless otherwise specified. Underlined passages in the original letters are reproduced in italics. The enclosures mentioned in the letters, almost without exception, have not been preserved. Circumstances and background information discussed in the Translator's Introduction and in Dr. Grasberger's Preface are not mentioned again in the annotations.

Biographical information regarding persons is annotated when the name is mentioned for the first time in the text of the letters. Names of Köchert family employees and friends mentioned in the text are omitted, as well as those persons otherwise untraceable.

The numbers of the following annotations refer to the numbers of the letters.

1. Arnfels in Styria, located between Windischgraz (Wolf's birthplace; now Slovenj Gradec) and Leibnitz.
2. Wolf is accompanying his brother-in-law—his sister Modesta's husband, Josef Strasser—to Bruck.
3. The brothers Joseph and Franz Schalk became acquainted with Wolf's songs in 1887. In particular, Joseph Schalk (1857–1900), professor of piano at the Vienna Conservatory and artistic director of Vienna's academic Wagner Society, actively promoted his friend's work. The *Eichendorff-Lieder* are dedicated to him and Franz Schalk (1863–1931),

the renowned conductor.—Wolf had been composing the *Goethe-Lieder* since October 27, 1888.

4. In connection with correcting the proofs during the printing of the *Eichendorff-Lieder*, Wolf refers to "Die Zigeunerin"; the lieder were published by C. Lacom (Vienna) in September 1889.—Miss Park is the Köchert children's English teacher.—Heinrich Köchert, the husband of Melanie Köchert.

5. Wolf had known the singer Amalie Materna (1847–1918) since 1882; he requested her, without success, to sing his songs.—Wolf had been working on the *Spanisches Liederbuch* since October 28, 1889. He would write "Bitt' ihn, o Mutter" later in the afternoon of November 26.

8. Wolf was orchestrating the Mörike song "Er ist's" during this month.

9. A hidalgo is a Spanish nobleman.—Wolf signs his name here in the diminutive.

11. *Dem Vaterland,* written by German painter and poet Robert Reinick (1805–1852), was composed as a song on May 12, 1890, and arranged by Wolf soon afterward for men's chorus and orchestra; for a short time it was given the title *An das Vaterland;* there were three versions of the work in this form (1890–1898).—The well-known Wagnerian singer Ferdinand Jäger, who was teaching voice in Vienna, had put himself at the service of Wolf's music since December 1888 and was greatly instrumental in its promotion.

12. The attorney Heinrich Rauchberg, a friend of Wolf's since 1880. His review of the *Mörike-* and *Eichendorff-Lieder* ("Neue Lieder und Gesänge") in the *Österreichisch-Ungarische Revue* (Austrian-Hungarian Review), Vol. 8 (1889–1890), is the first discussion of Wolf's songs.—Opera plans are again in the foreground, as a result of the connection with Detlev von Liliencron (1844–1909), German poet drawn to Wolf's songs by Schalk's and Conrad's articles. (He later wrote a poem, "An Hugo Wolf," which appeared in his next volume.) Texts under consideration were Shakespeare's *Midsummer Night's Dream* and *The Tempest;*

Wolf turned down a *Buddha*, penned by Grohe's friend Karl Heckel, the Mannheim music publisher.—Dr. Oskar Grohe, a lower-court judge in Mannheim, was in touch with Wolf by letter beginning in April 1890 and belonged thereafter to his circle of close friends.—In 1882 Wolf became friends with Bruckner's pupil Friedrich Eckstein, a Viennese music-lover of wealthy background; see Eckstein's memoirs *Alte unnennbare Tage* (Vienna, 1936). The Eckstein family had a summer house in Unterach.— Gustav Schur, bank official, long-standing treasurer of Vienna's academic Wagner Society and the first treasurer of the Hugo Wolf Society in Vienna. He negotiated with Schott Publishers regarding the printing of the *Spanisches Liederbuch* and was also involved in the opera plans as librettist.—Joseph Schalk published two important essays: "Neue Lieder, neues Leben," in the newspaper *Allgemeine Zeitung* (Munich) on January 22, 1890 (Supplement No. 18); and "Hugo Wolf," in *Der Kunstwart* (Munich), 1890, No. 11. The article in the Munich *Allgemeine Zeitung*, in particular, evoked a large response and won the composer a circle of South German friends (above all Emil Kauffmann in Tübingen and Oskar Grohe in Mannheim).—Michael Georg Conrad (1846–1927), friend of Liliencron, publisher of the periodical *Die Gesellschaft* (Munich), the main publication of the young naturalistic movement in German literature, brought out a review in 1890 of the *Mörike-Lieder* on p. 770 of the journal.—Brahms had set Liliencron's "Auf dem Kirchhofe" (Op.105, No. 4) and "Marienkätzchen" (Op. 107, No. 4).—Wolf began the compositions from Swiss writer Gottfried Keller's *Alte Weisen* in Unterach on May 25. The undertaking gave him trouble; the manuscript of "Wandl' ich in dem Morgentau" is dated June 8, but the song was still not completed on June 16.

14. The *Alte Weisen, Sechs Gedichte von Keller* (Gottfried Keller, 1819–1890) are finished. the reference is to the Keller poem "Wie glänzt der helle Mond."

15. Theodore Köchert, brother of Heinrich Köchert.—The

Stadelmanns were the owners of the house in Rinnbach where Karoline Köchert, Heinrich Köchert's mother, lived in the summer.

16. Rudolf von Larisch, civil servant, art enthusiast, and later professor at the Vienna Kunstgewerbeschule (School for Applied Arts) and the Academie der bildenden Künste (Academy of Visual Arts); a close friend of Wolf.—"Wisst ihr (weisst du), wie das ward?": *Götterdämmerung*, Act 1.—Brahms had set four of Gottfried Keller's poems: "Salome" (Op. 69, No. 8), "Abendregen" (Op. 70, No. 4), "Therese" (Op. 86, No. 1), and "Hochzeitslied" (cantata for four voices and piano). Wolf selected the first lines as titles after all ("Du milchjunger Knabe" and "Singt mein Schatz").—The negotiations with Schott continue.

17. Hermann Bahr, "Pantomime," in *Deutschland*, Vol. 1 (1889–1890), pp. 748–749. Arnold Böcklin (1827–1901) was a Swiss painter known for paintings of moody land- scapes and sinister allegories.—Friederike Mayer, a young mezzo-soprano.

18. Dr. Wilhelm Dlauhy, physician and Heinrich Köchert's brother-in-law.

19. University professor Dr. Alois Höfler, philosopher and pedagogue; strongly influenced by Wagner.—University professor Dr. Joseph Freiherr von Schey, lawyer, married to Henriette Lang, Melanie Köchert's sister. Wolf took a trip to Kövecses in Hungary on September 10.

22. This letter arrived in Ebensee on September 23, 1890, ac- cording to the postmark.

23. Ignaz Brüll (1847–1907), successful Viennese opera com- poser (*Das goldene Kreuz*, among others).—Grohe had sent his own songs for an opinion.

25. Wolf is undertaking his first trip to Germany.—Provincial Court Counselor Dr. Viktor Boller, chairman of Vienna's academic Wagner Society.

26. Hermann Levi (1839–1900), conductor, *Hofkapellmeister* (court conductor) in Munich until 1896.—Wagnerian bari- tone Eugen Gura (1843–1906).—It was customary in Vi- enna to fill the pauses between groups of songs (which al- lowed the singer to rest) with piano playing, performed by

young and old.—Heinrich Porges (1837–1900), music critic and choral conductor in Munich.—Oskar Merz, opera critic for the newspaper *Münchner neuesten Nachrichten*.

28. Wilhelm Förstler (1885–1912), conductor of the Stuttgart Liederkranz.—*Dem Vaterland*, the title of Reinick's poem, was Wolf's eventual choice of title.—Wilhelm Speidel (1826–1899), teacher at the Stuttgart Conservatory, brother of Ludwig Speidel, critic working in Vienna.—Tübingen music director Emil Kauffmann (1836–1909), in correspondence with Wolf since March 1890, eventually formed an untroubled friendship with the young composer twenty-four years his junior.

29. Dr. Wilhelm Schmid, professor of classical philology.

30. . . . *Da klingt schon viel Jahr kein Glas* (No glass clinked here for many years).—Mörike wrote five Peregrina poems on the episode of his passion for Maria Meyer. Wolf set two of them.—Jean Paul (pseudonym for Johann Richter, 1763–1825), German writer.—Friedrich Hölderlin (1770–1843), German poet; insane from 1802, except for brief periods. The folkloric Feuerreiter (fire-rider) was gifted with the power of detecting distant fires to which he was irresistibly drawn. Forbidden to extinguish these fires by magic, Mörike's fire-rider chose to disobey and suffered disastrous consequences.

31. Dr. Alfred von Domaszewski, relative of Wolf's Viennese friends, the Werner family (Perchtoldsdorf).—*Sause- und Brausewind:* from the Mörike setting "Lied vom Winde."—*Epheuwand:* from the Mörike setting "An eine Äolsharfe."—*Aus alten Märchen . . .:* from Schumann's *Dichterliebe* (Heine), No. 15,—In his letters Wolf often used a row of dashes to indicate the passage of time.

32. Felix von Weingartner (1863–1942), conductor and composer, *Hofkapellmeister* in Mannheim, 1889–1891; from 1891 on, *Kappellmeister* at the Königliche Oper (Royal Opera) in Berlin.—Gustav Schur had laid the groundwork for the negotiations with Schott Publishers (see n. 12).— Franz Wüllner (1832–1902), conductor and composer, active in Cologne since 1884.

34. Hans Schuster, concertmaster at the Mannheim National

Theater.—Singer August Livermann, on the roster at the Mannheim Theater, 1890–1892.—Tenor Albert Mittelhauser, in Mannheim, 1890–1892.—Dr. Ludwig Strecker (1853–1943), head of B. Schott's Sons Publishers.

35. *Christnacht*, for vocal solists, chorus, and orchestra (see n. 44).—The work performed was by Kaspar Jakob Bischoff (1823–1893).—Eugène Ysaÿe (1858–1931), Belgian violinist, conductor, and composer.—Alexander Borodin (1833–1887), Russian composer.—Wagner changed the name Veit Hanslick to Sixtus Beckmesser (see Hanslick, n. 37).—Engelbert Humperdinck (1854–1921) was an editor for Schott Publishers. His opera *Hansel and Gretel* received its first performance in Weimar in 1893.

37. Cologne physician Dr. Hermann Wette (1857–1919), prominent dramatist and reciter, wrote dialect poetry and was married to Humperdinck's sister Adelheid.—Alexander Strakosch (1845–1909), eminent representative of the art of recitation, active for many years in Vienna.—Eduard Hanslick (1825–1904), influential Viennese music critic and friend of Brahms, rejected Wagner and Bruckner.—Ludwig Speidel (1830–1906), theater and music critic as well as feature columnist in Vienna.—Otto Neitzel (1852–1920), German composer and music critic.—August Lesimple (1827–1909), chairman of Cologne Wagner Society.

41. *Dem Vaterland* (Robert Reinick) for men's chorus and orchestra (see n. 11).—The Viennese publisher C. Lacom, who brought out the *Eichendorff-* and *Goethe-Lieder.*—The music to Ibsen's *The Feast at Solhaug*, in German translation *Das Fest auf Solhaug*, was composed in 1890–1891, commissioned by the Burgtheater; premiere November 21, 1891.

42. *Alte Weisen* (Keller; see n. 12) was published by Schott after the *Spanisches Liederbuch*.

43. Wolf's second trip to Germany.

44. *Christnacht*. Hymn (words by August von Platen) for vocal soloists, mixed chorus, and orchestra, composed 1886–1889; premiered April 9, 1891, by Weingartner in his final concert in Mannheim before starting his new position at the Berlin Opera. The work was published by Lauterbach

& Kuhn in 1903.—Ferdinand Langer, second *Kapellmeister* at the Mannheim National Theater.

45. Karl Stieler (1842–1885), Munich essayist, poet, and travel writer.—Peter Cornelius (1824–1874) was as talented a poet as he was a composer *(Barbier von Bagdad)*.

46. "Zitronenfalter im April": title of Mörike setting.—Karl Bernhard Öhn, bank official and member of Vienna's academic Wagner Society.

47. Felix Mottl (1856–1911), active as a conductor in Bayreuth, Karlsruhe, and Munich; acquainted with Wolf since their days at the Vienna Conservatory.—Oskar von Chelius (1859–1923), German officer and composer.—Hermann Götz (1840–1876), German composer of *Der Widerspenstigen Zähmung (The Taming of the Shrew)*, comic opera.

48. The diplomat Wilhelm Eduard von Schön (1851—1933).

51. Karl Frank, *Kapellmeister* at the Mannheim National Theater.

55. Music pedagogue Otto Lessmann (1844–1918), owner and editor of the *Allgemeine Musik-Zeitung* (Berlin), 1881–1908.

56. Viennese sculptor Johannes Benk (1844–1914).—Presumably Wolf had read La Rochefoucauld's (1613–1680) *Maxims*.

58. Wolf is in Bayreuth for the fifth time.—Conductor Ferdinand Löwe (1865–1925), who was active primarily in Vienna.—Hans Freiherr von Wolzogen (1848–1938), editor of the *Bayreuther Blätter*, arts critic and playwright.—Hermann Winkelmann (1849–1912), heldentenor and well-known Wagnerian singer.—Gustav Holländer (1855–1915), professor of violin at the Cologne Conservatory.

60. Viennese pianist and critic Hans Paumgartner (1843–1896) had been the leader of the opposition in 1888 against promoting Wolf in Vienna's academic Wagner Society.

61. Renowned Wagnerian singer Rosa Sucher (1849–1927).—Fritz Plank (1848–1900), respected interpreter of baritone roles at Bayreuth.—"O diese Sonne!" *Tristan und Isolde*, Act 3.

62. Four songs in the *Italienisches Liederbuch* (first part) were composed in Döbling, December 2–4, 1891.

63. Wolf has written out the last nine lines of the seventeen-line Mörike poem he set in October 1888.
64. Wolf's third trip to Germany. Ferdinand Jäger, along with Friederike Mayer, was supposed to have sung in a *Lieder-abend* at the Berlin Singakademie, with the composer as accompanist. Jäger canceled his appearance, however.— "Romance," Op. 138 ("Flutenreicher Ebro"), by Robert Schumann, "An die Leier" by Franz Schubert, "So lasst uns wandern" by Johannes Brahms.—Concert management Hermann and Louise Wolff; see Edith Stargardt-Wolff, *Agents of Great Musicians* (Wiesbaden, 1954).—Hint-erbrühl is a scenic area in the Vienna Woods.—Heinrich Grahl, Berlin concert tenor.
65. Franz Betz (1835–1900), renowned Wagnerian singer (the first Hans Sachs, 1868, in Munich).—Nikolaus Rothmühl (a pupil of Viennese voice teacher, Josef Gänsbacher) and Elisabeth Leisinger, were on the roster at the Berlin Opera.—Richard Genée (1823–1898), librettist (for Johann Strauss, Millöcker, and others), *Kapellmeister*, and composer.—Richard Sternfeld (1858–1926), historical researcher and author of works on Beethoven, Wagner; leading member of the Berlin Wagner Society.—Lawyer Rudolf Freiherr von Seckendorff, on the board of directors of the General Richard Wagner Society. Frau Schmid-Lafourcade, a friend of Frau Grohe.—Franz and Frieda von Lipperheide, well-to-do owners of a Berlin fashion magazine, were to become special patrons. Wolf later completed *Corregidor* at their castle (Matzen) near Brixlegg in Tyrol.—Bote & Bock, important Berlin publishers.—Wolf hoped to find a librettist in Hermann Sudermann (1857–1928), whose *Frau Sorge* had impressed him very much.
66. Frau Begas-Parmentier, Berlin painter of the Begas family of artists.
67. Hermann von Helmholtz (1821–1894), famous physicist who also wrote pioneering treatises on musical acoustics and aesthetics in music.—Therese Rothauser, mezzo-soprano at the Berlin Hofoper (Court Opera).
68. Oskar Eichberg (1845–1898), director of a music school, conductor, and critic; enthusiastic Wagner supporter.

69. Jettka Finkenstein, contralto at the Hoftheater (Court Theater) in Darmstadt, lieder singer only since 1891.—Gustav Schönaich (1841–1906), very friendly with Wolf between 1877 and 1883, then turned against Wolf's music when he became music critic for the *Wiener Allgemeine Zeitung.*—M. Gaigg is Marie Gaigg, peasant proprietor of the house rented in Rinnbach by the Köchert family; also the assumed name under which letters were sent by Wolf to Melanie via general delivery.

70. Swiss Dr. Heinrich Welti (1859–1937), music critic in Berlin since 1890; his wife, Emilie Herzog, was active as a singer at the Berlin Hofoper beginning 1889.

72. On Schalk, see n. 12; Emil Kauffmann's review of the *Goethe-Lieder* appeared in the *Allgemeine Zeitung* (Munich) on November 22, 1890; Kauffmann discussed the *Spanisches Liederbuch* in the *Musikalisches Wochenblatt*, Vol. 22 (1891), pp. 290–292.—Lawyer Dr. Otto Gumprecht (1823–1900) resided in Berlin as a writer on music.

74. Rudolf Genée (1824–1914), Berlin playwright, journalist, and reciter (primarily of Shakespeare's dramas).—Ernst von Wildenbruch (1845–1909), the Prussian national dramatist during the Wilhelminian period.—Major Hippolyt de Vigneau, later *Intendant* (manager) of the Weimar Hoftheater.

75. Paul Meyerheim (1842–1915), Berlin painter.—Fritz Mauthner (1849–1923), writer and philosopher.—Siegfried Ochs (1858–1929), conductor and composer, distinguished himself especially as a choral conductor in Berlin with first performances of works by Bruckner, Wolf, and Reger.—Friederike Gossmann (1838–1906), actress, married since 1861 to the diplomat Anton Graf Prokesch von Osten.—Ernst Freiherr von Wolzogen (1855–1934), storyteller and dramatist.

78. Louise Kaulich, Hofoper singer; Felix Kraus, young concert singer; Philipp Forstén, concert singer.—The music to *Fest auf Solhaug* was performed under the baton of Joseph Schalk in conjunction with the International Music and Theater Exhibition on June 15, 1892; Hofoper singers Anna Warnegg and Felix Kraus took part.

82. Adalbert Karobat, manager of the Hotel Post in Traunkirchen and chairman of the Music Society.

84. "Max Stirner" was the pseudonym of Kaspar Schmidt (1806–1856), German philosophical writer and translator of Adam Smith's *Wealth of Nations* and champion of radical egotism whose works inspired many 19th- and 20th-century anarchists; Wolf was reading *Der Einzige und sein Eigentum (The Individual and His Property)* (1845).

85. Secondary school professor Hermann Schickinger from Linz.

86. Wolf is back home for the first time since 1889.—Orcus, name of the Roman god of the dead and, by extension, of the underworld.—The Köchert family is building a summer house ("Puchschacher") in Traunkirchen.—Fräulein Hermine is the daughter of Frau J. Prey, an employee of Melanie Köchert's parents.

87. Paul Heyse (1830–1914), one of the most prolific followers of Classicism and Romanticism; his translations of Italian literature have proved truly enduring.—Siegfried Ochs had agreed to a performance of *Elfenlied* (women's chorus and orchestra, with soprano solo: a setting of "You spotted snakes" from *A Midsummer Night's Dream* in German translation) and *Feuerreiter* (for chorus and orchestra) with the Philharmonic Chorus in Berlin.—Heinrich Gottinger, director of the Graz Theater at that time, as well as baritone at the opera.—Sophie Wiesner, a singer in Graz.

88. The composer is in Graz to accompany a Wolf *Liederabend*, which took place December 1.—Julius Stinde (1841–1905), mainly a satirist, also a dialect poet.—Josef Purgleitner managed the Hirschenapotheke (pharmacy) in Graz with his brother.—Dentist Dr. Heinrich Potpeschnigg, excellent musician and one of Wolf's best friends in his final years.—Martin Plüddemann (1854–1897), voice teacher after 1889 at the Styrian Music School in Graz.—The husband-and-wife singers August Krämer–Maria Widl, who had performed in the first Wolf *Liederabend* in Graz in 1890.—Friedrich von Hausegger (1837–1899), lecturer in music history at the University of Graz and author of important writings on musical aesthetics.

90. Architect Friedrich Hofmann, chairman of the Graz Richard Wagner Society.—Henriette ("Hansi") Schey was Melanie's sister and wife of Joseph von Schey.—Wolf's sisters Katharina (1865–1944) and Adrienne (Jenny) (1867–1923) lived with their mother; the oldest sister, Modesta (1852–1922), had married Josef Strasser; however, the marriage was subsequently dissolved. Alphonsa is one of Modesta's five children.

92. Franz Schalk was *Kapellmeister* in Graz at this time.—Wilhelm Kienzl (1857–1941), the conductor of the Styrian Music Society in Graz since 1886.

94. Brother Max Wolf (1858–1915).

95. Wolf had begun a trip to Berlin on January 4 (Anton Bruckner was on the same train) to attend a performance of *Feuerreiter*, *Elfenlied*, and songs with orchestra prepared by Siegfried Ochs, along with Bruckner's *Te Deum*.—Eugène d'Albert (1864–1932), pianist, at that time still a composer of instrumental music, later an opera composer.—Anna Corver sang "Margit's Ballad" from the score to Ibsen's *Fest auf Solhaug;* Jeanette de Jong sang the solo in *Elfenlied.*—"Anakreon's Grab" was performed by Georg Ritter.—Music-loving Prince Bojidar Karageorgievich, a cousin of Serbia's future King Peter, had accompanied Bruckner to Berlin; he was also acquainted with Wolf.

96. Friedrich Spielhagen (1829–1911), noted storyteller as well as translator, dramatist, and lyricist.—Ernst Otto Nodnagel (1870–1909), lieder singer, composer, and music author.—Adalbert Goldschmidt (1848–1906), composer, friend of Wolf's during their Vienna Conservatory days.—Karl Muck (1859–1940), eminent conductor, at that time *Hofkapellmeister* in Berlin and later conductor of the Boston Symphony. Wolf had become acquainted with him during the period of his unsuccessful conducting stint in Salzburg.—Lilli Lehmann (1848–1920), one of the greatest singers of her time.

97. Lieutenant Colonel von Selzam, chairman of the Wagner Society in Darmstadt, had offered to arrange a Wolf concert in Darmstadt.—The diary was destroyed by Melanie Köchert after Wolf became ill.

98. Vitzliputzli: military god of the Aztecs.—Bruckner dedicated some of his works *ad majorem Dei gloriam*.

99. Wilhelm Tappert (1830–1907), music critic and music author.

100. Paula Conrad, very popular Viennese-born actress.—Arthur Vollmer, on the roster at the Berlin Hoftheater since 1874.—See René Ternois, *Zola et son temps* (Paris, 1961), on van Santen-Kolff.—Wagner's settings of five Mathilde Wesendonck poems.

101. Erich Schmidt (1853–1913), professor of German philology, in particular a Lessing and Goethe researcher.—Ida Becker, a relative of Grohe's wife.—Julius Schulhoff (1825–1898), pianist.—*Elfenlied* was published by Fürstner in 1894, *Feuerreiter* in the same year by Schott.—Leoncavallo's *I Medici* (1888), the first and only opera composed of a trilogy commissioned by Ricordi.—Anton Bruckner never married.—Possibly Marie Gaigg is the name he meant: see n. 69.

102. Paul Schlenther (1854–1916), influential theater critic.—Gerhart Hauptmann (1862–1946), German writer awarded Nobel prize in literature (1912).—Stuttgart lawyer Hugo Faisst, a recent correspondent of Wolf's; as a lieder singer he promoted the art of his new friend and was an especially avid supporter of him in the following years.

103. Sculptor Reinhold Begas (1831–1911).—Heinrich von Kleist (1777–1811), considered the first great German dramatist of 19th century, was also a poet and prose writer.

105. Wolf met the Mainz mezzo-soprano Frieda Zimmer (professional name Zerny) and fell in love with the pretty singer of his songs. Perhaps it was an attempt to find in the experience a release from the unbroken two-year period of creative stagnation. In any case, letters to the singer clearly combine the personal bond with his artistic concerns. Wolf acknowledged the latter without hesitation when things became strained in June 1894 and his creative spirit was still musically stagnant. In this same year he gradually but determinedly ended the relationship.—Richard Senff, conductor of the Darmstadt Mozart Association and lieder singer.—Richard Voss (1851–1918), free-lance writer, storyteller, and dramatist (pseudo-Romantic style).

106. Emil Steinbach (1849–1919), *Kapellmeister* in Mainz.—

Fritz Volbach (1861–1941), conductor and music scholar, then director of the Mainz Liedertafel (choral society).

108. Pauline Merk, concert singer in Stuttgart.

110. Theodor Billroth (1829–1894), pioneer surgeon, very musical, friend of Brahms and Hanslick. Mention must be made here of the Brahms-Wagner controversy during this period and the enmity of its partisans. Prominent Viennese music critic Eduard Hanslick (see n. 37) was a strong Brahms supporter and anti-Wagnerian; Wolf was a passionate Wagnerian who expressed his disdain for Brahms's music at every opportunity.—Ernst Kraus, heldentenor at Mannheim beginning in 1893 and later at the Berlin Hofoper.

113. Wolf had met the Marchese Silvio della Valle di Casanova, a poet and patron of the arts, through the Klinckerfuss family.—Degerloch, a suburb of Stuttgart.—Apollo Klinckerfuss, the Stuttgart representative for the Bechstein and Blüthner companies, and his wife, Johanna (a Liszt pupil), were especially cordial to Wolf; a small romance developed between Wolf and the nineteen-year-old daughter Margarete (see Margarete Klinckerfuss, *Aufklänge aus versunkener Zeit*, Urach, 1948), who later became a well-known pianist.

114. Wolf was giving a concert in Graz with Faisst and Frieda Zerny.

116. Henriette Faisst in Heilbronn, his friend's mother.—Secondary school professor Dr. Edwin Mayser, a good musician, later active in the Hugo Wolf Society founded by Faisst in Stuttgart.—Viennese singer Rudolf Oberhauser, engaged for a long time at the Berlin Hofoper.—Wolf was working on the second version of *Dem Vaterland* for men's chorus and orchestra.

118. Mascagni's opera *L'amico Fritz* was composed in 1891.

120. The Swiss poet Gottfried Keller was first state secretary in Zurich from 1861 to 1876.—Robert Franz (1815–1892), primarily a composer of songs.

121. The fourth President of the French Republic, Sadi Carnot, was stabbed to death by an Italian anarchist.

123. Eduard Kremser (1838–1914), chorus master of the Vienna Men's Glee Club.

124. Beckmesser's "noble air" is sung in Act 2 of Wagner's *Meistersinger.*—"Wächterlied auf der Wartburg" (Scheffel), song from 1887; the arrangement for men's chorus and orchestra remained a fragment.

125. The Werner family, in whose Perchtoldsdorf country home Wolf had composed 116 songs; Wolf had made music with Mitzi, the daughter of the house, as early as the Mayerling days.—Franz Mögele (1834–1907), Viennese opera and operetta composer.—Wagnerian singer Marianne Brandt (1842–1921), Kundry in the first performance of *Parsifal*, resided in her hometown of Vienna after 1890 as a voice teacher.

127. Georg Scherer (1828–1909), literature professor and librarian in Stuttgart, after 1881 in Munich; publisher, poet, translator.—Jens Peter Jacobsen (1847–1885), Danish novelist and poet; introduced and led Naturalist movement in Denmark.

128. Wolf is with Grohe at Schloss Matzen near Brixlegg in Tyrol as the Lipperheides' guest.—Paul von Szczepański (1855–1924), editor for periodicals and storyteller.—Elsa Jäger, Ferdinand Jäger's eldest daughter.

129. Professor Huppert from Prague, a friend of Lipperheide.

130. Wilhelm Gericke (1845–1925), conductor of the concerts of the Society for the Friends of Music in Vienna. Wolf had sent in the choral arrangements of *Elfenlied* and *Feuerreiter;* both pieces were performed at the society's concert on December 2, 1894.

132. Wolf has returned to Matzen.—The line drawing is the opening of Wolf's song "Das verlassene Mägdlein" (Mörike).

133. Eduard Grützner (1846–1925), Bavarian painter of scenes of wine-induced conviviality.—The Rolandsbogen is a large stone arch built near the hunter's cottage at the request of Baron von Lipperheide.—English philologist Alois Brandl (1855–1940).

134. Painter Karl Rickelt, a nephew of Baron Lipperheide.

135. Beginning in 1885, Wolf was one of the unconditional supporters of Anton Bruckner. After their joint concert in Berlin on January 8, 1894, there ensued a friendly association. Wolf had sent congratulations on the occasion of Bruckner's birthday and received the following written reply:

Greatly honored Master and Colleague!
 Your very kind letter pleased me immeasurably! I thank you from the bottom of my heart for your wishes, which I devotedly return to you in kind! May God protect you always and lead you along the loveliest, though at the same time most difficult artistic pathway! My state of health, unfortunately, is incurable! Sometimes a little better, then worse again! May you, honorable sir (dearest friend), remain in good health, and well disposed toward me, just as I also respect you most devotedly. If bad weather should come, I'll go to Vienna.
 In most faithful love and respect   Your Bruckner
Steyr, Sept. 23, 1894

Wolf is reading Rudolf Krauss's *Mörike als Gelegenheitsdichter* (Stuttgart, 1894).

136. Karl Stauffer-Bern (1857–1891), painter and etcher, whose passionate life of feeling also found expression in poetry; see O. Brahm, *Karl Stauffer: Sein Leben, seine Briefe, seine Gedichte* (Berlin, 1892).—Dr. Robert Defregger, a son of the Austrian painter Franz Defregger (1835–1921).

138. Hermann Zumpe (1850–1903), *Hofkapellmeister* in Stuttgart, was preparing *Elfenlied* and *Feuerreiter;* performance on January 29, 1895.

142. *Mittag—die Stund ist da: Parsifal,* Act 3.

144. August Labitsky (1832–1903), conductor of the Karlsbad spa orchestra.

145. Edwin Bormann (1851–1912), dialect poet from Saxony (pseudonym Bliemchen), advocate for the Bacon-Shakespeare theory.

147. Paula Mark, Hofoper singer in Vienna.—Fräulein von Spurny from Graz, singer, performed for the Graz Wagner Society.

148. Wolf has moved to Perchtoldsdorf in order to write his op-

era *Der Corregidor,* using the libretto written by Rosa Mayreder.

153. *Glück auf zum Meistersingen: Die Meistersinger,* Act 1.

155. Rosa Mayreder (1858–1938), married to the architect Karl Mayreder, was at first a painter, later a pioneer in the women's movement. She wrote stories and essays and created for Wolf the libretto for *Corregidor* after Pedro de Alarcón's novella *The Three-Cornered Hat.* Wolf rejected the libretto in 1890, but now it was able to ignite his fantasy.

158. Finance official Richard Hirsch, member of the Vienna Wagner Society.—*Die Lachtaube,* operetta by Otto Rehberg, music by Eugen von Baund.

164. Kauffmann's review in the *Musikalisches Wochenblatt* (Leipzig) of February 28, 1895, is included in *Collected Articles on Hugo Wolf,* No. 2 (Berlin, 1899), pp. 4–8.

166. Wolf incorporated "In dem Schatten meiner Locken" and "Herz, verzage nicht geschwind" into *Corregidor.*

169. Wilhelm Meinhold (1797–1851), *Maria Schweidler, die Bernsteinhexe;* in addition to the novel, which became famous, Meinhold also wrote poems and novellas.

175. Elisabeth Förster-Nietzsche, *Das Leben Friedrich Nietzsche,* Vols. 1–2 (1895–1904).

176. Lino is Karl Mayreder, husband of Rosa Mayreder; his watercolor *Hugo Wolf in the Hunter's Cottage at Matzen, Working on 'Corregidor'* became very well known.—Polyhymnia, Muse of singing, rhetoric, and mime.—The words *'gegenseitigen" (Beziehungen)*—"mutual" (relations)—were written over with the word *freundlichen* (friendly).

177. Richard Spur, initially a painter, later a civil servant, was very musical and belonged to the Schalk brothers' inner circle of friends.

178. Hugo Röhr (1866–1937), first *Kapellmeister* at the Mannheim National Theater in the years 1892–1896, conducted the first performance there of *Corregidor* (June 7, 1896).

180. Emil Heckel (1831–1908), music-store owner and publisher in Mannheim who, with his son Karl, promoted the composer extensively in the final years. *Corregidor,* the *Manuel Venegas* fragment, the second part of the *Italienisches Liederbuch,* and the *Michelangelo-Lieder,* among others, were

brought out by Heckel.—Wolf also negotiated with Brock-
haus Publishers in Leipzig concerning *Corregidor,* as well
as with the Viennese publisher Josef Eberle.

181. Mime: *Siegfried,* Act 1.—Georg Pierson, artistic secretary,
later (1896) director of the General Management Office of
the Royal Theater in Berlin.

182. "Am besten wenn ich *ihn* . . ." (*Die Meistersinger,* Act 2).—
Leonore Baroness Bach sang these three Wolf songs on
November 16, 1895, in the Brahmssaal of the Musikverein
(concert hall in Vienna).

188. Guy de Maupassant (1850–1893) was a friend of Hermine
Lecomte du Nouÿ. Madame Lecomte had published her
books, originally anonymously, in which Maupassant more
or less played a role. This was the case, also, with *Amitié
amoureuse,* an epistolary novel, in all likelihood the book
in question here.

189. Bernhard Pollini (1838–1897), *Intendant* of the Hamburg
Opera.—Gustav Mahler was engaged at this time in Hamburg. There must have been a certain contact with his
friend from conservatory days, because the Vienna Stadt-
bibliothek (City Library) has a letter of Mahler's dated
September 3, 1895, to Natalie Bauer-Lechner, who also
knew Wolf, in which he says, "Above all, let Wolf know
that he should send his opera *to me,* if he cannot or does
not want to have it done elsewhere. If it is in my power,
I'll make sure that it is given the performance; i.e., *if* it
seems to me to be worthy of performing. You don't have
to pass on this last comment, or rather clothe it in a somewhat less dubious form."

190. Jakob Julius David (1859–1906), writer and journalist in
Vienna; Wolf was thinking of working with him on an opera.—Hans Pfitzner (1869–1949) wrote music to Ibsen's
Fest auf Solhaug in 1889–1890; Wolf had composed music
for the same work for the Viennese Burgtheater in 1890–
1891 (first performance, November 21, 1891; the score was
published by Heckel in 1903). Pfitzner's music was heard
for the first time on November 28, 1895, in the first German performance of the drama, in Mainz.

191. The Graz copyist Bernhard Maresch was busy producing

the *Corregidor* material under the direction of friend Potpeschnigg.

193. "Bei Sedan" is presumably to be found in the first of two collections of novellas by Richard Voss (see n. 105), published in 1889 and 1898. Available reference materials list it under the author's numerous works as a *Schauspiel* (play), published in 1895. Sedan was the scene of the defeat of the French in the Franco-Prussian War (1870).—Wilhelm Jahn (1834–1900), director of the Vienna Hofoper from 1881 to 1897.

195. Wolf was in Matzen from May 16 to December 28, 1895.

196. Wolf is beginning to compose the second part of the *Italienisches Liederbuch*.

197. "Ich liess mir sagen und mir ward erzählt, der schöne Toni hungre sich zu Tode" and "Schon streckt' ich aus im Bett die müden Glieder."

198. Teacher Paul Müller in Berlin, who founded the Berlin Hugo Wolf Society.—The variant refers to No. 9 of the *Goethe-Lieder* ("Mignon").

204. Thanks to the generosity of his circle of friends, Wolf was finally able to obtain his own flat (Vienna IV, Schwindgasse 3); he moved into it on July 4, 1896.—Brother Gilbert Wolf (1862–1938) lived after 1894 in Vienna, very comfortably situated.—*Eugénie Grandet*, a novel by Honoré de Balzac.

205. The "other" song is "Wenn du mich mit den Augen streifst."—Edmund Hellmer (1873–1950), lawyer, son of sculptor Edmund Hellmer (1850–1935), who also belonged to the inner circle of friends and created the tombstone in the Zentralfriedhof (Main Cemetery) after Wolf's death.—Sculptor Viktor Tilgner (1844–1896) was the creator of the Mozart Monument in Vienna and many other monuments.

207. The second song is "Wenn du mich mit den Augen streifst" (see n. 205).

210. Wolf traveled to Stuttgart on May 12, 1896, and remained there until May 17. The piano score to *Corregidor* had just been published, and Wolf traveled on to Mannheim in order to attend the rehearsals for the premiere (June 7).—

Wolf knew the Lambert family and the Degerloch publisher Adolf Nast from the time of his trip to Germany in 1894.

211. Banker Hermann Hildebrandt, one of the Mannheim patrons.

212. Helene Hohenleitner had great difficulties with her role.—*Intendant* Dr. August Bassermann.—Anna Reiss, grand ducal *Kammersängerin* (chamber singer; title bestowed by the government upon a respected singer), of Baden, belonged to the Mannheim circle of patrons.

213. Hans Rüdiger, at the Mannheim National Theater, 1891–1903; and Joachim Kromer, active there 1895–1922.—Wolf took his own bathtub with him when he traveled.

214. Anna Sorger, at the Mannheim National Theater, 1884–1898.—Hugo Becker (1864–1941), world-renowned cellist, son of acclaimed Mannheim-born violinist Jean Becker (1833–1884) and brother of Jeanne Becker, married to Grohe since 1891.—Hans von Bülow (1830–1894), German pianist and conductor; married (1857) to Liszt's daughter Cosima, who later married Wagner.

216. Archduke Karl Ludwig (1833–1896), younger brother of Austrian emperor Franz Joseph I.

217. The premiere of *Corregidor* was a great success, despite unfavorable rehearsal circumstances; the opera was repeated on June 10, but Wolf had already gone to Stuttgart.—Dr. Alois Obrist (1867–1910) was *Hofkapellmeister* in Stuttgart, 1895–1900.

218. Eugen Staegemann (1845–1899), director of the Stadttheater in Düsseldorf since 1891.—Kappellmeister Johann Nepomuk Fuchs (1842–1899) of the Vienna Hofoper, director of the Vienna Conservatory at the same time.

221. Tirso de Molina, born Gabriel Téllez (1571–1648), Spanish dramatist who introduced the character of Don Juan to literature in *El Burlador de Sevilla*.

222. Giambattista Piranesi (1720–1778), Italian architect and engraver (copperplate).—Presumably Anton Katzer (1863–1938), Viennese painter.

223. Wolf was recently invited to Matzen by Baron Lipperheide.—Jacobsen's novel *Fru Marie Grubbe* (see n. 127).

224. On the basis of the Mannheim performance, Wolf had made a revision in the *Corregidor* score.—C. G. Röder is engraving the second part of the *Italienisches Liederbuch* for Heckel Publishers.—[*Fru*] *Marie Grubbe* by J. P. Jacobsen (see n. 127).

228. Wolf became acquainted with Pedro de Alarcón's novella *Manuel Venegas* during his stay in Berlin in 1892. Various attempts on the part of his friends to write a scenario and libretto were found by him to be unsatisfactory and caused disagreements and difficulties. After the completion of *Corregidor*, Wolf took up the text once again and requested a libretto from Rosa Mayreder. The first act of the libretto was finished in March 1897 and satisfied him very much. However, he rejected the final work, completed in May. He turned then to the prehistorian Moritz Hoernes, who delivered the finished libretto to him on July 8. Wolf began the composition with the "Frühlingschor" (Spring Chorus) on July 29, 1897, and worked for ten days, had to stop, continued in August and then composed at a furious rate, even surpassing his *Corregidor* ardor. Wolf managed to wrest from himself thirty-three pages of piano score for the first act. September 18, 1897, was his last real working day; on September 19 he was seized by an attack of madness.—Edmund and Marie Lang, Melanie Köchert's brother and sister-in-law, longtime friends of Wolf.—Michael Haberlandt, Indologist, ethnologist, and student of folklore, belonged to the circle of friends in the final years of Wolf's life.—Franz Schaumann, chairman at that time of Vienna's academic Wagner Society, had adapted Alarcón's *Three-Cornered Hat* material for Wolf.—Mahler went to Vienna on April 27, 1897, conducted for the first time at the Hofoper on May 11, and then quickly climbed the ladder of his new sphere of activity. With Mahler's entrance into the association of the Vienna Hofoper, Wolf viewed the chances for his *Corregidor* as particularly favorable.

231. Joseph Schalk had married on July 12, 1896.—*Genoveva*, Schumann's only opera, written 1847–1849, premiered 1850 at Leipzig; *Iphigénie en Aulide* (Gluck), premiered

1774 at the Paris Opera; *Armida* (Haydn), premiered 1784 at Esterhaz, Hungary; *Armida* (Rossini), premiered 1817 at the San Carlo Opera, Naples; *Armide* (Gluck), premiered 1777 at the Paris Opera.

232. *Intendant* Krückl of the Strassburg Stadttheater was preparing a *Corregidor* production; it was presented on April 29 and May 13, but Wolf was not present.

233. Mödling manufacturer Walter Bokmayer, himself a singer, promoted Wolf's music by arranging *Liederabends*.

235. Prater: Viennese amusement park.—Ernst Otto Nodnagel's essay "Hugo Wolf, der Begründer des neudeutschen Liedes" (Hugo Wolf, the Originator of the New German Song) appeared in the *Magazin für Literatur*, Vol. 66, no. 25 (1897); Richard Sternfeld's article "Ein neuer Liederfrühling" (A New Spring-Season of Song) was printed in Vol. 61, no. 11 (1892), of the same periodical.

236. Wolf set three Michelangelo poems *(Michelangelo-Lieder)* to music between March 18 and 28, 1897.—Kobenzl, a popular Viennese hilltop overlooking city

240. The passage from *Die Meistersinger*, Act 1, reads *ein sau'res Amt u. heut' zumal*.

241. Vally Franck, daughter of a university professor, Paris-born and friends with Wolf in the years 1878–1881. The separation, initiated by Vally, was very hard on Wolf at the time.

242. Ferdinand Foll (1867–1929), solo repetiteur at the Vienna Hofoper and recital accompanist; friend of Wolf's.—Fritz Lang, a brother of Edmund.—Beckmesser in *Meistersinger*, Act 3. *"Schon gut der Witz'! Und genug der Streich'!"*

245. In this final letter Wolf drew a line in place of his signature.

CHRONOLOGY

1860   Born on March 13 in Windischgraz (now Slovenj Gradec, Yugoslavia).

1870   Attended Graz Gymnasium [secondary school] for one term.

1871   Attended Stiftsgymnasium St. Paul [Monastery School] in Carinthia.

1873   Attended Gymnasium in Marburg on the Drau.

1875   September: began studies at the Vienna Conservatory. Paid a visit to Richard Wagner in December at the Hotel Imperial.

1877   Composition of songs, piano and choral pieces, and first experiments with opera. Dismissed from the Vienna Conservatory. Became acquainted with Adalbert von Goldschmidt and his circle of friends. Infected with syphilis.

1878   *Heine-Lieder.* His first love: Vally Franck.

1879   String Quartet in D Minor. Disappointing visit to Johannes Brahms. Shared living quarters with Gustav Mahler. Introduction to Melanie Köchert.

1880   First visit to Perchtoldsdorf.

1881   Eichendorff choral pieces. *Kapellmeister* in Salzburg, November to January 1882. Break with Vally Franck.

1882   In Vienna for short term as recruit in Austrian army. First visit to Bayreuth in summer to see *Parsifal*. Acquaintance with Friedrich Eckstein. Beginning of relationship with Melanie Köchert.

1883   Work in Rinnbach on *Penthesilea*. Meeting with Franz Liszt.

1884   Composed incidental music for *Prinz Friedrich von Homburg*, play by Kleist. Employed (until April 1887) as music critic for "Wiener Salonblatt" (weekly newspaper). Shared living quarters with Hermann Bahr.

1885   First meeting with Anton Bruckner.

1886   Intermezzo in E-Flat for string quartet. Song settings of poems by Scheffel, Mörike, Goethe, Kerner, and Eichendorff. Began composition of oratorio *Christnacht*. Ceased work on *Penthesilea* following the Vienna Philharmonic's "reading" in October.

1887   *Italian Serenade* for string quartet (May). First songs published: *Sechs Lieder für eine Frauenstimme; Sechs Gedichte von Scheffel, Mörike, Goethe and Kerner*. Death of father, Philipp Wolf, on May 9.

1888   Composed 53 *Mörike-Lieder* from January to May in Perchtoldsdorf, October in Unterach. 12 *Eichendorff-Lieder* in Unterach. 25 *Goethe-Lieder* in Vienna/Döbling. Acquaintance with Joseph Schalk and Ferdinand Jäger.

1889   Composed additional 26 *Goethe-Lieder* in Döbling and Perchtoldsdorf. Began *Spanisches Liederbuch* in Perchtoldsdorf end of October, completed there in April 1890. Printing of Mörike, Eichendorff, and Goethe songbooks.

1890   Composed *Alte Weisen* (Gottfried Keller) in May-June. Began *Italienisches Liederbuch* in Döbling in September. Incidental music to Ibsen's *Fest auf Solhaug*. Trip to Germany in October. Made acquaintance of Liliencron in Munich, Kauffmann in Tübingen, Strecker (head of Schott Publishers) in Mainz. Contract agreement with Schott Publishers.

1891   Completion of *Italienisches Liederbuch*, Part 1 (22 songs), in December in Döbling. Premiere of oratorio *Christnacht* in Mannheim. Visits to Oskar Grohe in Philippsburg, Engelbert Humperdinck in Frankfurt.

1892   Extended lull in creativity. Trip to Berlin in February-
        March for two Wolf *Liederabends*.

1894   Second trip to Berlin in January. Successful perfor-
        mances of *Elfenlied* and *Feuerreiter* (choral versions).
        Friendship with Hugo Faisst in Stuttgart. Turbulent
        love affair with Frieda Zerny. Choice of opera libretto
        after desperate search.

1895   Began composing opera *Der Corregidor* in Perchtolds-
        dorf in April-May, completed composing and scoring
        in December at Matzen Castle in Tyrol.

1896   *Italienisches Liederbuch*, Part 2 (24 songs), March-April.
        Premiere of *Der Corregidor* in Mannheim, June 7. Move
        to first flat of his own in Vienna in July.

1897   *Drei Michelangelo-Lieder* in March. *Vier Lieder nach Heine,
        Shakespeare, und Lord Byron* published. Work on opera
        Manuel Venegas in summer. Altercation with Mahler
        (then music director at Vienna Court Opera) over possi-
        ble performance of *Corregidor*. Sudden nervous break-
        down. Committed to Dr. Svetlin's sanatorium Septem-
        ber 20.

1898   Released from sanatorium in January. Trip to Adriatic
        with sister and Melanie. Depression, then suicide at-
        tempt in Traunsee in October. Committed to insane
        asylum in Vienna, October 4.

1899–   Progressively worsening paralysis. Died February 22,
1903   1903. Funeral services at Votivkirche on Vienna's
        Ringstrasse. Burial in Zentralfriedhof, Vienna, next to
        Schubert and Beethoven.

BIBLIOGRAPHY

The Bibliography in the German-language edition has been adapted and supplemented by the translator.

LISTS OF COMPOSITIONS

"Verzeichnis seiner Werke" in Paul Müller, *Hugo Wolf*, Leipzig, 1907.

"Wolf's Compositions," in Frank Walker, *Hugo Wolf*, London, 1951; rev. ed., New York, 1968 (English); Graz, Vienna, Cologne, 1953 (German).

List of Compositions in *New Grove Dictionary of Music and Musicians*, "Hugo Wolf" entry by Eric Sams.

EDITIONS OF WORKS

Gesamtausgabe (Complete Works). Published by the International Hugo Wolf Society, edited by Hans Jancik (complete except for *Der Corregidor*).

Group I: Songs (Vol. 1–7: with piano accompaniment. Vol 8–9: with orchestral accompaniment).

Group II: Choral Works (Vol. 10: Male voice chorus with and without accompaniment. Vol. 11: Mixed chorus with and without accompaniment).

Group III: Works for the Stage (Vol. 12: *Der Corregidor* [opera]. Vol. 13: *Manuel Venegas* [opera fragment]. Vol. 14: Incidental Music).

Group IV: Chamber Music (Vol. 15: String Quartet in D minor, *Intermezzo in E flat, Italienische Serenade* [Serenade in G for string quartet]).

Group V: Orchestral Works (Vol. 16: *Penthesilea.* Vol. 17: *Symphonie in B (g),* Scherzo und Finale, *Italienische Serenade*).

Group VI: Piano Music (Vol. 18: Piano compositions).

Group VII: Supplement (Vol. 19: Unfinished compositions, sketches, supplements, addenda. Vol. 20: Iconography, Index of Manuscripts, General Index).

Nachgelassene Werke (Posthumous Works). Prepared for publication by Robert Haas and Helmut Schultz (Leipzig, Vienna, 1936–1938). This edition was never completed.

DISCUSSIONS OF WORKS

Gesammelte Aufsätze über Hugo Wolf. Foreword by Hermann Bahr. Vol. 1–2 (Berlin, 1898/99).

H. O. Hécaen, *Manie et Inspiration Musicale. Le cas Hugo Wolf* (Bordeaux, 1934).

Kurt Vargas, "Der Musikkritiker Hugo Wolf" (diss., Magdeburg, 1934).

Richard Batka, "Der Corregidor" (*Opernführer.* 26, Leipzig o. J.).

Edmund Hellmer, *Der Corregidor* (Berlin, 1900).

Georg Bieri, *Die Lieder von Hugo Wolf* (Bern and Leipzig, 1935) (*Berner Veröffentlichungen zur Musikforschung.* 15).

Eric Sams, *The Songs of Hugo Wolf* (London, 1961; revised 1983).

E. Stahl, "Die Jugendlieder Hugo Wolf" (diss., Göttingen, 1949).

R. Egger, *Die Deklamationsrhythmik bei Hugo Wolf* (Tutzing, 1963).

Anton Tausche, *Hugo Wolfs Mörikelieder* (Vienna, 1947).

Ursala Sennheim, "Hugo Wolfs Spanishches und Italienishches Liederbuch" (typed diss., Frankfurt, 1955).

Sonja Eisold, "Der Gehalt der Lyrik Mörikes in der Vertonung von Hugo Wolf" (typed diss., Freie Universität Berlin, 1956).

Karl Grunsky, "Hugo Wolf-Fest in Stuttgart." October 4–8, 1906. *Festschrift* (Stuttgart, 1906). Einführungen zu den Liederzyklen [Introduction to the Lieder Cycles]).

P. Cook, *Hugo Wolf's Corregidor* (London, 1976).

Karl Heckel, *Wolf in seinem Verhältnis zu Richard Wagner* (Munich, 1905).

Hugo Wolf issues of the journals *Die Musik*. 2 (1903), No. 12; *Österreichische Musikzeitschrift*. 8 (1953), No. 2; *Österreichische Musikzeitschrift*. 15 (1960), No. 2.

Mosco Carner, *Hugo Wolf Songs* (BBC Music Guides, London, 1982).

Deborah J. Stein, *Hugo Wolf's Lieder and Extensions of Tonality* (Ann Arbor, MI, 1985).

WOLF'S MUSIC CRITICISM

Hugo Wolfs Musikalische Kritiken. Edited by Richard Batka and Heinrich Werner (Breitkopf & Härtels Musikbücher. 15, Leipzig, 1911).

The Music Criticism of Hugo Wolf. Translated, edited, and annotated by Henry Pleasants (Holmes & Meier, NY, London, 1978).

LETTERS

"Hugo-Wolf-Rhapsodie. Aus Briefen und Schriften." Edited by Willi Reich, *Vom Dauernden in der Zeit*. 37 (Zürich, 1947).

Hugo Wolf: Familienbriefe. Edited by E. Hellmer, Breitkopf & Härtels Musikbücher. 17 (Leipzig, 1912).

Letters to Hugo Faisst (Stuttgart, 1904).

Oskar Grohe (Berlin, 1905)

Emil Kauffmann (Berlin, 1905)

Henriette Lang und Josef von Schey (Deutsche Musikbücherei. 48, Regensburg, 1913)

Rosa Mayreder (Vienna, 1921)

Paul Müller (in: *Jahrbuch der Musikbibliothek Peters*, 1904)

Heinrich Potpeschnigg (Stuttgart, 1923)
Frieda Zerny (edited by Ernst Hilmar and Walter Obermaier, published by Musikwissenschaftlicher Verlag, Vienna, 1978).

BIOGRAPHIES

Hugo Wolf: "Daten aus meinem Leben" (in: *Österreichische Musikzeitschrift*. 15 [1960], No. 2).
Ernst Decsey, *Hugo Wolf* Bd. [Vol.] 1–4 (Leipzig und Berlin 2, 1903–1906); 3. Auflage [Edition], 1 Vol., 1919; 7–12. Auflage, 1 Bd., 1921).
Eugen Schmitz, *Hugo Wolf* (Reclams Universalbibliothek, 4853, Leipzig, 1906).
Ernest Newman, *Hugo Wolf* (London, 1907, 1966 [English], Leipzig, 1910 [German]).
Zdzislaw Jachimecki, *Hugo Wolf* (Cracow, 1908 [Polish]).
Max Millenkovich, *Hugo Wolf* (Leipzig, 1912).
Karl Grunsky, *Hugo Wolf* (Leipzig, 1928) (*Die Musik*. 52).
V. B. Benvenisti, *Hugo Wolf* (Rome, 1931 [Italian]).
H. Schouten, *Hugo Wolf* (Amsterdam, 1935 [Dutch]).
Richard Litterscheid, *Hugo Wolf* (Potsdam, 1939) (*Unsterbliche Tonkunst*. 8).
Magda von Hattingberg, *Hugo Wolf* (Vienna, 1941 and 1953).
Alfred Orel, *Hugo Wolf* (Orpheus-Bücherei. 1, Vienna, 1947).
Frank Walker, *Hugo Wolf* (London 1951, New York, 1968 [English]; Graz, Vienna, Cologne, 1953 [German]). Grasberger notes: "definitive, comprehensive work."
Norbert Loeser, *Hugo Wolf* (*Componisten-Serie*. 31, Haarlem 1955 [Dutch]).
Dolf Lindner, *Hugo Wolf* (*Österreich-Reihe*. 96/97, Vienna, 1960).
Erik Werba, *Hugo Wolf* (Vienna, Munich, Zürich, 1971).
Kurt Honolka, *Hugo Wolf* (Stuttgart, 1988).

MEMOIRS

(Some with letters)
Michael Haberlandt, *Hugo Wolf. Erinnerungen und Gedanken* (Leipzig, 1903; Darmstadt, 1911).

Edmund Hellmer, *Hugo Wolf. Erlebtes und Erlauschtes* (Vienna, 1921).

Gustav Schur, *Erinnerungen an Hugo Wolf* (Deutsche Musikbücherei. 34, Regensburg, 1922).

Heinrich Werner, *Hugo Wolf in Perchtoldsdorf* (Deutsche Musikbücherei. 53, Regensburg, 1925). *Hugo Wolf und der Wiener academische Wagner-Verein* (Deutsche Musikbücherei. 60, Regensburg, 1925). *Hugo Wolf in Mayerling* (Breitkopf & Härtels Musikbücher. 21, Leipzig, 1913). *Der Hugo-Wolf-Verein in Wien* (Deutsche Musikbücherei. 35, Regensburg, 1922).

Friedrich Echstein: *Alte unnennbare Tage* (Vienna, 1936).

ICONOGRAPHY

Alfred von Ehrmann, *Hugo Wolf. Sein Leben in Bildern* (Leipzig, 1937).

GLOSSARY
of Frequently Mentioned Names

Bokmayer, Walter   Manufacturer in Mödling (near Vienna), amateur singer, furthered Wolf's career by arranging *Liederabends*

Boller, Viktor   Provincial court counselor, chairman of Vienna's academic Wagner Society

Dlauhy, Wilhelm   Physician, Heinrich Köchert's brother-in-law

Eckstein, Friedrich   Bruckner pupil, music-lover, intellectual from wealthy Vienna family

Faisst, Hugo   Stuttgart lawyer, lieder singer, strong promoter of Wolf's songs, close friend

Grohe, Oskar   Lower-court judge in Mannheim, frequent correspondent from 1890 on, close friend

Haberlandt, Michael   Viennese Indologist, ethnologist, belonged to circle of friends of Wolf's later life

Jäger, Ferdinand   Famous Wagnerian tenor, voice teacher in Vienna, significant in promoting Wolf's music

Kauffmann, Emil   Tübingen music director and journalist, one of Wolf's earliest German admirers, close friend of long duration

Köchert family   Heinrich, Melanie, and daughters Hilde, Ilse, and Irmina, as well as Heinrich's mother, Karoline ("Mama Köchert")

Lang family   Edmund and Marie, Melanie's brother and sister-in-law; Henriette (Lang) von Schey, Melanie's sister, was married to Joseph von Schey

Larisch, Rudolf   Public official, later professor at Vienna Academy of Visual Arts, good friend

Lipperheide, Baron Franz von and Baroness Frieda   Well-to-do owners of a Berlin fashion newspaper; special patrons of the composer; frequent hosts at Matzen Castle in Tyrol

Löwe, Ferdinand   Viennese conductor

Mauthner, Fritz   Writer and philosopher in Berlin

Mayreder, Rosa   Austrian writer and librettist for *Corregidor;* husband Karl, architect

Mottl, Felix   Conductor in Bayreuth, Karlsruhe, Munich; friend since Vienna Conservatory days

Muck, Karl   Court conductor in Berlin; acquaintance as of Wolf's Salzburg assignment

Müller, Paul   Berlin schoolteacher, founder of Berlin Hugo Wolf Society

Ochs, Siegfried   Conductor and composer, choral conductor in Berlin; premiered works of Wolf, Bruckner, and Reger

Potpeschnigg, Heinrich   Dentist in Graz, excellent musician, a best friend in later years

Rickelt, Karl   Painter, Lipperheide's nephew

Schalk, Franz and Joseph (brothers)   Viennese musicians: Franz, a well-known conductor; Joseph, professor of piano at the Vienna Conservatory and artistic director of Vienna academic Wagner Society; good friends

Schey, Joseph von   University professor, married to Melanie's sister Henriette

Schur, Gustav   Viennese bank official, treasurer of Vienna's academic Wagner Society and first Hugo Wolf Society

Sternfeld, Richard   Historical researcher and writer, Berlin professor, leading member of Berlin Wagner Society

Strecker, Ludwig   Director of B. Schott's Sons Publishers

Werner family   Heinrich, Marie, and children Heinrich and Mizzi; Viennese friends; owners of Perchtoldsdorf country house where Wolf composed 116 songs, including Mörike, Spanish, and Italian

INDEXES

INDEX OF COMPOSITIONS

The following compositions of Hugo Wolf are mentioned in Letters and Annotations as well as in the Insight into the Personality (numbers indicate pages).

GENERAL INDEX

The General Index contains the names of persons and places; page numbers for repeated mentions of names in the formal greeting at the conclusions of the letters are not listed.

Compositions of Hugo Wolf mentioned in the letters are compiled in the Index of Compositions.

The numbers indicate pages.